AF271381

THE KITCHEN

COOKBOOK

MELCHER
MEDIA

THE

KIMBAL MUSK

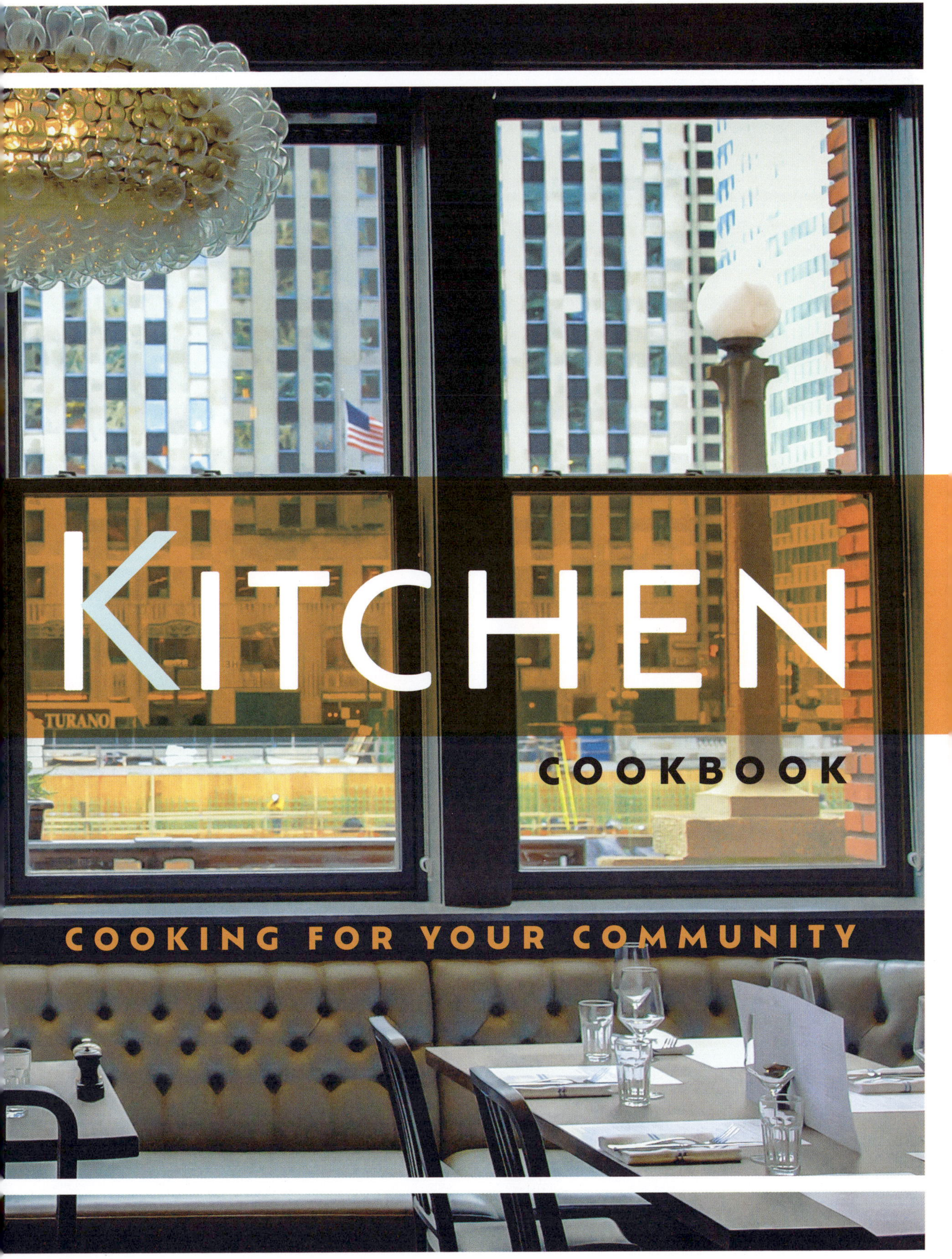

KITCHEN

COOKBOOK

COOKING FOR YOUR COMMUNITY

The Kitchen Cookbook:
Cooking for Your Community
© 2023 The Kitchen Café, LLC
All rights reserved.
www.thekitchen.com
Printed in China
ISBN: 978-1-59591-1315
10 9 8 7 6 5 4 3 2 1

Introduction by *Kimbal Musk*
Written with *Mariah Bear*
Recipe testing by *Leda Scheintaub*
Photographs by *Laurie Smith*
Design by *Roberto de Vicq de Cumptich*
Food styling by *Christine Albano*
Prop styling by *Nicole Dominic*

This book was produced by
Melcher Media, Inc.

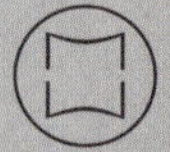

**MELCHER
MEDIA**

124 West 13th Street
New York, NY 10011
www.melcher.com

Founder and CEO:
Charles Melcher
Vice President and
COO: *Bonnie Eldon*
Editorial Director:
Lauren Nathan
Production Director:
Susan Lynch
Executive Editor:
Christopher Steighner
Senior Editor:
Megan Worman

Melcher Media
would also like
to acknowledge
the contributions
of *Cathy Dorsey,
Kevin Li,
Elisabeth March,
Sarah Scheffel, and
Anna Wahrman.*

THE KITCHEN

This book is dedicated to the people who have come through our doors at The Kitchen. For more than twenty years now, you all have sustained us, inspired us, and brought us joy. Thanks for being part of our community.

How I Started Cooking for My Community

▶**KIMBAL MUSK**

When I was young, I never expected that I'd become a chef. I always loved cooking for my family growing up, and for my friends in college, but never thought I'd go any further. I really did love cooking, though, and how it brought us together more often and more deeply than anything else. I love to have dinner with my wife Christiana and our four children every day. It's not always possible, but it is great when we do and it never gets old. Eating with your friends and family is the best.

When I was twenty-seven years old, the tech company I co-founded with my brother Elon was acquired for a large sum of money. I had conflicted feelings because I had envisioned myself working there for the rest of my life. I was young. So, when the acquisition happened, I decided not to stay in Silicon Valley. I moved to New York City to try Manhattan on for size.

In New York I was recruited by many startups to help them in different ways. But I found that going from building your own company to building parts of them for others is like drinking watered-down coffee. Not for me. With some prodding from Jen Lewin, my fiancée at the time, I went down the street to the French Culinary Institute to see what cooking programs they offered. After a few classes, I fell in love with the profession. I remember being screamed at by a French chef who was a foot shorter than me, his spittle landing on my face, and I was okay with it. I was there to learn, and I loved it.

Eighteen months later I graduated, in 2001, just before 9/11. I lived right by the World Trade Center and woke up to the sound of the first plane hitting the building. Jen and I narrowly escaped the white dust cloud of the first tower falling. As we ran uptown, away from the towers, we saw the second one fall as we reached Union Square. I'll never forget that moment when reality broke for me.

Jen and I made our way uptown to my mom's apartment, where we ended up staying for two weeks, sleeping on the floor until we got permission to return to our place in Lower Manhattan. My mom, Maye Musk, was a top dietitian in New York at the time. Through her connections she learned that the city was seeking volunteer chefs to cook for the firefighters and other first responders. She put in my name as a recommendation. Thousands of New York chefs wanted to volunteer, but for most they couldn't get access to go below the "security curtain" set up to keep unauthorized personnel away from the disaster site. My apartment at the time was below that line, so I was one of the few civilians allowed to work at Ground Zero. Since I already had that access and had just gotten my cooking diploma, I was welcomed as a volunteer. It was quite the honor, and it became one of the pivotal experiences of my life. It was through that experience that I truly came to understand the power of cooking to connect, honor, and serve.

For six weeks, we cooked sixteen hours a day. We served the firefighters world-class food, cooked by the best chefs on the planet—with me as one of the humble prep cooks supporting them. We'd watch the firefighters come in from digging through a giant pile of toxic rubble outside the gym-turned-cafeteria where we served them. Covered in white dust, they'd take off their outer shells and sit down to eat the food we'd prepared. It would start quietly. No one spoke at first. And then slowly over their 45-minute break we'd see life come back into their eyes. The food was a kind of nurturing, and we were so proud to do our small part for them. By the end of the break, they were talking loudly with each other, their energy visibly back. And then

they put their shells back on and headed back out to that giant pile of metal, still melting weeks after the Towers fell, to save American lives. Witnessing firsthand how food brought people together during such a traumatic time told me that I had to open a restaurant. I wanted to feel this community energy every day for the rest of my life.

With this new sense of mission, Jen and I left Manhattan and set out on a road trip around the country to find our next home. We wanted to settle in a town where we could eventually open a restaurant, as well as a place where we could raise a family. We found it in Boulder, Colorado, on a sunny, snowy day in February 2002. People often ask me why I live in Boulder. My answer is always, "'Have you tried Boulder?'" It truly is a wonderful town with delightful people, and I am proud to live here.

Very soon after we moved, we met Hugo Matheson in a chance encounter at Spruce Confections, a local coffee shop. He and I quickly found that we had some important things in common. We were both immigrants. He was from England and I was from South Africa. Plus we were both chefs. He was working at Mateo, a local French bistro, and I wanted to connect with local chefs. These simple connections were enough for Hugo to invite us to dinner that very evening. I was not used to such an off-the-cuff invitation (not exactly standard in New York City), but I have found that saying yes to life yields better, and definitely more interesting, results than saying no.

Clockwise from top left: Kimbal with his mother, Maye, and sister, Tosca; Maye, in the Kalahari Desert; Kimbal at seventeen with his cousin Russ; Kimbal cooking in Jasper, Canada; Elon learning a technique from his brother; Kimbal the year the restaurant opened.

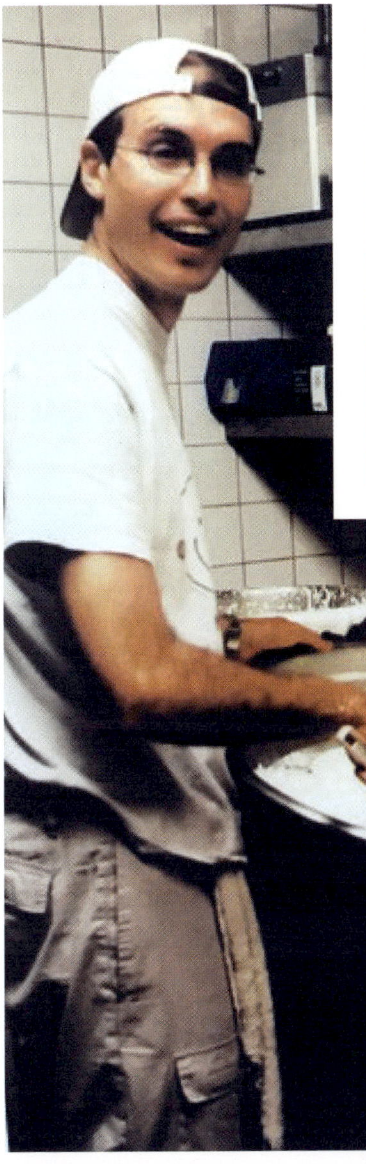

THE KITCHEN
COCKTAIL du JOUR
LAST
WORD

That evening, Hugo cooked us an unforgettable meal, completely unlike anything I had experienced in New York. Instead of using complicated French techniques, Hugo cooked with the flair of an Italian grandmother. He knew what he was doing and cooked from the heart without overthinking it. His background had been at the River Café in London, one of the originators of farm-to-table dining. Run by Ruth Rogers and Rose Gray, that restaurant showed London that it was possible to work directly with farmers—and that the results would be not just better food, but also a stronger community beyond the restaurant. The River Café's recipes are famous for their simplicity, showing off the quality of the ingredients first and foremost.

Hugo cooked wood-grilled striped sea bass with salsa verde (featured on page 173), and a side of braised eggplant (or, as Hugo and the rest of Europe call it, aubergine). For dessert, he'd made fresh panna cotta with poached strawberries. After years of complex recipes like duck à l'orange (still one of my favorite French dishes), I was taken aback by how good his simple cooking was. I asked him if I could come work for him as a line cook.

I worked with Hugo at Mateo for $10 an hour and learned everything I could. He was a great manager and we got to know each other as friends outside of work. Jen and I started to look into opening the restaurant we'd been dreaming of, and it was only natural to ask him to join us in that venture.

My vision was of a little bistro serving exquisite, innovative plates, with a vibe that was less white tablecloths and dinner jackets and more like one of the lively, fun neighborhood restaurants I'd loved in New York. Jen wanted to create a space that would feel equally welcoming to a CEO and to a local carpenter hungry after a day's work. And Hugo's vision was to embrace our local farmers and expand our connections. Together we created The Kitchen, Boulder's Community Bistro. Located on beautiful West Pearl Street in downtown Boulder, our original restaurant is still kicking butt twenty years later.

The Kitchen, American Bistro, opened in March, 2004. We hit a nerve with Hugo's style of cooking and Jen's upscale yet easy design. For the first year, I was Hugo's sous-chef, and we both worked the line five to seven days a week. It was one of the most fun years of my life, and I still love watching our chefs on the line to this day. A year later, we decided to open the cocktail lounge, Upstairs. That was when I stepped back from the line to concentrate on growing the business. I had largely traded my life in tech for the culinary world, but I never lost my interest in and connection to Silicon Valley's kind of open-minded, "let's try it and see if it works" culture of innovation. To this day, I love a good cooking or bartending hack, and I encourage my chef teams to play around with ingredients and presentations, then bring the best results to our tasting and brainstorming sessions.

Meanwhile, Hugo was building trust with local farmers, getting them to agree to deliver fresh produce to our restaurant. We told them that as long as they delivered by 4 p.m., we'd get their food on the menu that evening. My main claim to fame back then was helping our farmers become more tech-savvy. I remember going to Best Buy with one of our farmers, helping him choose a computer, and then setting it up for him at his home. It seems funny to say, but going from paper orders and invoices to email was a game-changer for the farm-to-table movement.

FOR THE FIRST YEAR,
I WAS HUGO'S SOUS-CHEF,
AND WE BOTH WORKED THE LINE
FIVE TO SEVEN DAYS A WEEK.
IT WAS ONE OF THE
MOST FUN YEARS
OF MY LIFE.

We wrote a new menu every day back then. Hugo and I would look at the ingredients delivered from the farmers and start to browse cookbooks (The River Café's was one of our go-tos) and make up the day's menu. It was fun, and every day was a cooking adventure. We were cooking for our community—and we loved it!

We started supporting a local gardening organization in Boulder and volunteering on school planting days. Watching the kids plant a seed, then water and care for it as the green sprout emerged from the ground, was so moving for me. We were helping kids connect to real food and build a love for getting outside in the garden. Harvest days at schools were the best—seeing a kid pull out a huge orange carrot from the ground was like witnessing a magic trick. Inspired by this experience, Hugo and I co-founded Big Green (see page 120 for more info), which now supports hundreds of grassroots organizations around the country who believe growing food changes lives. Our goal is to get everyone in America growing food.

Another piece of our mission is to make the restaurant business as sustainable as we can. Early on, we connected with a company that takes our used frying oil and converts it to biodiesel. We were the first wind-powered business in Colorado. We also strive for a zero-waste kitchen—using ingredients creatively to minimize waste and composting whatever we can't use. In the beginning, these initiatives felt revolutionary. Today, thankfully, more and more restaurants are taking similar actions.

Now, twenty-plus years on, here I am writing a cookbook for our beloved guests and anyone who loves to cook for their friends and family. Jen has moved back to New York to focus on her art. Hugo has since retired. And The Kitchen keeps going in Boulder, Denver, Chicago, and (as this book goes to press) Austin, Texas. Each restaurant still has that feeling we hope to share with guests. First dates begin at The Kitchen, strangers become friends, and more than one marriage proposal has happened over a glass of bubbly and a shared plate of fries.

The Kitchen of today is defined by the joining of two incredible restaurateurs, Sam Hallak and Michael Bertozzi. After fifteen years of hands-on management, we brought on Sam to run operations and Michael to run culinary. Michael's food is influenced by his upbringing in Peru, which also has a strong Japanese community. Prior to joining The Kitchen in 2019 he was a top chef in Atlanta. Together, with our farm-to-table roots, his Peruvian/Japanese love for high-flavor shared plates and his Southern training, we serve up flavor-popping seasonal American shareable plates.

We love seasonal food because nothing beats fresh fish or ripe produce, American because we get to pick from the cuisines of the world and make them our own, and shared plates because breaking bread with your family and friends is a cornerstone of a good life.

One of my heroes is Anthony Bourdain. I actually went to his talk in New York in 2000 at the National Arts Club. He was really funny and entertaining. It's quite possible that his book, *Kitchen Confidential,* was the tipping point that made me enroll in cooking school. His advice is still what I live by today: Don't be afraid, get excited, and cook with love.

Enjoy!

Kimbal

"Pablo Picasso
once beautifully said,
'The meaning of life is to
find your gift. The purpose of
life is to give it away.'
I believe food is a gift we give
ourselves three times a day.
Cooking food for
others is a joy and a gift
I give my community."

Essential Tools for Your Kitchen

Every chef you ask will almost certainly have a different list of tools and kitchen equipment they rely on most—but only slightly different. Despite the thousands of appliances, gadgets, and traditional hand tools out there, the basic kit tends toward the minimal. If your home kitchen already has everything on this list, you're in good shape. If not, and if you're looking forward to cooking your way through this book with us, take a look at the items you're missing and think about adding them to your collection. Always go for the best-quality implements you can reasonably afford—reasonably being the key word. You don't need a $2,000 hand-wrought Damascus steel chef's knife (though they are pretty cool). But please don't buy your most important knife at the dollar store either. There's a wide world in the middle, and if you're unsure, check out recommendations and reviews online or visit a specialty cooking store to check out your options.

CHEF'S KNIFE: A classic chef's knife is 8 to 10 inches long, with a sharp point and wide, flat blade. This is the multitasking knife you'll rely on to chop vegetables, slice meat, chiffonade herbs, and even smash garlic with the flat of the blade. You want it to feel absolutely natural in your hand.

SILICONE SPATULA: There is almost nothing you can't cook with a silicone spatula. The flat edge at the bottom ensures you can scrape the bottom of the pan and the silicone texture lets you get the round sides of the pan. The silicone also is easy on nonstick pans and will make them last longer.

A THICK-BOTTOMED LARGE PAN: The thick bottom heats up evenly to relatively high temperatures and holds the heat well. Use a pan like this to sear meat, caramelize onions, stir-fry fresh veggies, or bake a frittata. Choose between cast iron or stainless steel, and don't pinch pennies.

BLENDER: A high-quality home blender is useful for so many applications beyond smoothies. You might also want to check out handheld immersion blenders, which can be used to puree and emulsify soups, sauces, and desserts right in the cooking or serving vessel.

FLAT-EDGED WOODEN SPOON: A humble, unassuming kitchen basic that can last for years with just a little care, the simple wooden spoon is invaluable for stirring, scraping, mixing, and serving. Flat-edged wooden spoons as opposed to rounded have the advantage of being better suited at scraping up the flavorful bits on the bottom of the pan.

METAL TONGS: Made from stainless steel,

these are indispensable for general kitchen tasks like flipping meats, handling veggies like asparagus, and picking up food from hot pans or the deep fryer. The good ones have rubber sides and tips and are worth the expense.

VEGETABLE PEELER:

The most versatile option is what's called a Y-peeler, with a sturdy, easy-to-grip handle and the blade held between two arms at the top (the Y). The setup allows you to exert varying pressure depending on whether you need to shave ribbons of cheese, slice a dainty strip of lemon rind, or peel a thick-skinned gourd.

NONSTICK SKILLET:

You can use your cast-iron pan for virtually every stovetop task, but a good nonstick pan is great for browning veggies, reducing sauces, and of course frying or scrambling eggs.

MEDIUM SAUCEPAN:

The absolute workhorse of a home kitchen, this is the pan you use to boil water or broth, warm up sauces, and just about everything else. Get one with a tight-fitting lid and sturdy enough construction that sauces can simmer without worry of burning.

MICROPLANE GRATER:

This handheld "rasp-style" zester is ideal for anything that needs to be grated very finely, such as garlic cloves, nutmeg, or fresh ginger. It's also excellent for zesting citrus and shaving fluffy clouds of Parmesan over a finished plate.

DIGITAL SCALE:

A digital food scale is useful in general, but especially so when you're in our baking section. Make sure and get one that can switch back and forth between metric and imperial measurements.

BOX GRATER:

This is your standard four-sided kitchen grater. It can be used to grate, zest, shred, or slice, depending on which side you use.

SPICE GRINDER:

Freshly ground spices are more brightly and deeply flavored than pre-ground ones. You can use a mortar and pestle to grind them old-school, but we like the small electric grinders that can often resemble coffee grinders.

FOOD PROCESSOR:

This multitasking utility player can save you time and effort grinding, chopping, mincing, kneading, pureeing, and much more.

STAND MIXER:

If you're planning to do much baking, pasta making, or other tasks that involve mixing dry and wet ingredients, even a lower-priced stand mixer can be a game-changer.

MEASURING SPOONS AND CUPS:

For dry ingredients, go for sturdy stainless-steel cups and spoons. Make sure they're clearly marked or stamped so that you'll be able to tell the measures apart even after they've been washed multiple times. For liquid measures, use a Pyrex measuring cup with a spout for easy pouring.

ROLLING PIN:

An old-fashioned solid wood rolling pin is your best choice as an all-around tool for rolling out dough of all sorts evenly.

LE CREUSET DUTCH OVEN:

Le Creuset makes a wide range of pans, but the Dutch oven is the one chefs consider indispensable for simmering, braising—even frying and baking bread.

You could say that the cocktail list is your first taste of where The Kitchen's spirit really shines. Anchored in the tried-and-true with some unexpected twists, our specialties are fresh, seasonal, innovative, inviting, and, most of all, tasty.

Nothing beats a well-made margarita when you are entertaining. You can make it in batches and it's the ultimate crowd-pleaser. We are proud of our Marg (page 38) at The Kitchen—a classic with a spin that brings in fresh orange juice for a drink that's as fresh as a summer afternoon.

My personal favorite is the "Perfect" Negroni recipe (page 47), which drinks more easily than a typical Negroni and works well mixed in batches for a larger group. "Perfect" is in quotes here because there is really no such thing as perfect, but after many years of experimenting, I like this recipe a lot and think you will too.

On the pages that follow, you'll find a selection of some of our favorite cocktails, which we hope will inspire you to start having your own gatherings at home. On that note, you'll also find batch recipes for entertaining in style and a blueprint for creating your own signature combinations. The evening is young. Put on your favorite tunes, mix up a glass of something wonderful, and step into The Kitchen.

Cocktails

Basic Bar Tools and Techniques

There's a mystique surrounding bartending that can be a little intimidating to the beginner—but it doesn't have to be. In the pages that follow, we'll demystify basic mixology, share some essential tools, give you the know-how you need to mix delicious drinks at home, and even develop your own signature cocktails. For starters, here's a quick roundup of the tools and techniques we use every day in The Kitchen's bar—and some hacks for mixing excellent drinks without them.

Handy all-in-one kits make setting up your home bar a breeze; look for them in any good cooking or specialty store or order a well-reviewed one online. Be sure that any kit you buy includes, at a minimum, a good quality stainless-steel Boston shaker (also referred to as a shaking tin), a double-jigger measure, fine and coarse strainers, a long bar spoon for mixing, and a pair of ice tongs.

To level up, a stirring beaker is a powerful addition to any bar setup. A heavy glass vessel with a handy pouring spout, these beakers make it easy to mix two or more drinks at once and decant them smoothly into individual glasses.

When it comes to crafting citrus garnishes, you'll want a good vegetable peeler at the very least. To take your garnish game up a notch, a channel knife (also known as a citrus zester) is the professional's choice.

As for glassware, ten different experts will likely give you ten different lists of essentials, but the basics are the same. Here's what we recommend:

WINEGLASS: Wine aficionados don't limit themselves to one type of glass, but for mixed drinks, the most basic one will do you right.

MARTINI GLASS: This iconic glass's conical shape allows the spirits to open up after pouring, while the long stem lets you hold your drink without your hands warming the glass—important since there's no ice to keep martinis and similar drinks chilled.

ROCKS: Also known as an old-fashioned glass, the rocks glass is a short, sturdy tumbler generally used for more spirit-forward drinks served over ice.

COUPE: Essentially a small, shallow bowl on a stem, the coupe is incredibly versatile. Originally created as a Champagne glass in the 1700s, it is now used for virtually any mixed drink served "up," which is to say not over ice. (For bubbly, however, a flute is your best option.)

HIGHBALL OR COLLINS GLASS: These are technically two different glass types, although they are similar enough that they're often used interchangeably. Tall and straight sided, both variations are perfect for mixed drinks involving soda or tonic because the shape preserves the carbonation.

Three Parts Make a Whole

n this chapter, you'll find recipes for some of our most beloved cocktails. But if there's one thing we hope you'll take away—even more than the recipes—it's a sense of fun and the freedom to experiment. Here's a simple, almost infinitely adaptable formula to get you started: Three parts make a whole. Almost any cocktail out there is made up of three main ingredients: the main spirit, the sweetener (often in the form of a liqueur), and the sour or bitter component. You can mix and match different spirits, syrups, and citrus juices within this formula to find combinations you like.

MIXING UP LARGE-BATCH COCKTAILS

When you shake a cocktail, you're not only mixing the ingredients but also chilling them and adding a last little bit of dilution to soften the edges of the spirit. For large-batch cocktails, you can get the same effect without shaking twenty margaritas one after another (or finding the world's largest mixing tin!). All it takes is a little math and some very cold water. Don't worry, you won't weaken the drinks by adding water, but you will save yourself a whole lot of shaking.

How much water to add? That's where the math comes in. A shaken cocktail gains about 30% more volume from the ice that breaks up in the shaker. To mimic this, total the volume of all the liquid ingredients in your batch, figure out what around 30% of that total would be, and then add that much water to your big batch. This accomplishes the dilution part of what shaking would do.

You don't have to be super-precise about any of this. If your guests prefer a stronger drink, know that it's easier to dilute a strong drink in the glass than to doctor the whole thing back up, so err on the side of slightly less dilution. Once you've figured out how much water to add, start with a little less and taste before proceeding. If it's still too strong, add another splash of water and mix well. Now pop the batch into the fridge so it's nice and cold when you serve it at your gathering.

SIMPLE SYRUP

Makes approximately ½ cup

¾ cup granulated sugar
¾ cup water

Put the sugar and water into a small saucepan and bring to a boil. Reduce to a simmer and stir for 1 to 2 minutes until the sugar dissolves completely. Remove from heat and let cool to room temperature before decanting into a covered jar. Keep your syrup refrigerated until you're ready to use. It will keep, tightly sealed in the refrigerator, for about a month.

You can size this recipe up or down as needed—just use equal measures of sugar and water and follow the same preparation method.

One fun hack is to replace the water in this recipe with an equal measure of tea to create an infused syrup. Just steep a tea bag in hot water, then use that as the water in this syrup recipe. Some of our favorite options include chamomile, mint, and chai, as their distinct flavors complement a range of spirits.

The Kitchen Martini

Manzanilla sherry to rinse
2 ounces (¼ cup) gin or vodka
¾ ounce (1½ tablespoons)
   dry vermouth
¼ ounce (1 tablespoon)
   Cocchi Americano
Lemon, to garnish

A great martini is a hallmark of any good restaurant. This recipe is the result of twenty years of experimentation. It is our special take on this absolute classic. The Cocchi Americano, an aromatized and fortified wine, adds a touch of bitter citrus, and the sherry brings a light nuttiness when you raise the glass for that first sip. Pick your gin based on how floral you like it, and your vodka on how smooth and neutral it is. However you make it, this martini is delicious.

1. Grab your favorite martini or coupe glass and pour just a splash of the sherry into it. Roll it around to coat the glass's interior, then discard any excess that has pooled in the bottom.

2. Combine all of the other ingredients in a stirring beaker with ice and stir until thoroughly chilled, about 40 seconds. Strain the drink into your glass and garnish with a lemon swath, rolled up and neatly pinned with a cocktail pick, before you drop it into the glass (see sidebar).

While spirits like gin and vodka have a virtually infinite shelf life, that's not the case with fortified wines, which contain less alcohol. The vermouth, Cocchi Americano, and sherry will keep only for about a month in the fridge once opened. If you really love your martinis, or are planning drinks for a party, you'll be able to use the bottles up quickly. Otherwise, if you have one of these fortified wines hanging out in your fridge for a while, take a whiff first; if it smells off, discard it.

CUTTING A ZEST GARNISH

A citrus garnish twist dresses up the glass while also adding a subtle pop of flavor to your cocktail. A twist can range from the simple to the elaborate, depending on the drink and your personal sense of style. A lemon swath, rolled and twisted over your drink, adds a hit of aromatic complexity and deliciousness. Here's how to do it right.

Using a channel knife or vegetable peeler, cut a swath of peel approximately 1 inch wide by 2 inches long. Try to avoid getting too much of the bitter white pith along with the yellow peel. Hold the swath over your glass with the peel side facing the surface of the cocktail, then gently twist and squeeze the peel to express the citrus oils into your glass. To serve, neatly roll the swath up, skewer it with a cocktail pick, and drop it lightly into the drink.

Almost Summer

½ ounce (1 tablespoon) Aperol

½ ounce (1 tablespoon)
St-Germain

½ ounce (1 tablespoon)
Lillet Blanc

½ ounce (1 tablespoon)
lemon juice

½ ounce (1 tablespoon)
Simple Syrup (page 25)

Club soda, chilled, to finish

Fresh orange, to garnish

This refreshing and easy-drinking cocktail is our take on the Aperol spritz, a sparkling drink invented in Venice and sipped throughout Italy when the languid heat of summer approaches. Here, we add some springtime notes with uniquely floral St-Germain liqueur, crafted from hand-picked elderflowers. Crisp, light Lillet Blanc lends subtle herbal and citrus flavors, while club soda brings the fizz.

1. This festive, sparkling drink might seem like it belongs in a champagne flute, but serving it in a wineglass gives the flavors room to shine. Fill a standard wineglass about halfway full of ice, then add the alcoholic ingredients, lemon juice, and simple syrup. Give it a good stir, then top off with club soda.

2. To make the garnish, use a vegetable peeler to cut a swath of orange peel approximately 1 inch wide and 2 inches long. Fold and squeeze the swath, with the peel side facing the glass, to express the citrus oils for added aromatic complexity and deliciousness, then drop it in the glass.

APERITIVO WITH FRIENDS

Italians tend to drink their spritzes in the evening after work with some light snacks. This is their version of happy hour, the aperitivo. If you have a garden or deck, head out there. If not, bring the springtime inside with fresh flowers and seasonal shared plates. This recipe yields ten cocktails; you can scale it up as large as you need for your party, just use equal amounts of each ingredient.

5 ounces (½ cup +
2 tablespoons) Aperol

5 ounces (½ cup +
2 tablespoons) St-Germain

5 ounces (½ cup +
2 tablespoons) Lillet Blanc

5 ounces (½ cup +
2 tablespoons) lemon juice

5 ounces (½ cup +
2 tablespoons) Simple Syrup
(page 25)

Club soda, to finish

Fresh oranges, for garnish

1. Combine the alcoholic ingredients, lemon juice, and simple syrup in a large pitcher and stir well. To serve, fill wineglasses about halfway full of ice, then pour about 2½ ounces (1/3 cup) over the ice (about half a standard wine pour), top with club soda, and garnish with orange swaths (see step 2 above) if desired. (You can skip this step if you want to get back to the party. We promise nobody will mind.)

These days, Jen Lewin is an internationally known artist whose interactive light sculptures exist at the intersection of art, technology, conservation, and collective action. Her background is in architecture, robotics, and art, and her mission is "Connecting Community Through Art." Jen's work is not only beautiful but also deeply entwined with sustainability and creative reuse. This is true when the medium is 22,000 pounds of plastic trash gathered from polluted beaches for the massive, immersive piece *The Last Ocean,* and it's true of the reclaimed wood in The Kitchen's upcycled fixtures. When Jen, Kimbal, and Hugo founded The Kitchen in Boulder, one of Jen's guiding principles was to create a place where a Fortune 500 CEO and a local farmer would feel equally welcome. The spaces are open, friendly, and unpretentious. Fans of her art might be most drawn to the gorgeous lighting design, but her handiwork is everywhere. Though she and Kimbal are no longer a couple, she's still a close friend and you can see her ongoing influence in the beautiful chandelier lights at all The Kitchen restaurants.

SHINE
A LIGHT

A Little Farther Southside

1¼ ounces (2½ tablespoons) pisco

¾ ounce (1½ tablespoons) cachaça

¾ ounce (1½ tablespoons) lime juice

¾ ounce (1½ tablespoons) Simple Syrup (page 25)

3 or 4 mint leaves, plus sprig of mint, to garnish

Club soda, to finish

Fresh lime wheel, to garnish

THE OG

Curious about how Al Capone drank his Southside? Leave out the pisco, cachaça, and club soda, and instead substitute 2 ounces (about a quarter cup) of your favorite gin. Enjoy over ice, remember to pay your taxes, and try to stay off the FBI's Most Wanted list.

Al Capone, Chicago's most famous gangster, ruled the city's South Side during Prohibition. Legend has it that his gang's favorite way to enjoy their bathtub gin was in a sweet cocktail they called a Southside. This riff on that drink gives a shout-out to The Kitchen's Windy City location, but with spirits from just a little farther south. How far? Well, we combine pisco, a Peruvian brandy that dates back to the sixteenth century, with cachaça, a Brazilian spirit made from sugar cane. Together, they add wild, brambly fruit notes to this unique cocktail.

1. Fill a rocks or collins glass with ice immediately before mixing your cocktail.

2. Next, combine the spirits, lime juice, syrup, and mint leaves in a mixing tin with ice to fill. Cover and shake thoroughly for about 10 seconds, then strain into your glass.

3. Top it with a couple splashes of club soda and give it a quick stir; garnish with the lime wheel. The amount of club soda is up to you. More soda yields a lighter and longer drink while with less you get a brighter and punchier drink. Start with a light hand and increase as desired, tasting with each splash to find the right balance. Crafting the perfect cocktail often involves a fair bit of sampling. We've never heard anyone complain about that requirement.

Picnic with Hemingway

This play on a classic daiquiri leans into fresh basil's floral qualities while balancing a sweet and spicy ginger liqueur (we like Domaine de Canton or Stirrings) with aromatic Suze bitters for a touch of spice and bitter citrus. The pineapple juice cuts through it all to keep things easy and fun, with a tropical flair.

1. Rip the 4 basil leaves in half and toss them into the mixing tin before adding the rest of the ingredients, then fill the rest of the tin halfway with ice.
2. Cover and shake thoroughly, for about 10 seconds, then pour through a fine strainer into a martini glass.
3. Float a whole basil leaf on top of the drink and enjoy, preferably in the company of cats.

4 leaves Thai basil, plus one additional leaf per drink for garnish

1 ounce (2 tablespoons) white rum

½ ounce (1 tablespoon) ginger liqueur

½ ounce (1 tablespoon) Suze gentian liqueur

¾ ounce (1½ tablespoons) lime juice

½ ounce (1 tablespoon) pineapple juice

½ ounce (1 tablespoon) simple syrup

KNOW WHEN TO STIR In most cases, liquor-forward drinks such as martinis are stirred for best results, and drinks featuring fruit juices and strongly flavored mixers are shaken.

SHAKE IT UP Pour your ingredients into the shaking tin, fill the rest of it with ice, and make sure the top is on securely. Keeping one hand on the tin's top half, grab the bottom with your other hand. Holding it at shoulder height, shake vigorously for a count of ten or until the outside of the shaker is cold and frosty.

STRAIN AFTER MIXING Shaking your drink with ice chills it to the perfect temperature and barely dilutes it. You'll want to strain out any remaining ice before it melts any further, so have a strainer and glass waiting for you to pour the drink right away. Discard any ice shards in the strainer and dump out whatever remains in the tin. If the drink is to be served over ice, strain it over fresh cubes—never over the dregs from the shaker.

KEEP IT CHILL Every drink looks more elegant, keeps cold longer, and tastes brighter and stronger when served in a well-chilled glass. Pop glasses into the freezer at least 30 minutes, or up to 2 hours, before you need them. Pull them out one at a time just before mixing each guest's drink for optimal chill. We like to chill our rocks glasses as well—both for uniform fanciness and to keep the ice from melting too quickly and diluting the drink.

A LITTLE FARTHER SOUTHSIDE
ZERO-PROOF PINEAPPLE SPLASH
PICNIC WITH HEMINGWAY

KIMBAL'S INFINITE PLAYLIST

Walking into The Kitchen feels like a gently immersive experience. We welcome our community in with a warm, friendly light-bathed space, wonderful smells, the hum of a dozen or more lively conversations, and always an intriguing soundtrack. We work with music professionals who help us curate the restaurant's playlist, based on songs that Kimbal has chosen over the years, with community input, to subtly set a mood that's fun and upbeat without distracting too much from the important matters at hand—friends and food. Scan this code to check out our current Spotify playlist and start it up for your guests if you like. Or make your own mix to get pumped up while you cook, and a slightly mellower set for dining and conversation.

Zero-Proof Strawberry Fizz

1 ounce (2 tablespoons)
    Strawberry Thyme Syrup
    (recipe follows)
1 ounce (2 tablespoons) lime juice
2 ounces (¼ cup) ginger beer
2 ounces (¼ cup) club soda
Lemon wheel, to garnish
Thyme sprig, to garnish

We review our drinks menu seasonally, and we'll always keep the menu flexible enough to take advantage of the best local produce. One year, everything just came together—we were ready to refresh the zero-proof menu for summer right as the most amazing strawberry season began. That inspired our Strawberry-Thyme Syrup, a community favorite that tastes like pure, unfiltered summer.

1. Start by filling a rocks or Collins glass with ice. Next, combine the syrup and lime juice in a mixing tin. Add ice to fill, cover, and shake thoroughly for about 10 seconds. Strain into your glass, top with the ginger beer and club soda, and give it a quick stir to fully incorporate all of the flavors. Garnish with a lemon wheel and a sprig of thyme slid into the glass and serve.

STRAWBERRY THYME SYRUP

1 pound frozen strawberries
⅓ ounce (about 3 tablespoons
    torn) fresh thyme sprigs
16 ounces (2 cups) water
2 cups granulated sugar

1. Roughly chop the strawberries, then place them in a pot with the thyme. Add the water and bring to a boil. Once a boil is reached, reduce heat to a simmer, cover, and let simmer for 45 minutes, stirring occasionally. A white foam may develop on the surface. This is normal—just grab a large spoon and scoop it away as needed.

2. After 45 minutes, add the sugar. Increase the heat to medium-high and stir until sugar has fully incorporated, then remove from heat and strain into a container with a tight-fitting lid, such as a mason jar. The syrup will keep tightly sealed in the refrigerator for up to a month.

IT'S PARTY THYME!

Mix up a batch of Strawberry Fizz for a brunch or garden party. Or bring the components to a picnic and assemble the drinks fresh for friends and family. This recipe yields ten cocktails, and you can scale it up as large as you need for your party; just multiply each ingredient by the same number to keep the proportions balanced.

1. Combine the syrup, lime juice, and water in a large container and chill in the fridge for about an hour or until cold. For each serving, pour approximately 2½ ounces (about a third of a cup) of the chilled mixture over ice, top with club soda and ginger beer, and enjoy! For more on this batch technique, see page 24.

10 ounces (1¼ cups)
Strawberry Thyme Syrup
(recipe on preceding page)
10 ounces (1¼ cups) lime juice
6 ounces (¾ cup) water
Ginger beer, to finish
Club soda, to finish

Zero-Proof Pineapple Splash

¾ ounce (1½ tablespoons)
pineapple juice
¾ ounce (1½ tablespoons)
cranberry juice
¾ ounce (1½ tablespoons)
lemon juice
¾ ounce (1½ tablespoons)
Agave Syrup (page 38)
Club soda, to top
Rosemary sprig, to garnish
Lemon wheel, to garnish

With its refreshing interplay of sweet and tart fruit juices, aromatic fresh rosemary, and a bright hit of citrus, this is the playful yet sophisticated nonalcoholic sipper you've been looking for. We use agave syrup as an all-natural vegan sweetener that's twice as sweet as sugar, making it a tasty option for anyone trying to cut down on sugar and processed carbs. You can purchase agave syrup in well-stocked grocery stores, online, or use the recipe on page 38 to make it fresh in small batches.

▼

Fill a wineglass halfway with ice. Next, combine the pineapple, cranberry, lemon juices, and syrup in a mixing tin with ice. Cover and shake for about 10 seconds. Strain into the wineglass and top with about 2 ounces (¼ cup) of club soda, or to taste, depending on whether you prefer a lighter drink or one with brighter and punchier flavors. Garnish with a sprig of rosemary and a lemon wheel, then enjoy!

The Kitchen Marg

Kosher salt

Fresh lime wedge

Lime wheel, to garnish

Orange wedge, to garnish

2 ounces (¼ cup) blanco tequila

1 ounce (2 tablespoons) lime juice

½ ounce (1 tablespoon)
   Agave Syrup (recipe follows)

¼ ounce (½ tablespoon)
   orange juice

Nothing says party like a pitcher of margaritas. Get the fiesta started with a single, perfect marg (as we like to call them for short) for yourself, or dive right in with the friends-and-family-ready batch recipe below. The version we serve at The Kitchen uses house-made agave syrup and a little fresh OJ instead of Cointreau or triple sec, which makes for a lighter, brighter, and tastier drink.

1. To rim the glass, pour out a little kosher salt onto a small plate, then take your favorite rocks glass, moisten the rim with a lime wedge, and dip half of it onto the plate to coat.

2. Fill the glass with ice, then slide your lime wheel and orange wedge down the glass's side so that the ice will hold the garnishes neatly in place.

3. Combine the rest of the ingredients in a mixing tin with ice to fill, then cover and shake for about 10 seconds.

4. Strain into your prepped rocks glass and serve. For extra style points, submerge half of each citrus garnish in the cocktail and leave half above the surface. (Alternatively, if you prefer your Marg served up, as pictured at right, then strain into a chilled martini glass that has been rimmed with salt.)

AGAVE SYRUP

Light agave nectar

Water

You can buy agave syrup in most health food and grocery stores, but this fresh version is easy to make, and in the precise quantity you want. Note that the terms "agave nectar" and "agave syrup" are often used interchangeably by importers and bottlers, so check to be sure what you're buying is pure, light agave nectar.

1. Combine equal parts water and light agave nectar in a medium saucepan and heat over medium-high, stirring until totally incorporated. It will keep tightly sealed and refrigerated for up to 1 month.

HERE'S HOW TO SCALE IT UP

THE BIG BATCH MARG

20 ounces (2½ cups) blanco tequila

10 ounces (1¼ cups) lime juice

5 ounces (½ cup + 2 tablespoons) Agave Syrup (page 38)

2½ ounces (4½ tablespoons) orange juice

11¼ ounces (1¼ cups + 2½ tablespoons) water

Now is the time to break out your favorite pitcher. (We love our colorful ceramic ones from Mexico.) This recipe yields ten cocktails and is easy to scale up as large as you need for your party—no fancy math required. Just multiply each ingredient by the same number (so if you want to make twenty margaritas, for example, you'll want 5 cups of tequila, 2½ cups of lime juice, and so on).

1. Combine all of the ingredients in a large container, then chill in the fridge until very cold, at least an hour. Rim your glasses as described above, add ice, and pour a little more than 4 ounces (a half cup) over the ice. ¡Salud!

Kanroku Manhattan #3

1¼ ounces (2½ tablespoons) mezcal

¾ ounce (1½ tablespoons) Japanese whiskey

½ ounce (1 tablespoon) Pedro Ximénez sherry

¼ ounce (½ tablespoon) Amaro Nonino

¼ ounce (½ tablespoon) sweet vermouth

Lemon, to garnish

The classic Manhattan is a simple, whiskey-forward drink that's been an American favorite since the 1880s. Here, we take it on the road for a little smoky and spicy kick from Mexican mezcal and Japanese whiskey. Amaro Nonino, a bitter liqueur made from grappa, adds citrus notes to complement the spirits' smoke, while the sherry and vermouth soften and sweeten it all with beautiful hints of chocolate and raspberry.

1. Combine all of the ingredients in a stirring beaker with ice to fill and stir for about 40 seconds. Strain into your favorite martini glass, garnish with a lemon flag (see below) resting on the rim, and serve.

LEMON FLAG

To make a lemon flag, start by cutting a lemon swath (page 26), then use a small, sharp knife to cut it into a trapezoidal shape, with a small incision in the middle. Hold the flag over your drink and pinch it gently to express lemon oil across the cocktail. Finish by folding it in half peel-side out and place it on the rim of the martini glass, using the incision in the middle to hold it in place.

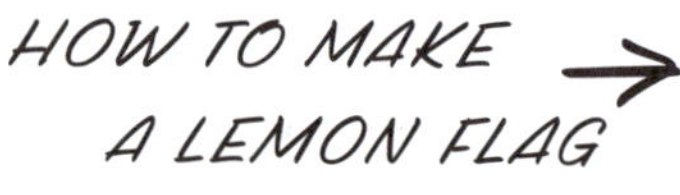

Coffee with Alexander

1¼ ounces (2½ tablespoons) brandy

¾ ounce (1½ tablespoons) Kahlúa

¾ ounce (1½ tablespoons) Frangelico

¼ ounce (½ tablespoon) heavy cream

1 egg white (see opposite page for technique)

Ground nutmeg, to garnish

Finely ground coffee, to garnish

Lemon, to garnish

A classic Brandy Alexander gets its sweetness from crème de cacao; here, we've replaced the chocolate liqueur with Kahlúa and Frangelico. The resulting drink is like a hazelnut cappuccino that is truly living its best life. Shaking up an egg white with the ingredients creates a beautiful soft foam that feels amazing on the tongue and provides a sumptuous bed for the nutmeg-and-coffee garnish. Any good brandy will work here; we like to use St-Rémy VSOP.

1. Combine the brandy, both liqueurs, the heavy cream, and the egg white in a mixing tin, fill with ice, then cover and shake for about 20 seconds.

2. Separate the two tins and strain the cocktail from one to the other. Dump the ice out of the first tin, then put them back together and shake again without any ice (what bartenders call a "dry shake") for another 30 seconds. Then separate the tins again and pour through a fine strainer into a martini glass.

The dry shake is the step that yields that nice pillow of foamy egg white on the top of your drink. The harder you shake, the thicker that pillow will be, so experiment a bit to get it the way you like.

3. Garnish with a pinch each of nutmeg and finely ground coffee sprinkled lightly over the foam. (If you don't have any ground coffee, ground cinnamon is a good substitute.)

4. To finish off the cocktail, cut a long, thin strip of lemon peel, rotating the fruit over your drink as you cut in a spiral around the widest part of its midsection (keep going to create a longer spiral if you're feeling fancy!). As soon as you begin to cut, you will see citrus oils practically jumping off the peel, and you want to shower your drink in that beautiful aromatic oil.

5. Take your strip of lemon peel and twirl it into a spring-shaped coil with your hands, applying a bit of pressure to help keep it twisty. If you want a tighter spring shape, wrap the cut strip of peel around a chopstick, press, and then slide the chopstick out. Rest the garnish on the rim of the glass, so that most of it is floating lightly across the surface of the drink.

SEPARATING YOUR EGG WHITES

Separating an egg white from its yolk may seem tricky if you've never done it before, but once you learn how, you'll be looking for excuses to make meringues and custards just to wow friends and family with your mad skills. Both of the methods below are equally good; it's really just a matter of which you prefer.

Gently crack an egg on the rim of a small glass or metal bowl, rotating it to create an even line around the center. Once you have created a good crack, hold the egg over the bowl and gently separate the top of the shell from the bottom, making sure that the yolk remains nestled in the bottom shell. The white should naturally drain into the bowl. To make sure you get it all, carefully pass the yolk from shell to shell until all of the white has separated into the bowl.

Alternatively, crack the shell in half as in the method above. This time, carefully deposit the entire egg into the bowl, making sure not to break the yolk. Using your dominant hand, gently scoop up the yolk with your ring, middle, and index fingers and hold it over the bowl. Your fingers will act like a strainer, keeping the yolk suspended on your hand while the white slides between your fingers and back into the bowl.

LEARN HOW TO SEPARATE YOUR EGG WHITES

THE KITCHEN
MARTINI
KANROKU
MANHATTAN #3

COFFEE W/
ALEXANDER

BARTENDER'S CHOICE:
Kimbal's Perfect Negroni
THIS APERITIVO WILL "OPEN UP" YOUR APPETITE.

Kimbal's Perfect Negroni

As you might have read in this chapter's introduction, Kimbal has been experimenting with this classic Italian cocktail for years. There is no such thing as a perfect Negroni, which is part of the fun. But, as of the writing of this book, Kimbal thinks this is about as good as it gets. Unlike our other recipes, the specific brands and ingredients in the recipe really matter.

Negronis usually contain equal parts gin, Campari, and semi-sweet vermouth. This version replaces the Campari with a more bitter digestif made in Colorado by the Leopold Brothers. The Cappelletti, made with a secret family recipe in Italy for generations, balances out this increased bitterness and brings in a delightful flavor not found in your standard Negroni. Dolin's dry vermouth mellows it out, for an easy-drinking summer afternoon cocktail.

Fill a rocks glass with ice, then combine the liquid ingredients in a stirring beaker with ice and stir thoroughly for about 40 seconds. Strain the Negroni into the prepared glass with fresh ice. (Alternatively, if you prefer your Negroni served up, then strain into a chilled glass without ice.) Garnish with a twist of orange (page 26 for technique) on the rim, just dipping down into the drink, and serve.

1 ounce (2 tablespoons) CapRock gin

½ ounce (1 tablespoon) Leopold Bros. aperitivo

½ ounce (1 tablespoon) Aperitivo Cappelletti

¾ ounce (1½ tablespoon) Dolin's dry vermouth

¼ ounce (½ tablespoon) Dolin's sweet vermouth

Orange twist, for garnish

WATCH HOW TO MAKE AN ORANGE TWIST

NEGRONIS FOR ALL!

For a sophisticated, convivial gathering, mix up a pitcher of Negronis for your guests. For the cocktail hour, Italians often enjoy their Negronis paired with a charcuterie board, since salty meats and mature cheeses like pecorino or blue cheese play nicely with the cocktail's bitter notes. This recipe will yield ten cocktails.

1. Combine all of the ingredients in a large container and chill in the fridge for about an hour or until cold. For each drink, serve approximately 4 ounces (½ cup) over ice and enjoy the party.

10 ounces (1¼ cups) CapRock gin

5 ounces (¾ cup) Leopold Bros. aperitivo

1 cup water

5 ounces (¾ cup) Aperitivo Cappelletti

7½ ounces (just under a cup) Dolin's dry vermouth

2½ ounces (a bit over a quarter cup) Dolin's sweet vermouth

GIFFARD
CACAO
KAHLÚA
THE ORIGINAL
BAR BOOK
The Comprehensive Guide
TO OVER 1,000 COCKTAILS

Thinking back to that first meal Chef Hugo cooked for me (see story on page 64), the whole sea bass was delicious, but it was the salsa verde that really took it up a level. Bright green and herbal, with just the right amount of salt from the anchovies, it was surprising and delightful. We want you to learn how to level up your cooking like this, to surprise and delight everyone at your table. If there is any section you should spend extra time on in this book, this is it. The sauce, condiment, and topping recipes in this chapter will help you add incredible flavor and zing to anything you cook—from this book and beyond. These flavor boosters provide a fun way to impress your guests and turn even the simplest snack into something unforgettable.

Every recipe in this chapter is used in one or more recipes in the book, but we urge you not to stop there. Is the Roasted Garlic Aioli (page 59) a perfect accompaniment to our Steak Tartare (page 216)? Absolutely. Is it also an excellent dip for vegetables or french fries? Do we even need to ask?

We give you the tools you need to customize almost everything based on your preferences, lifestyle, or dietary needs. Build a meal plan around the cooking of one basic dish—a whole roasted chicken or a head of cauliflower, for example—and dress it up differently every day of the week.

Condiments, Toppings & Sauces

Bright & Herbal

I t seems like every culinary culture around the world has its favorite herb-forward sauces. They offer brightly flavored ways to dress up a neutral staple like pasta or bread and, when shimmering with vinegar, they can serve to offset rich cuts of meat. These are some of our favorite global variations on the green theme.

GREEN OLIVE–LEMON SALMORIGLIO

A staple Sicilian and Calabrian condiment frequently served with fish, salmoriglio gets an extra depth of flavor in our version thanks to the addition of preserved lemons and green olives.

Makes about 1 cup

3 preserved lemons
1 cup Castelvetrano olives, pitted and roughly chopped
¼ cup finely chopped fresh parsley
¼ cup finely chopped fresh oregano
½ teaspoon red chile flakes
½ cup extra-virgin olive oil

1. Slice the preserved lemons in half, remove the seeds and flesh, then finely dice the peels.

2. Combine the remaining ingredients in a medium bowl, add the preserved lemon peels, and stir to thoroughly combine. Cover and refrigerate until ready to use. Remove from the refrigerator 1 hour before serving. The salmoriglio can be made ahead; it will keep tightly sealed and refrigerated for up to a month.
• TRY THIS WITH
Salmon with White Bean Ragout (page 164)

ARUGULA PESTO

Keep this one thick and creamy if you're using it on our gnocchetti (page 126), to ensure the right consistency once you stir in the cream. Otherwise, if you're using it as a dip, loosen it up a bit by adding olive oil and/or lemon juice to taste.

Makes about 1 cup

4 ounces arugula
4 ounces Parmesan cheese, grated (1 cup plus 3 scant tablespoons)
¾ cup (2 ounces) walnuts, toasted
2 garlic cloves, peeled
3 tablespoons fresh lemon juice, or to taste
½ teaspoon salt, or to taste
½ cup extra-virgin olive oil

Combine the arugula, cheese, walnuts, garlic, lemon juice, and salt in a food processor and process until smooth. With the motor running, slowly add the oil through the hole in the lid and continue to process until smooth. Taste and add more salt and/or lemon juice if needed. You can make the pesto 2 to 3 days ahead of using it.
• TRY THIS WITH:
The Kitchen Gnocchetti Plate (page 126)

CHIMICHURRI

Argentina's favorite condiment is popular throughout Latin America and beyond as a topping for steaks and roasted sausages, poultry, and seafood.

Makes about 2 cups

3 shallots, chopped
1 Fresno chile, seeded
    and chopped
3 garlic cloves, smashed
    and peeled
1 bunch cilantro, leaves and
    tender stems chopped
1 bunch flat-leaf parsley,
    leaves chopped
2 tablespoons fresh
    oregano leaves
1 teaspoon salt, or to taste
1½ cups extra-virgin olive oil
3 tablespoons red wine vinegar,
    or to taste

Combine the shallots, chiles, garlic, cilantro, parsley, oregano, salt, and 1 cup of the oil in a food processor and process until the ingredients are finely chopped to a uniform texture. With the motor running, slowly pour in the remaining ½ cup oil through the hole in the lid, then add the vinegar and pulse a few times to combine. Taste and add more salt and/or vinegar if needed. Chimichurri will keep tightly sealed and refrigerated for up to 2 weeks.

• TRY THIS WITH
Grilled Kansas City Strip Steak (page 225)
Whole Roast Chicken (page 177)

SALSA VERDE

We use this Italian green sauce to top meats, spread on sandwiches, and anywhere else we would like its intense flavors.

Makes about 1 cup

1 cup lightly packed fresh
    flat-leaf parsley leaves
½ cup lightly packed
    fresh oregano leaves
2 tablespoons brined capers,
    drained then minced
½ (2-ounce) can anchovies
    in oil, drained
Zest of 1 lemon
½ teaspoon red chile flakes
2 medium garlic cloves
2 tablespoons red wine vinegar
1 cup extra-virgin olive oil
Salt & freshly ground black
    pepper

1. Bunch the parsley leaves together using your non-dominant hand and carefully tuck your fingers inwards. Slice the parsley finely, making sure not to cut back through it multiple times, which would mince it. What you're looking for is thin ribbons (aka a chiffonade). Cut the oregano into a fine chiffonade in the same manner. Place the herbs in a medium bowl, then add the minced capers.

2. Finely chop the anchovy fillets, then use the flat side of your knife to smash the fillets against the cutting board to form a paste. Continue gathering and smashing the anchovy fillets until they are smooth. Scrape the anchovy paste off the cutting board with your knife, place it in the bowl with the herbs and capers, then add the lemon zest and chile flakes.

3. Using a Microplane, grate the garlic cloves into the mixture, starting with the tip end and discarding the root end. Stir in the vinegar, then whisk in the oil until you have a smooth, homogenous mixture. The salsa verde will keep tightly covered and refrigerated for up to 2 days.

• TRY THIS WITH:
Creamy Burrata and Grilled Sourdough Focaccia (page 103)
Charred Bass (page 173)
Whole Roast Chicken (page 177)
Pulled Pork (page 201)
Peruvian Lamb Sirloin over Hominy (page 211)

HACK: Blitz all the ingredients in a food processor, pulsing a few times to keep it a rough chop of the herbs.

TAMARIND CHUTNEY
SALSA VERDE
CHIMICHURRI
ROMESCO
SALMO-RIGLIO
SALSA ROJA
TOMATO JAM

Tomatoes for All Seasons

Tomatoes make a wonderful base for sauces and condiments because they preserve and can so well, letting you enjoy the taste of summer all year long.

ROMESCO

Catalonian fishermen have been using this smoky, complex sauce for centuries with seafood. As its popularity spread throughout Spain and beyond, many chefs have discovered how it enhances their favorite fish as well as poultry, meats, and vegetables.

Makes about 2 cups

1 Roma tomato (about 5 ounces)

3 garlic cloves, peeled

2 Fresno chiles, seeded

1 small yellow onion, roughly chopped

¼ cup almonds

⅓ cup extra-virgin olive oil

4 ounces piquillo chiles or roasted red bell pepper

¼ cup Focaccia (page 231) or other bread scraps (stale is fine)

2 tablespoons sherry vinegar, or to taste

1 teaspoon smoked paprika

1 teaspoon salt, or to taste

1. Preheat the oven to 325°F.

2. Place the tomato, garlic, Fresno chiles, onion, and almonds on a baking sheet and roast, stirring once or twice, until the almonds, onion, and garlic are browned and the chiles and tomatoes are slightly wrinkled, 20 to 30 minutes. Remove from the oven and cool completely.

3. Transfer to a blender, add the remaining ingredients, and blend until almost smooth; you want to retain a little texture. Taste and add more salt and/or vinegar if needed. The romesco will keep tightly covered and refrigerated for up to 3 weeks.

• TRY THIS WITH: *Grilled Ranch Steak and Catalan Spinach (page 218)*

TOMATO JAM

Preserve the very spirit of summer tomatoes with this savory jam that enlivens everything you top with it, from grilled cheese to scrambled eggs to lentil soup.

Makes about 3 cups

1 tablespoon grapeseed or other neutral oil

1 medium yellow onion, roughly chopped

4 garlic cloves, roughly chopped

⅓ cup white wine

3 tablespoons sherry vinegar, or to taste

2 quarts campari or cherry tomatoes, chopped

Zest of 1 lemon

Juice of ½ lemon

½ cup packed light or dark brown sugar, or to taste

¼ teaspoon salt, or to taste

1. Heat the oil in a large saucepan over medium heat. Add the onion and garlic and cook for about

Continued

5 minutes, until softened without taking on any color. Add the wine and vinegar, raise the heat, and cook until most of the liquid has evaporated, about 5 minutes.

2. Add the tomatoes, lemon zest, lemon juice, and brown sugar. Bring to a simmer and cook for about 30 minutes, until the tomatoes have completely broken down and the mixture has thickened to a jam consistency with the oil starting to separate out.

3. Transfer to a blender and blend until smooth. Taste and add more salt, sugar, or vinegar if needed to get a good balance of flavor. Cool completely. The tomato jam will keep tightly covered and refrigerated for up to a week.

- TRY THIS WITH
  Beef Short Ribs with Taleggio Cream (page 217)

SALSA ROJA

The centerpiece of our chilaquiles (page 184), salsa roja is a spicy take on a tomato sauce that can enliven any Tex-Mex dish or serve as an unexpectedly piquant pasta sauce.

Makes about 6 cups

2 jalapeño chiles

4 dried guajillo chiles (about ½ ounce)

2 tablespoons grapeseed or other neutral oil

1 large onion, cut into medium dice

¼ cup thinly sliced garlic

1 teaspoon ground coriander

1 teaspoon ground cumin

1 teaspoon chile powder

2 (28-ounce) cans diced San Marzano tomatoes

2 teaspoons salt, or to taste

½ teaspoon freshly ground black pepper

1. Heat a cast-iron skillet or other heavy pan over medium-high heat and, when hot, add the jalapeño chiles and pan-roast them, turning them with tongs until they are well-charred on all sides, about 10 minutes. Remove the charred jalapeño chiles to a bowl, cover with a heat-safe plate, and leave for about 5 minutes to steam. Add the dried guajillo chiles to the pan and cook until they darken in color, flipping them a few times, about 3 minutes. Remove from the pan. Peel the charred skin from the jalapeños, remove the stems and seeds, and roughly chop them. Remove the stems from the guajillo chiles, remove the seeds, and tear the chiles into pieces.

2. In a medium saucepan, heat the oil over medium heat. Add the onions and garlic. Cook until the onions are translucent without taking on any color, about 5 minutes. Add the coriander, cumin, and chile powder; cook for 2 minutes. Add the tomatoes. Rinse out the tomato cans with a couple of tablespoons of water and add this to the pan. Add the jalapeño chiles, guajillo chiles, salt, and pepper and bring to a simmer. Cover and simmer for 1 hour, then puree with an immersion blender on high speed or in a regular blender or food processor until smooth. Taste and adjust the salt if needed.

3. The salsa keeps tightly covered and refrigerated for 3 to 5 days and can be frozen for up to 6 months.

- TRY THIS WITH:
  Chilaquiles with Chicken (page 184)

Aiolis & Mayos

Garlic-spiked aioli is what your ordinary mayonnaise wants to be when it grows up. And plain mayo, boosted with other flavors, is an equally versatile condiment. The range of possible embellishments is almost infinite, limited only by your imagination and the ingredients you have at hand. Use these anywhere you'd use any other mayo—in sandwiches, to top meats and vegetables, or as a dip.

COMEBACK SAUCE

Makes about ¾ cup

½ cup mayonnaise

2 tablespoons Heinz Chili Sauce

1 tablespoon ketchup

1½ teaspoons fresh lemon juice

⅛ teaspoon smoked paprika

½ teaspoon Worcestershire sauce

⅛ teaspoon hot sauce

¼ teaspoon garlic powder

¼ teaspoon onion powder

¼ teaspoon mustard powder

¼ teaspoon salt

⅛ teaspoon freshly ground black
   pepper

Combine all the ingredients in a small bowl and whisk until fully incorporated. The sauce will keep tightly covered and refrigerated for up to 2 weeks.

• TRY THIS WITH
The Kitchen Burger (page 221)
The Kitchen Fries (page 80)

YUZU KOSHO MAYO

We love the big flavor of red yuzu kosho, a Japanese condiment made from red chiles and fermented, citrusy yuzu fruit. It's sold as a paste; find it at specialty shops or online.

Makes about 2¼ cups

2 cups mayonnaise

½ cup red yuzu kosho

2 tablespoons sriracha hot sauce

1 tablespoon fresh lime juice

In a medium bowl, whisk together all the ingredients. The sauce will keep tightly covered in the refrigerator for up to 1 week.

• TRY THIS WITH
Halibut Steaks Glazed with White Ponzu Sauce (page 170)

ROASTED GARLIC AIOLI

Makes about 1 cup

1 cup mayonnaise

¼ cup Roasted Garlic Paste
   (page 73)

1 teaspoon Dijon mustard

1 teaspoon fresh lemon juice

¼ teaspoon salt, or to taste

Combine all the ingredients in a medium bowl and whisk to combine. Taste and add more salt if needed. The aioli will keep tightly covered and refrigerated for up to 1 week.

• TRY THIS WITH:
Steak Tartare with Chicharrons (page 216)

CURRY MAYO

Makes 1 cup

1½ teaspoons curry powder

1 cup mayonnaise

1 teaspoon fresh lime juice,
   or to taste

Continued

Add the curry powder to a small skillet set over low heat and toast until fragrant, about 2 minutes. Put the mayonnaise in a large bowl. Whisk in the curry powder and lime juice. Taste and add more lime juice if needed. It will keep tightly covered and refrigerated for up to 1 week.

• **TRY THIS WITH:**
The Kitchen Fries (page 80)

JALAPEÑO AIOLI
Makes about 1¼ cups

¼ cup minced Pickled Jalapeños (page 67), or use store-bought
2 tablespoons Roasted Garlic Paste (page 73)
1 tablespoon fresh lime juice, or to taste
1 cup mayonnaise
Salt, to taste

In a medium bowl, whisk together all the ingredients. This mayo will keep tightly covered in the refrigerator for up to 1 week.

• **TRY THIS WITH**
Fish "Tacos" (page 158)

SAFFRON AIOLI
Makes about 1½ cups

2 tablespoons fresh lemon juice
⅛ teaspoon saffron threads
1 large garlic clove, peeled
½ teaspoon salt, plus more to taste
½ teaspoon Dijon mustard
2 large egg yolks
¾ cup grapeseed or other neutral oil
½ cup extra-virgin olive oil

1. In a small cup, combine the lemon juice and saffron. Set aside for 20 minutes as you wait for the saffron to bloom, or infuse, the lemon juice.

2. On a cutting board, smash the garlic and salt together with a fork to form a paste.

3. Combine the saffron-infused lemon juice, garlic paste, mustard, and egg yolks in a food processor and blend to combine. With the motor running, slowly drizzle the grapeseed oil in through the hole on the top, first drop by drop and then in a slow, steady stream. Then drizzle in the olive oil, continuing to blend until smooth. Taste and season with more salt if needed. The aioli will keep tightly covered in the refrigerator for up to 1 week.

• **TRY THIS WITH:**
Fresh Mussels in Spicy Chorizo Broth (page 154)

HONDASHI MAYO

Hondashi, a seasoning based on dried bonito tuna, is often used in Japanese cooking to brighten flavors and add a salty element. In the West, it's mainly known as a shortcut base for miso soup. You can find Hondashi powder in specialty stores or online.

Makes 1 heaping cup

2 tablespoons Hondashi
1 tablespoon fresh lime juice, or to taste
1 tablespoon sriracha hot sauce, or to taste
1 cup mayonnaise
2 tablespoons finely diced green onion (white and green parts)
2 tablespoons finely diced red onion

In a medium bowl, stir the Hondashi with the lime juice and sriracha until dissolved. Add the mayonnaise, green onion, and red onion. Whisk to combine. It will keep tightly covered in the refrigerator for up to 1 week.

• **TRY THIS WITH**
Lobster Rolls with Old Bay Chips (page 148)

YUZU KOSHO MAYO
HONDASHI MAYO
SZECHUAN CHILI CRISP
SAFFRON AIOLI
CURRY MAYO
CORIANDER CHUTNEY
COMEBACK SAUCE

Asian Flavors

We're lucky to have learned so much from talented and generous members of our global community, including Indian neighbors who've shared their favorite chutneys, Japanese colleagues who taught us how to use traditional ingredients that are less commonly seen in the U.S., and street food vendors from all over who introduced us to new and inspirational flavors.

KABAYAKI SAUCE

Also known as eel sauce, kabayaki gives grilled unagi sushi rolls their salty-sweet flavor and caramelized sheen. It's also used to season rice and cooked seafood of all kinds.

Makes about ½ cup

½ cup mirin

2 tablespoons sake

¼ cup sugar

½ cup tamari or other soy sauce

Combine the mirin, sake, and sugar in a small pot, set over medium heat, and stir until the sugar dissolves. Add the tamari and simmer over low heat for about 20 minutes, until it thickens to a consistency similar to syrup. Cool completely.

The sauce will keep in the fridge for 1 week.

- TRY THIS WITH
  Grilled Oysters (page 161)

MISO SAUCE

Shiromiso, or white miso, has a short fermentation time, resulting in a relatively sweet taste and light umami. This sauce provides a fantastic way to punch up almost any roasted vegetable, or, as a salad dressing or dip.

Makes about ½ cup

⅓ cup white miso

¼ cup extra-virgin olive oil, or more if needed

Zest and juice of 1 large lemon, plus more juice as needed

1 teaspoon red chile flakes

2 large garlic cloves, grated with a Microplane

In a medium bowl, combine all the ingredients and whisk until thoroughly incorporated. The miso sauce should have the consistency of a creamy dressing. Add a little more oil to reach that consistency if needed. Taste and add more lemon juice if needed. This sauce can be stored tightly sealed and refrigerated for up to 1 week.

- TRY THIS WITH
  Charred Broccolini (page 111)
  Roasted Vegetable and Chicken Salad with Freekeh (page 188)

TAMARIND CHUTNEY

Sweet and tangy tamarind paste is almost always sold in 14-ounce blocks, but if you find it in the 7-ounce size needed for this recipe, go for it. Otherwise, you can either double the recipe if you're feeding a bigger group or freeze the other half of the package well wrapped in plastic for up to 6 months. You'll find tamarind paste in Indian or Latin specialty stores, or online.

Makes about 2 cups

½ block (14 ounces) seedless tamarind, roughly chopped

½ cup sugar

3 tablespoons peeled and finely diced fresh ginger

2 cups water, or as needed

In a medium saucepan, combine all the ingredients and bring to a simmer over medium-low heat. Simmer for 30 minutes, using a spoon to break up the block of paste, until the mixture is fully incorporated. Remove from heat and cool slightly, then transfer to a blender and blend until smooth with a glossy texture. Add more water if the mixture is too thick. Strain, then store in a container in the refrigerator until ready to use. The chutney will keep tightly sealed and refrigerated for up to a week.

- TRY THIS WITH
Grilled Halloumi Cheese on Roasted Garlic Naan (page 138)
Crispy Cauliflower Korma (page 117)

CORIANDER CHUTNEY

Coriander, known in the U.S. as cilantro, is a foundational Indian spice, and this chutney adds a sweet, spicy, sour zing to everything from traditional curries to bruschetta, grilled sandwiches, and rich, roasted meats. This recipe uses Himalayan black salt, which is kiln-fired with charcoal and spices for a unique color and flavor popular in much of South Asian cooking. You can substitute Himalayan pink salt, although the flavor won't be as complex.

Makes about 1 cup

1 teaspoon ground cumin seeds

1 teaspoon ground coriander seeds

1½ teaspoons finely chopped peeled fresh ginger

1 large jalapeño chile, roughly chopped

4 cups packed chopped fresh cilantro leaves, including the tender stems

3 tablespoons fresh lemon juice, or to taste

1 tablespoon sugar, or to taste

2 tablespoons water, or as needed

¼ teaspoon Himalayan black salt, or to taste

In a small skillet, toast the cumin and coriander over medium heat, stirring constantly, until you start to notice their aroma, about 3 minutes. Remove from the heat and transfer to a food processor. Add the ginger, chile, cilantro, lemon juice, sugar, water, and salt and blend until smooth. Taste and add more lemon juice, sugar, and/or salt as you like, plus more water if needed for a spreadable consistency. The chutney is best the day it is made but will keep tightly covered and refrigerated for up to 3 days.

- TRY THIS WITH
Grilled Halloumi Cheese on Roasted Garlic Naan (page 138)
Crispy Cauliflower Korma (page 117)

SZECHUAN CHILI CRISP

Inspired by Szechuan street food, we developed this sauce by means of a lot of experimentation and tasting to get it right. Use it anywhere you might use sriracha or other hot sauces: over eggs, in stir-fries, or use it on meat or vegetables. This recipe is easily doubled.

Continued

Makes about ¾ cup

¾ cup grapeseed or
  other neutral oil

1 cinnamon stick

3 star anise pods

2 medium shallots, very
  thinly sliced

4 medium garlic cloves,
  very thinly sliced (yields
  about 2 tablespoons)

1-inch piece fresh ginger,
  peeled and minced (yields
  about 1 tablespoon)

2 tablespoons red chile
  pepper flakes

1 tablespoon tamari or
  other soy sauce

1 teaspoon sugar

1. In a small saucepan, combine the oil, cinnamon stick, and star anise. Bring to a simmer over medium heat, then reduce the heat and maintain a low simmer for 30 minutes. You should see scattered bubbles as it simmers and infuses the oils with the spicy flavors.

2. Remove the cinnamon and star anise from the oil using a slotted spoon or tongs, then discard.

3. With the oil still at a low simmer, add the shallots and garlic. If the mixture starts to bubble vigorously, take the pan off the heat briefly until it subsides. Make sure the heat is at the lowest setting to avoid burning the shallots and garlic. Fry until the shallots and garlic are golden brown and crispy looking, about 10 minutes. Remove them with a slotted spoon to a paper towel–lined plate to dry.

4. Place the ginger, red chile flakes, tamari, and sugar in a mason jar or other heatproof vessel, then slowly strain the hot oil into the jar over them. Stir until the mixture is smooth and homogenous, then let cool to room temperature.

5. Gently fold in the fried shallots and garlic, again stirring until the mixture has a smooth consistency. Cover and leave overnight to let the flavors mingle before using. The oil will keep tightly sealed for up to 1 week at room temperature or 1 month in the refrigerator.

• TRY THIS WITH
Roasted Delicata Squash with Miso Squash Puree (page 99)
Rice Middlins with Poached Eggs and Kimchi (page 142)
Steak Tartare with Chicharrons and Roasted Garlic Aioli (page 216)

A FORTUITOUS MEETING

As The Kitchen's co-founder Hugo Matheson recalls, he was sitting outside a Boulder coffee shop one day when a remarkably handsome Labrador retriever trotted up to say hello. The dog's owners, Kimbal and Jen, apologized. But Hugo responded that he loved a big, sturdy Labrador, as it made him a little homesick for the working dogs he'd grown up with in Britain.

With that, the three started chatting and soon discovered their shared interest in food and cooking—a conversation that quickly led to the invitation to Hugo's for dinner that night. As Hugo (pictured at right) tells it, "People get amazed by the story, but I feel like I've met a few people in my life like that, just randomly starting to chat to people. I always like meeting people for who they are, as opposed to what they do." The friendship sparked that night led to Kimbal and Hugo hanging out together and taking long walks during which they talked about anything and everything. Those talks eventually led to their cofounding The Kitchen with Jen.

Though Hugo has stepped back from the restaurant's daily operations in recent years, the long walks and deep connections continue. Throughout this book you'll see Chef Hugo come up, since he played a fundamental role in developing many of The Kitchen's signature recipes (including the salsa verde on page 54).

Pickled Veggies

A FEW PICKLING TECHNIQUES

Vinegar pickling is a relatively quick and easy way to preserve vegetables of all sorts. Pickled vegetables have their own unique flavor and texture profiles, generally retaining some crunch, eye-catching color, and a unique sweet-acid tang while the process also tempers the bite of raw onions or peppers.

PICKLED GREEN ONIONS

During the brief period of the year when fresh ramps are available, we use this recipe to preserve them. Use them much as you would green onions.

Makes 1 quart

16 whole green onions (about 8 ounces)
2 cups rice vinegar
1 cup water
⅓ cup sugar
2 tablespoons salt

1. Cut off and discard the roots from the green onions. Trim and reserve enough of the green tops so that the onion stalks fit bulb-side down when standing up in a 1-quart mason jar, leaving 2 inches of headroom. Pack the jar with the onion stalks, then arrange the reserved green tops around the whole bulbs to tightly fill the jar. (If it's not tight, the onions can float to the top after the brine is added.)

2. Combine the vinegar, water, sugar, and salt in a medium saucepan and bring to a simmer over medium heat. Lower the heat and simmer until the sugar and salt dissolve. Remove from the heat and cool to room temperature.

3. Pour the brine over the green onions, cover, and refrigerate for a minimum of 6 hours before using. The pickles will keep tightly covered and refrigerated for up to 1 month.

• TRY THIS WITH *Baby Lettuce Cups with Crispy Quinoa (page 93)*

PICKLED RED ONIONS

We add these to salads, sandwiches, and burgers for a pop of color and a sweet-acidic crunch. You can also try them on top of tacos or avocado toast, or stirred into a grain bowl.

Makes 3 pints

2 cups rice wine vinegar
1 cup water
½ cup sugar
2 tablespoons salt
2 large red onions, cut in half lengthwise and thinly sliced

1. In a medium saucepan combine the vinegar, water, sugar, and salt and bring to a simmer over medium heat. Simmer until the sugar and salt dissolve, about 5 minutes.

2. Divide the sliced onions evenly among 3 pint-sized mason jars. Pour the vinegar mixture evenly over the onions and set aside until cooled to room temperature. Cover and refrigerate for at least 12 hours

before using. The pickled onions will keep tightly covered and refrigerated for up to 1 month.

- TRY THIS WITH
  The Kitchen's Greek Salad (page 84)
  Crispy Cauliflower Korma (page 117)
  Grilled Halloumi Cheese on Roasted Garlic Naan (page 138)
  Fish Tacos (page 158)
  Chilaquiles with Chicken (page 184)

PICKLED JALAPEÑOS
Makes 1 quart

15 to 20 fresh jalapeño peppers (about 12 ounces)
1½ cups rice vinegar
¾ cup water
6 tablespoons sugar
1½ tablespoons salt

1 Slice the jalapeños, retaining the seeds and membranes.

2. Combine the vinegar, water, sugar, and salt in a medium saucepan, bring to a simmer over medium heat, and simmer until the sugar and salt dissolve. Remove from the heat and cool to room temperature.

3. Pack the jalapeños in a quart-sized mason jar and pour the pickling liquid over the sliced jalapeños, leaving an inch or so of headspace. Cover and refrigerate for at least 48 hours before using. The pickles will keep tightly covered and refrigerated for up to 1 month.

- TRY THIS WITH
  Jalapeño Aioli (page 60)

A SEA OF SALTS

Throughout history, salt has been both a necessity and a luxury. In our modern world, grocery stores carry a sometimes bewildering array of colors and textures to choose from. Here are the variants you'll see in these pages and how we use them.

KOSHER SALT: At The Kitchen, we prefer this coarser flake of sea salt to use in recipes for its texture and because it doesn't contain iodine, which some sensitive palates can detect as a slight bitterness. It is also sold by the box and very useful when cooking in large batches for your community. If you are only going to have one salt in your pantry, this is the one.

MALDON SALT: Hand-harvested from the British shore by the same family for over one hundred years, Maldon salt is one of those ingredients that cost more, but it is worth it because you don't need much to benefit from its unique taste and texture. Lightly sprinkle Maldon flakes over a finished dish to brighten flavors and add a satisfying crunch.

HIMALAYAN PINK SALT: Harvested from rocks rather than the sea, this salt boasts a distinctive color that comes from natural trace minerals, which can also add a very subtle flavor. This salt can be used in place of table salt, but given that it costs quite a bit more, it's mainly used as a finishing touch.

HIMALAYAN BLACK SALT: Unlike pink salt, this rock salt has high enough levels of trace minerals to impart a distinct flavor, often very slightly influenced by naturally occurring sulfates. It is often cured with charcoal to intensify the color and flavor, and to add depth and umami.

Salad Dressing and Marinades

I f you think about it, vinaigrettes and marinades inhabit a Venn diagram with a lot of overlap. In each, acid from vinegar, citrus, or both is mixed with good oil and finished with herbs and spices. Most vinaigrette-style dressings can be used as marinades without any changes. However, marinades can have a different flavor balance (they're not intended to be served as is), so if you're using one preparation to do double duty, taste and adjust the flavors before using it to dress a salad or vegetables.

HONEY THYME VINAIGRETTE

Makes about 2 cups

1 cup grapeseed or
   other neutral oil

4 garlic cloves, minced

2 shallots, minced

1 tablespoon dried thyme

¼ cup honey

Zest and juice of 2 lemons,
   or to taste

1 teaspoon Dijon mustard

2 tablespoons white
   balsamic vinegar

½ teaspoon salt, or to taste

1. In a small saucepan, combine the oil, garlic, shallots, thyme, honey, and lemon zest. Cook over the lowest heat setting for about 20 minutes, or until the garlic and shallots are lightly browned. If the mixture is starting to bubble too vigorously or the garlic is browning too fast at any point, briefly remove the pan from the heat. Once the garlic and shallots are lightly browned, remove the pan from the heat. Let cool to room temperature and then strain, discarding the solids.

2. In a blender or food processor, blend the lemon juice, mustard, vinegar, and salt to combine. Slowly drizzle in the infused oil through the hole in the lid, blending until creamy and smooth. Taste and add more lemon juice and/or salt if needed. The vinaigrette will keep tightly covered and refrigerated for up to 2 weeks.

• TRY THIS WITH
Baby Lettuce Cups with Crispy Quinoa (page 93)

LEMON AND WHITE BALSAMIC VINAIGRETTE

Makes about 1½ cups

¼ cup fresh lemon juice

¼ cup white balsamic vinegar

1 tablespoon honey

1½ teaspoons Dijon mustard

1 cup grapeseed or other
   neutral oil

Salt to taste

Combine the lemon juice, vinegar, honey, and mustard in a blender and blend until thoroughly combined. With the motor running, slowly drizzle in the oil until it is all added and the vinaigrette is emulsified. Season with salt.

The vinaigrette will keep tightly covered and refrigerated for up to 2 weeks. If it separates, return to the blender and blend until emulsified.

• TRY THIS WITH
Scallops with Celery Root Puree (page 167)

OREGANO VINAIGRETTE
Makes about 1 cup

¼ cup red wine vinegar
1 tablespoon agave nectar
2 teaspoons Dijon mustard
1 garlic clove, peeled
1 tablespoon dried oregano, preferably Sicilian
½ teaspoon salt
¼ teaspoon freshly ground black pepper
¾ cup Garlic Oil (page 73) or grapeseed or other neutral oil

Combine the vinegar, agave, mustard, garlic, oregano, salt, and pepper in a blender or food processor and blend until smooth. With the motor running, slowly add the oil through the hole in the top until emulsified. The vinaigrette will keep tightly covered and refrigerated for up to 2 weeks.

• TRY THIS WITH
The Kitchen's Greek Salad (page 84)

BLACK GARLIC CAESAR DRESSING

The sharp flavor of fresh garlic is balanced by the sweet, preserved black garlic in this sophisticated take on a traditional Caesar dressing.

Makes about 2 cups

1 large egg yolk
2 tinned anchovies
¼ cup grated Manchego cheese
¼ cup red wine vinegar
1 tablespoon fresh lemon juice
3 black garlic cloves, peeled
2 fresh garlic cloves, peeled
1 teaspoon Dijon mustard
1 teaspoon Worcestershire sauce
Large pinch of red chile flakes
1 teaspoon salt, plus more if needed
¼ teaspoon freshly ground black pepper
1½ cups grapeseed or other neutral oil

In a blender, combine all the ingredients except the oil and blend until smooth and fully incorporated. With the motor running, slowly drizzle in the oil until the dressing is emulsified and smooth. Taste and add more salt if needed. The dressing will keep tightly covered and refrigerated for up to 1 week.

• TRY THIS WITH
Black Caesar Salad with Smoked Trout (page 83)

CUMIN-LIME DRESSING
Makes about 1¼ cups

1 medium shallot, chopped
2 tablespoons chopped fresh cilantro
1 garlic clove, peeled
1 small serrano chile, stemmed and roughly chopped
1 teaspoon ground cumin
¾ teaspoon sugar
½ teaspoon salt
¼ teaspoon freshly ground black pepper
¼ cup fresh lime juice
2½ tablespoons rice vinegar
1 cup grapeseed or other neutral oil

Combine all the ingredients except the oil in a blender or food processor and blend until smooth. With the motor running, slowly drizzle in the oil in a steady stream until emulsified. The dressing will keep covered and refrigerated for up to 1 week.

• TRY THIS WITH
Sweet Corn Bhel (page 113)

CHECK OUT THIS VINAIGRETTE TRICK

BLACK GARLIC PUREE
ROASTED GARLIC CONFIT
HONEY-THYME VINAIGRETTE

ROASTED
GARLIC OIL
CUMIN-LIME
DRESSING
ROASTED
GARLIC
ACHAAR

Garlic with Everything

Garlic's flavor can be sharp, subtle, or almost sweet, depending upon how it is prepared. Here are some of our favorite garlic concoctions.

BLACK GARLIC PUREE

Black garlic is a traditional East Asian preparation in which garlic cloves are aged and preserved, allowing the garlic's natural sugars to develop. It has a mild flavor with notes of caramel and licorice that go well in a wide range of marinades and sauces. Look for it in Asian grocers or online.

Makes about 1¾ cups

1 cup tamari or other soy sauce

1 cup sherry vinegar

½ cup black garlic cloves

¼ cup sugar

1 teaspoon red chile flakes

Combine all the ingredients in a medium saucepan and bring to a simmer over medium heat. Reduce the heat to low and simmer for 15 minutes, then transfer to a blender and blend until smooth. Transfer to a container, cool, and refrigerate for up to 2 weeks.

• TRY THIS WITH
Porterhouse Steak and Roasted Mushrooms (page 214)

GARLIC BUTTER

Makes about 1 cup

2 medium heads garlic

1 cup (2 sticks) unsalted butter

Separate the garlic cloves, smash each one with the flat side of a chef's knife, and remove the peel. In a small saucepan, melt the butter over low heat. Add the smashed garlic cloves and let cook until the garlic softens. Remove the pan from the heat. Once the mixture is cool enough, pour it into a blender or food processor. Blitz the mixture until it is completely smooth. The garlic butter will keep, tightly covered in the refrigerator, for up to 2 weeks

ROASTED GARLIC ACHAAR

This piquant, spicy condiment is also called "garlic pickle" in Indian cuisine, and it is traditionally eaten as a flavor enhancer for a meal of rice, curry, dal, and yogurt. Try it as a base for pizza or pasta sauces, to spice up aiolis and marinades, or as a spread on naan or toasted and buttered bread.

Makes about 1 cup

6 Fresno chiles, stemmed and slit

¼ cup peeled, sliced fresh ginger

¼ cup grapeseed or other neutral oil

About 30 garlic cloves, peeled (about 1 cup)

1 teaspoon ground turmeric

3 tablespoons paprika

½ teaspoon fenugreek seeds

1 teaspoon black mustard seeds

1 tablespoon light or dark brown sugar

1½ teaspoons salt, or to taste

1 tablespoon fresh lemon juice

2 teaspoons distilled white vinegar

1. In a food processor, combine the chiles and ginger, then process into a paste.

2. Heat the oil in a small skillet over low heat. Add the garlic and cook, stirring frequently, until the cloves are golden brown, about 10 minutes.

3. Using a slotted spoon, scoop the garlic out of the oil and reserve. Add the turmeric, paprika, fenugreek seeds, and mustard seeds to the oil in the skillet and cook until the spices are fragrant. Add the chile-ginger paste to the oil and cook briefly, or until the raw smell of the ginger is gone.

4. Add the brown sugar and salt, remove the pan from the heat, and stir in the lemon juice and vinegar. Transfer to a food processor or blender, add back the reserved garlic, and process into a paste. Transfer to a container, preferably a mason jar with a tight-fitting lid, and keep in the refrigerator for up to a month.

• **TRY THIS WITH**
Crispy Cauliflower Korma (page 117)

ROASTED GARLIC CONFIT AND OIL

This simple preparation is a two-for-one: It delivers fragrant garlic-flavored oil and, as a bonus, garlic confit that you can puree and use to flavor aioli or hummus, mix into mashed potatoes, or spread on toasted sourdough bread

Makes about 2 cups oil and 1 cup garlic confit

1 cup peeled garlic cloves
2 cups grapeseed or other neutral oil, plus more if needed

1. Put the garlic in a small pot and add the oil. If the oil doesn't fully cover the garlic, add more until it does. Bring to a simmer over low heat and simmer for 30 minutes, or until the garlic has softened and is golden brown.

2. Cool completely, then cover and refrigerate until ready to use. It will keep for up to 2 weeks in the fridge, or you can freeze the oil and confit together in ice cube trays for at least a few months. Strain the garlic out when you are ready to use it.

• **TRY THIS WITH**
Halal Hot Sauce (page 181)
Oregano Vinaigrette (page 69)
Naan Tomato Tartine (page 114)
Grilled Halloumi Cheese with Naan (page 138)

ROASTED GARLIC PASTE

For a paste rather than a confit, this variation is your go-to.

Makes about ½ cup paste

1 cup peeled garlic cloves
Grapeseed or other neutral oil to cover (about 1 cup)

1. Bring the garlic and oil to a simmer over medium heat and then reduce to the lowest heat. Cook until the garlic is softened and golden brown, 20 to 30 minutes. If the oil starts bubbling vigorously, remove from the heat briefly, then return to low heat. Remove from the heat and cool completely.

2. Store the roasted garlic cloves in the oil, tightly sealed and refrigerated, for up to 2 weeks. When ready to use, strain out the garlic and blend to create a smooth paste. Reserve the oil as a flavorful substitute for a neutral oil in salad dressings and marinades.

• **TRY THIS WITH**
Roasted Garlic Aioli (page 59)
Jalapeño Aioli (page 60)

Seasonal Dessert Toppers

Our dessert menu changes over the year to make the most of each season's best, freshest produce. When you're looking for ways to jazz up your sweets, look to the following recipes. Mix and match them to embellish our cheesecake (page 269) or vanilla crémeux (page 254), as well as ice cream, pound cake with whipped cream, or pancakes and waffles for breakfast. These recipes are highly adaptable to whatever's in season, so think about creating your own signature treats by substituting the seasonal fruits you love most.

SPRING AND SUMMER

SLOW-ROASTED STRAWBERRIES
Makes about 1 cup

Zest of 1 lemon

¼ cup sugar

1 pound strawberries, cored and halved

1. Preheat the oven to 250°F.
2. Using your fingertips, rub the lemon zest into the sugar until fragrant, then toss the berries with the sugar. Line a large, rimmed pan with parchment paper, then pour the berries onto the pan and spread them out evenly. Bake for about 2 hours, turning a few times, until the berries are juicy and syrupy. Allow to cool before serving. The berries will keep tightly covered and refrigerated for 5 to 7 days.

• TRY THIS WITH
Vanilla Bean Crèmeux (page 254)

CHERRY COMPOTE
Makes about 1 cup

Zest of 1 orange

½ cup plus 2 tablespoons packed dark brown sugar

2 cups pitted black cherries, fresh or frozen

2 tablespoons orange juice

Pinch of salt

1½ teaspoons vanilla bean paste or 1 teaspoon vanilla extract

In a small saucepan, mix the orange zest with the brown sugar until fragrant. Add the cherries, orange juice, and salt. Cook over medium heat until the cherries begin to release their juices and the mixture turns thick and syrupy, about 10 minutes. Turn off the heat and add the vanilla. Allow to cool before serving. The compote will keep tightly covered and refrigerated for up to 2 weeks.

• TRY THIS WITH
Dark Chocolate Crèmeux (page 254)

BLUEBERRY CONFIT

Makes about 1½ cups

2 cups fresh blueberries

3 tablespoons water

2 tablespoons fresh lemon juice

¾ cup sugar

2 tablespoons plus 1½ teaspoons
 crème de cassis (optional)

1 teaspoon cornstarch

½ teaspoon vanilla bean paste or
 1 teaspoon vanilla extract

1. In a small saucepan set over low heat, combine the blueberries, water, and lemon juice. Cook, gently stirring occasionally, until the berries begin to release their juices, 2 to 3 minutes.

2. Stir in the sugar and simmer on low heat until the berries start to get saucy and glossy, 5 to 8 minutes. Pour the mixture through a strainer set over a small bowl to catch the liquid. Return most of the liquid to the pan, reserving 2 tablespoons in the small bowl. Add the crème de cassis (if using) to the reserved liquid in the bowl, then whisk in the cornstarch to create a slurry.

3. Pour the slurry into the liquid in the pan, bring to a simmer, and cook for 2 minutes. Add the cooked berries back to the pan and stir gently to coat and incorporate them into the sauce. Pour into a container, cool completely, then chill until ready to use. The confit will keep tightly covered and refrigerated for 5 to 7 days.

• TRY THIS WITH *Chèvre Cheesecake (page 269)*

STRAWBERRY AND PASSION FRUIT COULIS

Makes about 1 cup

½ cup plus 2 tablespoons
 strawberry puree

½ cup plus 2 tablespoons passion-
 fruit juice or puree

¼ cup plus 2 tablespoons sugar

¼ cup plus 2 tablespoons corn
 syrup

½ teaspoon vanilla bean paste or
 1 teaspoon vanilla extract

1. In a medium pot set over low heat, stir together the purees with the sugar and corn syrup. Cook until the sugar is fully dissolved, then stir in the vanilla. Allow the mixture to lightly simmer for 5 minutes, until it coats the back of a spoon.

2. Pour into a container and place a piece of plastic wrap or waxed paper directly onto the surface to prevent a skin from forming. Chill until set. The coulis will keep tightly covered and refrigerated for 5 to 7 days.

• TRY THIS WITH *Chèvre Cheesecake (page 269)*

FALL AND WINTER

ROASTED FIGS WITH ORANGE CARAMEL

Makes 2 cups

2 tablespoons light or
  dark brown sugar
Zest of 1 lemon
1 tablespoon balsamic vinegar
1 teaspoon vanilla bean paste or
  2 teaspoons vanilla extract
Pinch of salt
12 ounces (9 or 10) fresh figs,
  stemmed and halved lengthwise
Orange Caramel (recipe follows).

1. Preheat the oven
to 400°F.
2. In a large bowl, mix the
sugar with the lemon zest.
Add in the balsamic vine-
gar, vanilla, and salt. Mix
well, then toss the figs in
the mixture to coat.
3. Arrange the figs on a
baking sheet or small casserole dish, cut side up, in
a single layer. Bake for 15
to 20 minutes, until the
figs are jammy and syrupy.
Serve drizzled generously
with orange caramel. The
figs will keep tightly covered and refrigerated for up
to 1 week.

ORANGE CARAMEL

Makes 1 cup

½ cup orange juice
1½ cups sugar
2 tablespoon corn syrup
½ cup heavy cream
2 tablespoons unsalted butter
1 teaspoon vanilla bean paste or
  2 teaspoons vanilla extract
Pinch of salt

1. In a wide saucepan over
medium heat, stir together
orange juice, sugar, and
corn syrup. Swirl the pan as
the sugar begins to dissolve
and the mixture begins to
simmer. There's no need to
stir; just keep swirling the
pan. Keep a close eye on the
mixture as it simmers and
browns. The mixture will
turn a deep golden color
and begin to smell toasty.
2. As soon as the caramel
reaches an amber-honey
color, remove from the heat
and quickly whisk in the
cream and butter. The mixture will begin to seize up
a bit; stir until it's smooth.
Then stir in the vanilla
and salt. Allow to cool
before tasting. Add more
salt if desired. The caramel
will keep tightly covered
and refrigerated for up to
3 weeks.
• TRY THIS WITH
Chèvre Cheesecake (page 269)

PEARS POACHED IN WHITE WINE WITH CARDAMOM

Makes 8 pear halves

2 cups white wine
⅓ cup fresh lemon juice
2¼ cups sugar
8 cardamom pods
Zest strips from 2 lemons
  (peel with a peeler)
1-inch piece fresh ginger, thinly
  sliced
2 teaspoons vanilla bean paste or
  1 tablespoon vanilla extract
¼ teaspoon salt
4 Bosc pears

1. Mix the white wine,
lemon juice, and sugar in
a medium pot set over low
heat. Bring to a low simmer
and stir until the sugar
dissolves. Stir in the cardamom, lemon zest, ginger,
vanilla, and salt.
2. Peel and slice the pears
in half lengthwise. Use
a small cookie scoop or
melon baller to scoop out
their cores. Add the pears
to the wine mixture, bring
to a simmer, and cook on
low until the pears are just
tender enough to pierce
with a small paring knife,
about 30 minutes.
3. Turn off the heat and
allow the pears to cool in
the syrup for about 15 minutes. Then gently transfer

the pears and syrup to a medium container. The pears will keep tightly covered and refrigerated for 3 to 5 days. To serve, thinly slice the pears and use as a topping over cheesecake, ice cream, or other desserts.

- TRY THIS WITH
Vanilla Bean Crèmeux (page 254)

BLOOD ORANGE SLICES INFUSED WITH A HIBISCUS-PINK PEPPERCORN SYRUP

Makes about 2 cups

¾ cup plus 1 tablespoon blood orange juice

¾ cup plus 1 tablespoon brewed hibiscus tea

½ teaspoon ground pink peppercorns

1 cup sugar

1 tablespoon corn syrup

1 teaspoon vanilla extract

½ teaspoon cornstarch

4 blood oranges, cut into supremes (see page 133 for technique)

1. In a small pot, mix together ¾ cup of the blood orange juice and ¾ cup of the tea with the pepper, sugar, syrup, and vanilla. Mix the cornstarch with 1 tablespoon each of juice and tea to create a slurry. Bring the ingredients in the pot to a rolling simmer over medium heat, then whisk in the cornstarch slurry. Turn the heat to low and allow the mixture to steep and simmer gently for 10 minutes, until the syrup coats the back of a spoon. Pour into a heat-safe container and allow to cool completely prior to using. Keep chilled in the fridge until ready, up to 3 days.

2. To infuse the orange slices, gently toss them with the syrup. Allow to chill and infuse for at least 30 minutes, or overnight. The oranges will keep tightly covered and chilled in their syrup for up to 3 days.

- TRY THIS WITH
Dark Chocolate Crèmeux (page 254)

Chef Hugo really taught me the power of a good vegetable. From day one the freshest local fruits and vegetables have been central to our ethos. There's a graphic hanging in our Denver restaurant that kind of sums up our approach (see page 136). It depicts a small pig standing under a huge broccoli tree—illustrating the idea that the star ingredient, the center of attention in so many of our dishes is the vegetable. A fresh-from-the-farm carrot from your farmer's market is nothing like a generic grocery store carrot. In the opening years of The Kitchen we would sauté fresh halibut and serve it over pureed carrots from our local farm with nothing else (okay, maybe a squeeze of lemon), and it blew our guests away. We love this approach—take a humble vegetable and accent its flavors instead of smothering it in sauces.

Anne Cure from Cure Farm was one of our favorite farmers as we developed our menu. We'll never forget her spring mustard greens and how, for a few weeks every spring, we'd toss those greens in just lemon juice, salt, and olive oil for the best salad you've ever had.

Today The Kitchen continues our tradition of working with the best possible farmers locally and beyond, into our extended communities. We're proud of the small role we've played in helping bring the values of "farm to table" to the larger restaurant world.

Vegetables

The Kitchen Three-Day French Fries

Serves 4

2 pounds large russet potatoes

Peanut or other neutral oil

Salt

Finely minced chives and/or
  parsley, for topping (optional)

Garlic Butter (page 72), for
  topping (optional)

Here at The Kitchen, we envision virtually every dish as one to share, but some are almost impossible to keep to yourself, even if you wanted to. We could eat these hand-cut fries every day with just a sprinkling of salt and maybe a little chopped parsley. They're also incredible dipped into an aioli or flavored mayo (pages 59–60). Or, for a gloriously over-the-top experience, try them with Truffle Cream Sauce (page 179).

1. Fill a large bowl with cold water and set aside.

2. Day 1: Peel and rinse the potatoes. Next, cut each potato into 4 or 5 pieces lengthwise and then cut those pieces into ½-inch sticks. Add the potatoes to the bowl of cold water, place it in the refrigerator, and let them soak overnight. If you want to skip a day, let them sit for at least 3 hours before cooking.

3. Day 2: When you're ready to fry them, drain the water and lay the potato sticks on a baking sheet lined with paper towels. Pat them dry with more paper towels.

4. For the first stage, known as par-frying, pour enough oil into a large saucepan to come at least 3 inches up its sides, then affix a kitchen thermometer to the pan. Heat the oil over medium-high heat until the thermometer reads 275°F. Using a slotted spoon, add half of the potatoes to the oil and fry for 7 minutes. They should not begin to brown or show any color at all yet. Remove the potatoes from the pan and place on a fresh baking sheet. Bring the oil back up to 275°F and fry the rest of the potatoes the same way. Let the par-fried potatoes rest at room temperature until completely cool and then place them in the fridge overnight.

5. At this point you can proceed straight to the second fry to finish, or you can also freeze some or all of these par-fried potatoes for up to 3 months.

6. Day 3: Heat your oil until the thermometer reads 350°F. Once it's hot enough, add half of the par-fried potatoes and fry for about 5 minutes until nicely browned, very crispy on the outside, and tender on the inside. Remove to a paper towel–lined baking sheet and season liberally with salt. Repeat these steps to finish cooking the remaining fries.

7. Top each serving with the minced herbs and/or Garlic Butter, if you like. Serve with a dipping sauce such as those on pages 52–64.

Black Caesar Salad with Smoked Trout

A version of this salad was a big hit years ago when we first introduced it. Bringing it back to the menu was an exercise in collective memory. Nobody could find the original recipe, and everyone who'd eaten here since the beginning had a slightly different recollection of what had made this salad so special. This recipe reflects the best of those memories. It's a dream of a salad, with shiny black kale (called *cavolo nero,* in Italian), nutty Manchego, doubly garlicky dressing, and a handful of seasoned breadcrumbs in place of croutons. The smoked trout is a new addition and a shout-out to our Colorado home. It's the added protein you need to turn a memorable side into an unforgettable meal.

1. Put the kale in a large bowl with a cup of the dressing. Massage the dressing into the kale to thoroughly coat it, adding more dressing if needed. Gently add the smoked trout, taking care not to break up the pieces too much.
2. Season the salad with salt, divide into individual salad bowls, and grate a generous amount of cheese to cover each serving. Top with the breadcrumbs, finish with some black pepper, and serve.

LEMON GARLIC BREADCRUMBS

1. Preheat the oven to 350°F.
2. Place the panko in a medium bowl. Use a Microplane to grate the garlic into the panko, then zest the lemon into it. Add the salt and, using your hands, toss the breadcrumbs and work the lemon zest and garlic into them until completely incorporated.
3. Spread the mixture onto a small baking sheet and bake for about 5 minutes, then toss and bake for an additional 5 minutes, or until golden brown throughout. Cool completely. The panko will keep tightly covered in a cool, dry place for up to a month.

Serves 4

2 bunches black (lacinato) kale, stemmed and cut into chiffonade
Black Garlic Caesar Dressing (page 69)
12 ounces smoked trout, cut into large chunks
Salt, to taste
Manchego cheese, to top
Lemon Garlic Breadcrumbs (recipe follows)
Freshly ground black pepper, to taste

Makes 1 cup

1 cup panko breadcrumbs
1 garlic clove
Zest of ½ lemon
¾ teaspoon salt

83

The Kitchen Greek Salad

**Makes 1 plated salad,
easily multiplied**

1 slice feta cheese
(about 3 x 2 x ¼ inch)

½ Persian cucumber, thinly sliced

¼ cup Pickled Red Onion
(page 66)

1 large heirloom tomato, cut into
roughly 1-inch chunks

Salt

Sugar

4 cherry tomatoes, preferably
heirloom, cut in half

5 kalamata olives, pitted

3 pepperoncini

Oregano Vinaigrette (page 69)

Dried oregano, preferably
Sicilian, to garnish

Fennel pollen, to garnish

6 fresh parsley leaves,
torn, to finish

3 fresh mint leaves, torn, to finish

The idea behind this salad was to take the elements everyone loves most in a Greek salad and really punch them up, making sun-ripened tomatoes and a salty, perfect slice of feta the stars of the dish. If you want to make a more traditional salad, you can crumble the feta and add torn-up romaine lettuce—but try it our way first!

If you can't lay your hands on a Persian cucumber, you can use about a quarter of an English one instead. Fennel pollen is more commonly used in Italy, although Americans are becoming more aware of its subtle yet mesmerizing flavor, with hints of anise and honey, that can elevate savory and sweet dishes. Sometimes called "the spice of the angels," it is hand-harvested from foraged wild fennel in Italy and California. Look for it in food specialty shops or online—it's pricey, but we think you get what you pay for in this case. You can substitute ground fennel for a somewhat similar flavor if you wish.

1. Place the cheese in the center of a large, rimmed plate or large, shallow bowl, surrounded by cucumber slices. Place the pickled red onions near the rim of the plate in 3 separate piles, as though they were the points of a triangle.

2. Season the heirloom tomato chunks on a separate plate with pinches of salt and a scant amount of sugar, then scatter them, along with the cherry tomatoes, around the cheese slice.

3. Randomly but evenly distribute the olives and pepperoncini around the feta as well. Generously spoon the vinaigrette over the tomatoes and cucumbers. Garnish with the oregano and fennel pollen, then finish by scattering the parsley and mint over the plate. Serve immediately.

CRAGGY
CHUNKS OF
CHEESE
SOAK UP THE
DRESSING

Basil Salad with Stone Fruits

This decadent salad is one of Kimbal's favorites. Cherries are an easy fruit to find when you're buying from the grocery store, but look forward to substituting them with peaches and plums when they are in season at your farmer's market.

Combining stone fruit with the savory bite of Parmesan along with the kick from both basil and garlic makes for a dish that tastes like Italy on a plate. It's fresh and healthy with natural sugar, fat, and zest. Each bite hits a different note depending on what lands on your spoon. This dish gets better as it sits and macerates with the salt and lemon.

1. Chunk the Parmesan into small, irregular shapes: Using a large chef's knife, point the tip straight down into the block of cheese, plunge it in about a half-inch deep, then twist your knife so that the cheese breaks apart into chunks. You're looking for chunks with craggy edges as they bring texture to the finished dish.

2. Cut the fruit in half and take out the pits. If you're using peaches, cut the fruit into bite-sized chunks. If you're using cherries, just leave them in halves. Place the cut fruit in a large bowl.

3. Pick the basil leaves off of the stems, tear them in half, and add to the bowl with the fruit. Add the cheese chunks, garlic slivers, lemon juice, olive oil, and salt. Using your hands, toss everything together. Add pepper to taste. Toss again. Let the salad sit for at least 15 minutes before serving to allow the ingredients to macerate and let the flavors combine.

Serves 4–6 people

½ pound block Parmesan

1 pound cherries or stone fruit of choice (such as peaches or plums)

1 bunch basil

2 garlic cloves, sliced into thin slivers

2 tablespoons lemon juice

¼ cup extra-virgin olive oil

¼ teaspoon salt

Freshly ground black pepper, to taste

87

HOW TO CHUNK THE PARMESAN

Stroll down to the west end of the bustling Pearl Street pedestrian mall in Boulder, to a storefront that dates back to the early days of the 1900s. There, behind a simple gray door, is where it all began. This is the original restaurant location that Kimbal, his then-wife Jen, and co-founder Hugo opened back in 2004. The building is a cozy spot for a restaurant—and a reminder that Boulder's Wild West past was not so long ago. As recently as the 1980s, the space was the city's last pawn shop, and for many years before that it was a saloon. In the basement, we found an old, closed-off tunnel that, according to legend, may have served as a discrete way for ladies to travel from the saloon back to the nearby Boulderado Hotel after an evening's libations.

Today, the restaurant's front room beckons with its aged ceramic tile floor and a bar. Farther in, rough-hewn wood plank flooring complements the exposed brick walls. A comfortable, cosmopolitan vibe fills the air in this historic spot that has been deftly converted into a simple yet chic bistro. The cocktail lounge located directly above The Kitchen, aptly named Upstairs, opened in 2006 in a space that had last been an old bookstore. This more intimate room has a sleek yet friendly modern feel, with a fireplace that adds romance. When designing Upstairs, Hugo and Kimbal wanted staff and guests to simultaneously feel a sense of luxury and tranquility—a spot to kick back and have an innovative cocktail or a nice glass of wine with friends old and new.

Roasted & Pickled Beets w/ Labneh & Pistachio Granola

Serves 4

Roasted Red Beets (recipe follows)

Pickled Golden Beets
  (recipe follows)

Orange Vinaigrette
  (recipe follows)

Salt and freshly ground black
  pepper, to taste

1 cup Labneh (recipe follows)

2 oranges, peeled and sliced into
  wheels

About 1 cup Pistachio Granola
  (recipe follows)

¼ cup picked fresh dill

4 teaspoons minced fresh chives

1 pound red beets, scrubbed

1 pound yellow beets, scrubbed

4 tablespoons grapeseed or
  other neutral oil

1 teaspoon salt

½ teaspoon freshly ground
  black pepper

8 sprigs rosemary

4 thyme sprigs

2 bay leaves

2 cups water

The roasted and pickled beets complement each other's color and flavor and play off of the rich and tangy labneh and crunchy granola. And then it's all tied together with the clean, bright flavors of citrus and dill. You can roast the red and golden beets at the same time, if you like, and store the red beets in the refrigerator while the golden ones pickle overnight. Reheat the red beets just enough to take the chill off before assembling (try microwaving them for just 30 seconds or less, in batches). The granola and orange vinaigrette can also be made ahead, so all you need to do before serving is assemble it all on the plate.

Combine the roasted red beets and pickled golden beets in a large bowl and toss with orange vinaigrette, then season with salt and pepper. Using a large spoon, spread ¼ cup of the labneh over half of each of four plates. Neatly arrange the beets and orange wheels over the labneh in two layers to create height. Garnish each plate with about ¼ cup granola, 1 tablespoon dill, and 1 teaspoon chives and serve immediately.

ROASTED BEETS

1. Preheat the oven to 425°F.

2. We recommend cooking the two different batches of beets, red and yellow, at once, each in its own roasting pan. For each pan, toss the beets with 2 tablespoons oil, ½ teaspoon salt, and ¼ teaspoon pepper to coat well, then add 4 sprigs rosemary, 2 sprigs thyme, a bay leaf, and a cup of water to each. Cover the pans with aluminum foil and roast for about 1½ hours, until the beets are tender when pierced with a fork. Keep in mind that differently sized beets may need more or less time. If the center of a beet is difficult to pierce through, continue to roast, checking every 10 minutes.

3. Take the pans out of the oven and remove the foil. Peel the skin off the beets while they're still warm, then cut them into bite-sized half-wedges. Refrigerate the red beets while you prepare the yellow beets for pickling. (If you prefer, you can just make the yellow beets first, then bake the red ones the next day, before assembling.)

PICKLED YELLOW BEETS

1. While the beets are roasting, make your pickling brine in a container small enough that the beets will stay submerged in the liquid. Combine the warm water, sugar, and salt in your container and whisk to dissolve the sugar and salt. Then, whisk in the vinegar and orange juice.

2. Once the yellow beets have cooled, add them to the pickling liquid, cover, and refrigerate for at least 8 hours or overnight.

LABNEH

1. In a stainless-steel bowl, whisk together the yogurt, lemon juice, and salt. Line a strainer with cheesecloth, add the yogurt, and fold the cheesecloth over to cover it completely.

2. Place in the refrigerator and let it strain for 24 hours.

3. Remove the labneh from the cheesecloth to a bowl and whisk in the oil. Taste and add more oil and/or salt if needed. The labneh will keep tightly sealed in the refrigerator for up to 2 weeks.

ORANGE VINAIGRETTE

Combine all the ingredients in a jar with a tight-fitting lid and shake to combine and emulsify. The vinaigrette will keep tightly sealed in the refrigerator for up to 2 weeks.

Continued

1 pound roasted yellow beets (see above)

½ cup warm water

3 tablespoons sugar

1 teaspoon salt

½ cup champagne vinegar

½ cup orange juice

Makes about 3 cups

1 quart plain whole-milk Greek yogurt

1 tablespoon fresh lemon juice

1 teaspoon salt, plus more if needed

3 tablespoons extra-virgin olive oil, plus more if needed

Makes about ½ cup

¼ cup orange juice

¼ cup grapeseed or other neutral oil

1½ tablespoons apple cider vinegar

2 teaspoons agave nectar

¼ teaspoon salt

⅛ teaspoon freshly ground black pepper

PISTACHIO GRANOLA

1. Spread the quinoa on a baking sheet and toast, stirring once or twice until lightly browned, about 10 minutes. Remove from the oven and cool, then transfer to a large bowl.

2. Place the pistachios in a food processor and grind into medium pieces. Remove from the processor to a medium-sized mesh strainer to sift out any dust. Add to the bowl of quinoa, then add the salt.

3. In a medium saucepan, combine the brown sugar, agave, and oil and bring to a boil over medium-high heat, stirring constantly as the sugar melts. Don't get distracted—it can burn quickly. Pour the syrup over the pistachio mixture and immediately mix well with a silicone spatula.

4. Spread the granola in an even layer on a parchment paper–lined baking sheet and bake for 15 minutes, or until mostly set (it will set further as it cools). Remove from the oven and immediately stir with a silicone spatula to break it up. Cool, then break the granola into smaller pieces by hand. The granola will keep in a tightly sealed container in a cool, dry place for at least 2 weeks. If you have leftovers, use them to top breakfast cereal, sprinkle on a salad, or eat as a snack.

Makes about 4 cups

¾ cup dry quinoa

1½ cups whole raw pistachios

1 cup packed light or dark brown sugar

2 tablespoons agave nectar

¼ cup grapeseed or other neutral oil

½ teaspoon salt

Baby Lettuce Cups with Crispy Quinoa

This salad is a lot of fun as a shared dish at any potluck or communal dinner. The presentation in lettuce cups elevates an already delicious side salad into something extra-special. We switch the ingredients up as the seasons change—try peaches and feta in the summer and pears with gorgonzola in the autumn. In the early spring, for that brief, glorious window when ramps are available, we'll use them in place of green onions. We like Point Reyes's organic raw-milk blue cheese, but any good cheese that's firm enough to crumble will work.

▼

Lightly brush the inside of the lettuce cups with honey thyme vinaigrette and season with salt and pepper, then add ½ tablespoon pickled green onion to each cup. Combine the apple slices and fennel in a small bowl and toss with just enough dressing to lightly coat, then divide the apple-fennel mix evenly between the cups. Sprinkle 1 ounce of blue cheese crumbles into each cup, then top each with a half tablespoon of crispy quinoa. Drizzle a scant amount of vinaigrette over each cup, garnish with herbs, and serve immediately.

CRISPY QUINOA

The quinoa's moisture can cause the oil to spatter, so blot it well with paper towels before frying. You can scale up this recipe easily. You can use single-color quinoa, but we like the tricolor variety for its nutty flavor and varied texture (and because it looks cool).

1. Heat the oil in a medium sauté pan over medium heat. Add the quinoa and cook, stirring occasionally, until golden and crisp, 10 to 15 minutes. Place a strainer over a bowl and pour in the quinoa. Shake to drain off excess oil, then transfer the crispy quinoa to a plate lined with paper towels to drain further.

Serves 4

24 butter lettuce cups, chilled
Honey Thyme Vinaigrette (page 68)
Salt and freshly ground black pepper to taste
6 tablespoons thinly sliced Pickled Green Onions (page 66)
1 large apple, cored and cut into ¼-inch-thick slices
1 cup shaved fennel
4 ounces high-quality blue cheese, crumbled
6 tablespoons Crispy Quinoa (recipe follows)
Fines herbes or fresh flat-leaf parsley leaves, to garnish

Makes about 6 tablespoons

½ cup cooked tricolor quinoa
6 tablespoons grapeseed or other neutral oil

93

ROASTED BEETS AND LABNEH
BABY LETTUCE WITH CRISPY QUINOA

URFA CARROTS WITH
WHIPPED FETA

The Kitchen

Urfa Carrots with Whipped Feta

The joy of this dish is how it elevates the humble carrot to a starring role, slow-roasting it to bring out its natural sweetness and robust texture. You end up with carrots that are perfectly caramelized and fork tender. This recipe can be prepared as a side dish or as a hearty, satisfying main that would be especially appreciated by any vegetarian guests. Consider serving it alongside the traditional offerings of a big holiday dinner, taking advantage of the heirloom carrots that are available all winter. If you have leftovers, the marinade can be tossed with any roasted vegetable, the pistachios add a rich smokiness when sprinkled on salads or other veggies, and the whipped feta can be served on its own as a dip or slathered on warm, fresh bread. If time is tight, many of the components can be made a week or more ahead.

Makes about 1½ cups

1½ cups grapeseed or
   other neutral oil

¼ cup minced garlic

1 large shallot, minced

2 sprigs thyme

1 tablespoon ground urfa chile

1½ teaspoons dried sumac

1½ teaspoons Aleppo chile flakes

1½ teaspoon Italian red chile flakes

¾ teaspoon salt

½ teaspoon freshly ground
   black pepper

THE RIGHT WAY TO MINCE GARLIC

URFA MARINADE

1. In a medium saucepan, combine all the ingredients and bring to a simmer over low heat. Turn off the heat and steep at room temperature for 1 hour.
2. If you're not using this marinade right away, it can be stored tightly covered and refrigerated for up to 1 month.

SPICED PISTACHIOS

1. Preheat the oven to 350°F.
2. In a small bowl, toss the pistachios with oil to coat. Place on a small baking sheet and roast for about 5 minutes, until very lightly browned.
3. Remove the pistachios from the oven, transfer to a cutting board, and leave until cool enough to handle.
4. Once cooled, roughly chop the nuts and return them to the bowl. Add the smoked paprika, cayenne, and salt and toss to coat. Spread them on the pan again, return to the oven, and roast for another 2 to 3 minutes to allow the spices to sink into the pistachios.

Makes about ⅓ cup

½ cup shelled unsalted pistachios
   (about 2 ounces)

½ teaspoon extra-virgin olive oil

¼ teaspoon smoked paprika

⅛ teaspoon ground cayenne

¼ teaspoon salt

Continued

5. Remove from the pan to a plate and cool completely. The pistachios will keep tightly sealed in a cool, dark place for up to 2 weeks.

WHIPPED FETA

Makes about 1½ cups

8 ounces feta cheese (we use sheep's milk feta), crumbled, at room temperature
3 ounces cream cheese (½ cup), at room temperature

1. In the bowl of a food processor, pulse the feta cheese until only small crumbs remain. Add the cream cheese and process for 4 to 5 minutes, scraping down the sides of the bowl as necessary, until the mixture is super creamy.
2. This will make a bit more of the final product than you need for this dish. It will keep tightly sealed in the refrigerator for up to 1 week.

URFA CARROTS

4 large carrots, peeled and root ends trimmed
2 tablespoons grapeseed or other neutral oil
½ cup Urfa Marinade (recipe on preceding page)
Salt
1 cup Whipped Feta (recipe above)
Spiced Pistachios (recipe above)
Sesame seeds, to garnish
Torn fresh cilantro leaves, to garnish
Torn fresh mint leaves, to garnish

1. Preheat the oven to 400°F. Place the carrots in a baking pan, toss with the oil to coat, and add ½ cup water. Cover with foil, and roast for 10 minutes. Then remove the foil, rotate the pan, and roast for another 10 minutes, or until a carrot is easily pierced with a knife. If the carrots aren't done and are starting to brown, cover them with foil again, add a little more water if the pan is dry, and roast for a few more minutes.
2. Remove the carrots to a cutting board, cool until you can handle them, then cut into large bite-sized chunks. Place the carrot chunks in a bowl and toss with the urfa marinade to coat. Add salt to taste.
3. Divide the whipped feta into 4 serving bowls and arrange the carrots on top. Drizzle with any urfa marinade left in the bowl. Top with the spiced pistachios, sesame seeds, cilantro, and mint and serve immediately.

SOME LIKE IT FRIED

At the restaurant, we fry the carrots for this dish instead of roasting them. The roasted version you see here is no less delicious—and a lot easier for many home cooks—but deep-frying gives the carrots a unique caramelized taste and melt-in-your-mouth texture that's hard to beat. If you want to replicate the restaurant technique at home, here's how:

Take a large, wide pot and pour grapeseed or another neutral oil into it, about 3 inches deep. Place the pot over medium heat and heat the oil to 350°F, as measured by a kitchen thermometer. Pat the carrots dry with paper towels carefully, add them to the oil, and fry until softened and caramelized, about 10 to 12 minutes. Remove the carrots from the oil using tongs, place on a cutting board, and cool until you can handle them. Cut into large bite-sized chunks and follow the rest of the recipe just as you would with the roasted option here.

Roasted Delicata Squash with Miso Squash Puree

This dish is beloved by our vegan guests and friends, as well as anyone craving an extravagantly creative way to enjoy delicata squash. The squash has two opportunities to shine in this plating of sweet, tender slices roasted to a perfect golden brown and served over a smooth, umami-rich puree. The real secret is our house-made Szechuan Chili Crisp. You can use high-quality premade chili crisp, but there's really nothing like our recipe for this dish.

MISO SQUASH PUREE

1. In a medium saucepan, heat the oil over medium heat until it shimmers. Add the squash, onion, and garlic and cook until the onion is translucent but not yet taking on any color. Add the coconut milk, miso, and lime leaf and bring to a simmer. Lower the heat slightly, cover, and cook until the squash is softened and can easily be pierced with a knife, about 20 minutes.

2. Remove the lime leaf and strain the mixture into a bowl, reserving the cooking liquid.

3. Transfer the solids to a blender and blend to a smooth, spoonable puree, adding as much of the reserved liquid as necessary to thin. Taste and add a little more miso if necessary for a rich, round flavor. Add the lemon juice, taste, and add more if it needs a hit of brightness. Keep warm until serving or cool, cover, and refrigerate for up to 3 days before serving. Reheat just before serving.

Continued

Makes about 1½ cups

1 tablespoon grapeseed or
 other neutral oil

1 medium unpeeled delicata
 squash (about 12 ounces), cut
 in half, seeded, then cut into
 1-inch cubes

½ cup chopped yellow onion

2 tablespoons roughly
 chopped garlic

About 1 cup coconut milk
 (enough to cover the squash)

1 tablespoon white miso,
 plus more as needed

1 makrut lime leaf

1 teaspoon fresh lemon juice,
 or to taste

2 medium delicata squash (about
    12 ounces each)
1 tablespoon plus ½ teaspoon
    grapeseed or other neutral oil
Kosher salt
½ cup Szechuan Chili Crisp
    (page 63)
3 tablespoons pumpkin seeds
Fresh cilantro leaves, to garnish
Flaky salt, to finish

ROASTED DELICATA SQUASH

1. Preheat the oven to 400°F and line a baking sheet with parchment paper or a silicone mat.

2. Trim the ends from the squash and cut in half horizontally, then scrape out the seeds and fibrous flesh. Place the squash cut side down on a cutting board and cut into ¾-inch half-moons.

3. Put the squash slices in a large bowl, add 1 tablespoon of the oil, toss to evenly coat, and sprinkle with kosher salt. Arrange the slices on a baking sheet in a single layer, making sure their edges don't touch, and roast until the slices are golden brown on the bottom, 10 to 12 minutes. Remove the pan from the oven and use tongs to carefully flip each slice. Return to the oven and continue to roast until the second side is golden brown but the squash still holds its shape, about 10 minutes.

4. While the squash is in the oven, toss the pumpkin seeds with the remaining ½ teaspoon oil, place them on a small baking sheet, and roast with the squash until browned, about 10 minutes. Remove from the oven and cool.

5. To serve, divide the squash puree among 4 plates, smoothing it with a spoon to make a bed for the roasted squash. Arrange the squash slices decoratively over the puree. Stir the chili crisp to make sure you get both oil and crispy bits in each spoonful. Drizzle each plate with 2 tablespoons of chili crisp. Garnish with the pumpkin seeds and cilantro. Sprinkle with flaky salt and serve immediately.

THE SECRET IS
OUR HOUSE
SZECHUAN
CHILI CRISP.

Creamy Burrata with Salsa Verde & Sourdough Focaccia

This simple yet impressive dish is a natural for casual sharing among family and friends gathered around a table. It's all about the interplay of textures and flavors—slices of charred sourdough focaccia, gooey cheese, and our bright, herbal salsa verde to cut through the richness and tie it all together. Gather friends and loved ones old and new around the table and dip to your heart's content.

Serves 4

12 pieces Sourdough Focaccia
   (page 231)
4 (4-ounce) rounds burrata
   cheese, at room temperature
Salsa Verde (page 54)
Maldon salt

1. Heat a grill or grill pan over medium heat. Add the focaccia and toast on each side until warmed and grill marked but not charred or burned. Note: Do not oil the bread before grilling; it has enough oil in it that adding more can cause the grill to flare and burn the bread.

2. To serve, place one burrata round in the center of each of 4 shallow bowls. Stir the salsa verde to make sure the sauce is homogenous. This is important because after sitting for any length of time, the herb mixture will settle to the bottom of the container, leaving the olive oil on top. Stirring it like this before serving ensures that each serving has an equal amount of oil and herbs. Using a large spoon, top each round of burrata with salsa verde. Sprinkle with salt and set the grilled focaccia to one side of the bowl. Serve immediately, while the bread is still warm.

Fresh Fava Bean and Pea Bruschetta

Serves 4

10 ounces fresh fava beans

10 ounces fresh English peas

Leaves from 1 bunch mint, sliced

¼ cup extra-virgin olive oil, plus more for drizzling

1½ teaspoons salt, plus more to taste

Zest of 2 lemons

Juice of ½ lemon, plus more if needed

1 cup Whipped Ricotta (page 116)

4 large slices of country bread, toasted

Toasted bread, once the humblest of breakfasts, has been having a fantastic glow-up for years now. Of course, the Italians have been eating some version of bruschetta in the form of toasted bread with olive oil and seasonal toppings since Ancient Rome. In our version, the fresh green flavors of fava beans, English peas, and mint celebrate the springtime with pure deliciousness. If fresh fava beans (sometimes called broad beans) aren't available, you can substitute an equal measure of fresh peas.

To plan how many fava pods you will need to yield 10 ounces of beans, figure that fresh young pods yield about a 2:1 ratio by weight; with older, more mature pods it's closer to 4:1. The pod shells are edible, but become tough and bitter as they mature, so for more mature beans, you'll want to shell them after cooking.

1. Bring a large pot of water to a boil and salt it. Add the fava beans and cook for 5 minutes, or until the beans under the skins are bright green and soft. Scoop the favas out of the water with a spider or slotted spoon into a colander. Once the beans have drained, transfer them to a clean kitchen towel to absorb the remaining water. Note that you should not "shock" either the beans or peas in a bath of cold water, just drain and dry. Remove the skins from the favas if desired.

2. Return the water to a boil, add the peas, and cook for about 5 minutes until they are bright green and tender. Scoop the peas out of the water to drain in a colander, then transfer to a second clean kitchen towel to absorb the remaining water.

3. Toss the fava beans and peas together in a large bowl with the mint, olive oil, salt, lemon zest, and lemon juice. Taste and add more salt and/or lemon juice if needed.

4. Spread the cheese over the toast, then top each toast with the fava and pea mixture. Drizzle with a little more olive oil, and serve.

ON THE MENU SINCE DAY ONE
THE KITCHEN

The Kitchen Tomato Soup

Some of our favorite dishes have become staple comforts and celebrations. These are the dishes you'll always find on the menu, every day of the year. That's true of our iconic fries (page 80) and of this simple, deeply flavorful soup. Warm, comforting, and easy to put together, this is what love tastes like on a chilly winter day. We're often asked to share the secret to this soup's popularity. Now, we love a cool kitchen hack as much as the next chef, but in this case, it really is this simple. Accompany a bowl with freshly toasted Sourdough Focaccia (page 231) or sip a cup with our Halloumi Naan (page 138) for a sophisticated take on the ultimate comfort-food lunch of tomato soup and grilled cheese. Believe it or not, you can also use this soup as the perfect tomato sauce for pizza. Snag a pre-made pizza crust from the store or slather it atop Naan (page 140), sprinkle with whatever toppings you like, bake till bubbly and enjoy!

Serves 4 to 6 (about 1½ quarts)

7 tablespoons unsalted butter
1 large onion (about 10 ounces),
  roughly chopped
4 garlic cloves,
  smashed and peeled
2 (28-ounce) cans
  whole Roma tomatoes
2 teaspoons salt, or to taste
2 tablespoons heavy cream
Extra-virgin olive oil, for drizzling
Thinly sliced fresh chives or
  parsley

HOW TO BLEND HOT SOUPS

1. In a large saucepan, melt the butter over medium heat. Add the onions and garlic and cook until the onions are just translucent, 5 to 7 minutes. Catch them before they start to brown at all.

2. Add the tomatoes and salt and bring to a simmer. Reduce the heat to low and cook uncovered, stirring occasionally, for 1 hour. It's this long, slow cooking—below a simmer—that brings out the tomatoes' sweetness and depth of flavor.

3. To finish, add the cream and puree with an immersion blender or, working in batches, transfer to a standing blender and blend until smooth. Spoon into bowls and top with a drizzle of oil and a scattering of chives or parsley. This soup will keep for up to 1 week in the refrigerator or up to 3 months in the freezer.

Gazpacho with Dungeness Crab Salad

Serves 4

Gazpacho

2 pounds beefsteak tomatoes,
blanched, peeled, cored, and
roughly chopped

2 red bell peppers, roasted,
peeled, seeded, and roughly
chopped (or use store-bought)

1 large jalapeño chile, roasted,
peeled, and seeded

½ medium red onion, roughly
chopped

2 garlic cloves, finely chopped

½ English cucumber, peeled
and roughly chopped

¼ cup sherry vinegar,
plus more if needed

½ cup extra-virgin olive oil,
plus more for drizzling over
finished soup bowls

2 teaspoons chopped fresh
tarragon leaves

1½ teaspoons salt,
plus more if needed

Tomato juice, as needed

Dungeness Crab Salad
(recipe follows)

Dungeness Crab Salad

12 ounces Dungeness crab

2 tablespoons fresh lemon juice,
or to taste

2 tablespoon extra-virgin olive oil

Salt and freshly ground black
pepper

Snipped fresh chives, to garnish

I n the fall and winter, our Tomato Soup (page 107) is the cozy, comforting dish that the entire community dreams of when they're not here enjoying a bowl of it. Once we start to get into spring, it's joined on our menu by this equally delicious way to celebrate the perfect tomatoes from our favorite farmers. In looking for a twist to take an already amazing soup into the stratosphere, we realized that the peak season for tomatoes just so happens to overlap with the Dungeness crab season. It turns out the two make an awesome match.

1. To make the gazpacho, combine all the ingredients in a large bowl and blend with an immersion blender to get a chunky but homogenous mixture. Taste and add more salt and/or vinegar if needed, and some tomato juice if the soup needs thinning. Refrigerate for a few hours or overnight so the flavors can mingle. Taste and adjust the seasonings again before serving.

2. To make the crab salad, put the crab in a medium bowl and add the lemon juice and oil. Season with salt and pepper. Toss to coat, taking care not to break up the crabmeat pieces too small. Taste and add more salt if needed.

3. To serve, ladle the soup evenly between 4 bowls and top each with a scoop of crab salad. Top with chives and finish with a drizzle of olive oil.

ROASTING THE PEPPERS
BRINGS OUT THEIR
SWEETNESS.

JUST FOUR
INGREDIENTS!

Charred Broccolini with Miso Sauce

This dish is an absolute feast for the senses, marrying together as it does the bright green broccolini with subtle smoke and char lines from the grill, umami-rich miso sauce, sharp cheese, and tangy lemon. If broccolini isn't in season, you can substitute any sturdy vegetable that you would put on the grill, such as asparagus or zucchini.

Serves 4

Salt

18 ounces broccolini, tough ends trimmed

Miso Sauce (page 62)

1½-ounce chunk Parmesan cheese

SEE HOW TO CHAR THE BROCCOLINI

1. Fill a large bowl with water and ice to make an ice bath before you begin preparing this dish.

2. Fill a large pot with water three-quarters full. Season heavily with salt, enough so it tastes like the ocean. Bring to a simmer over medium-high heat. Reduce the heat to keep a simmer going (it should not reach a rolling boil).

3. Working in batches, blanch the broccolini for 3 minutes, then remove it from the simmering water using tongs and immediately plunge it into the ice bath until completely cooled. Thoroughly strain the broccolini, shake off the cold water from the ice bath, and place it on a paper towel–lined baking sheet, then blot dry with more paper towels.

4. Next, heat a grill pan over high heat. Add the broccolini and give it a good char for 2 to 3 minutes on each side, until it has nice grill marks and is heated through, taking care not to let it burn. Toss the charred broccolini in the miso sauce to completely coat it.

5. Arrange the broccolini on plates with the florets all facing the same direction in a uniform formation at the center of the plates. Microplane the cheese over the top to completely coat from end to end. Serve immediately, before the cheese melts, so it keeps its fluffy presentation.

111

CORNFLAKES ADD
A SERIOUS CRUNCH!

Sweet Corn Bhel

Michael Bertozzi, The Kitchen's executive chef, fell in love with cooking at a young age. In particular, he remembers being surrounded by wonderful food at family gatherings. His father worked as a surgeon, which meant that he was exposed to kids from different cultures and their families. Sometimes he was fortunate enough to get invited to eat at his friends' houses. His parents taught him to always try everything that was offered at the table. It was that lesson that led him to be adventurous with food and sparked his love of global flavors. That sense of curiosity about taste combinations from near and far is what led him to riff on corn bhel, a mix of puffed rice, fresh vegetables, herbs, and spicy sauces that traditionally is sold as a snack in paper cones by street vendors in Mumbai. Michael developed this recipe that replaces the puffed rice with cornflakes. They add an unexpected crunch to every bite, and double up on the corn flavor. Serve this as a side salad, or as a communal plate with a basket of flatbread or pita chips to scoop it up. This recipe is truly glorious with sweet corn fresh from the field, but if you're craving it off season, you can swap in 3 cups of frozen corn kernels; just heat them up first in a skillet over medium heat, stirring constantly, until thawed and warmed.

Serves 4

4 large ears corn, with husks on

1 cup cornflakes, plus more for garnish

½ cup finely chopped red onion

1 cup finely chopped peeled and seeded cucumber

1 cup halved cherry tomatoes

1 cup finely chopped red bell pepper

½ cup roughly chopped fresh cilantro, plus more for garnish

¼ cup fresh mint leaves, cut into chiffonade

Cumin Lime Dressing (page 69)

Salt

Fresh lime juice

Microgreens for serving (optional)

1. Preheat the oven to 450°F.

2. Place the corn on a baking sheet in a single layer with at least 1 inch between ears. Roast for 40 minutes, then pull back the husks from one ear just enough to see if the kernels look puffed up and shiny, which means they're done. Remove the corn from the oven and cool, then remove the husks. Stand each husked ear on end in a large bowl and use a sharp chef's knife to cut the kernels from the cob.

3. Add the cornflakes, red onion, cucumber, cherry tomatoes, red pepper, cilantro, and mint to the bowl and toss to combine. Add the dressing and toss to coat. Season with salt and lime juice if needed. Divide into bowls and garnish with cornflakes, cilantro, and microgreens, if you like.

Naan Tomato Tartine

Serves 4

4 heirloom cherry tomatoes,
 quartered or cut into eighths,
 depending on size

Marinated Tomatoes (recipe
 follows)

¼ cup sherry vinegar

Kosher salt, to season

4 Naans (page 140) parbaked

Tomato Caramel (recipe follows)

Whipped Ricotta (recipe follows)

Fennel pollen, to garnish

Maldon salt, to garnish

Fresh basil leaves, torn if large

Extra-virgin olive oil

▶ **Makes about ½ cup**

2 teaspoons grapeseed or other
 neutral oil

1 large garlic clove, peeled

1 cup canned plum tomatoes

1 teaspoon dried oregano

1 teaspoon dried basil

½ teaspoon red chile flakes

1 cup sugar

½ teaspoon fennel seeds

One of the great things about the restaurant world is the way it can foster community among chefs. You might be surprised to learn that many chefs are happy to share their secrets and bounce ideas around with each other. In fact, this recipe is the result of one such collaboration. One night years ago, The Kitchen's executive chef, Michael Bertozzi, was dining at a restaurant in Atlanta when a fellow chef served him a chocolate dessert accompanied by a caramel sauce that had an intense flavor and color. Michael had to know the secret ingredient. It turns out it was a vegetable—beets. This inspired Michael to ask himself what else in the garden could be made into caramel? That's the spark that led to this dish, in which a caramel made from canned tomatoes plays off heirloom tomatoes at their height of freshness.

▼

1. Combine the fresh heirloom tomatoes and marinated tomatoes in a large bowl and toss with the vinegar. Season with salt and set aside.

2. Heat a grill pan over medium-high heat. Add the parbaked naans and cook until the flatbreads are heated through, with some grill marks on both sides. Cool for about a minute, then spoon the whipped ricotta over the naans and spread it to completely cover them (you can also use a piping bag for the cheese, if you prefer). Arrange the mixed tomatoes on top of the ricotta, then drizzle with the tomato caramel. Garnish with fennel pollen, Maldon salt, and basil and finish with a drizzle of oil. Serve immediately.

TOMATO CARAMEL

1. Heat the oil in a small saucepan over medium heat. Add the garlic and cook until fragrant, 2 to 3 minutes. Add the tomatoes and crush them with a spoon. Add the oregano,

Continued

basil, and chile flakes, bring to a simmer, and simmer for 5 to 10 minutes to combine the flavors.

2. Meanwhile, in a medium saucepan, heat the sugar over low heat, stirring with a silicone spatula, until the sugar melts and lightly caramelizes to a blond color. Turn off the heat and add half of the tomato puree and the fennel—stand back, as it will splutter—and stir vigorously to combine. Add the rest of the puree and thin with warm water if needed to reach a syrupy consistency. Strain through a fine-mesh strainer. Store tightly sealed at room temperature (so the caramel does not set) for up to a week. Thin with water if needed before using.

WHIPPED RICOTTA

> **Makes about 1 cup**
> 1 cup whole milk ricotta cheese
> 2 tablespoons heavy cream
> 1 teaspoon salt, or to taste

Combine the ricotta, cream, and salt in the bowl of a stand mixer fitted with the whisk attachment or use a handheld electric mixer. Whisk on high speed until the ricotta is light and fluffy, about 3 minutes.

MARINATED TOMATOES

24 cherry tomatoes, preferably heirloom

About ¼ cup Roasted Garlic Oil (page 73), or enough to cover the tomatoes

1. Bring a large pot of water to a boil over high heat. Fill a large bowl with ice and water and set aside.

2. Using a sharp knife, make an X in the bottom of each cherry tomato to pierce the skin. Add the cherry tomatoes to the boiling water and boil for 2 to 3 minutes to loosen the skins. Remove with a slotted spoon and plunge into the ice-water bath. Remove from the water and gently peel the skins. Place the tomatoes in a bowl, add the oil, and gently toss to coat.

Crispy Cauliflower Korma

This dish started with a challenge: Kimbal asked Chef Michael Bertozzi to come up with a delicious shareable plate that his wife, Christiana, would love. It needed to be vegan, gluten free, and dairy free. Ask any of our guests who know the menu by heart to name their favorites, and even the meat lovers in the crowd tend to place this dish in their personal pantheons. The recipe isn't difficult, but it does have a lot of components. Ideally, you'll be able to set aside the better part of a day to craft this—and hopefully recruit a little help. You can also save time by making the tamarind chutney and roasted garlic achaar up to a week ahead, the korma sauce 2 days ahead, and the coriander chutney the morning of the big event. Note that you'll need to make the pickled onions a couple of weeks ahead.

CAULIFLOWER KORMA SAUCE

In a medium saucepan, combine all the ingredients and bring to a simmer over medium heat. Cover, lower the heat a little, and simmer until the cauliflower is soft enough to be easily pierced with a knife, about 20 minutes. Strain the mixture into a bowl, reserving the cooking liquid. Place the solids in a blender and blend until smooth, adding cooking liquid as needed until the sauce is thick enough to coat the back of a spoon. Taste and add more salt if needed.

Makes about 4 cups

1½ pounds cauliflower, cut into florets

1 (14-ounce) can unsweetened coconut milk

1½ tablespoons yellow curry paste

3 tablespoons Roasted Garlic Achaar (page 72)

2 teaspoons light or dark brown sugar or jaggery

2 teaspoons salt, or to taste

HERB SALAD

Make the herb salad just before serving: Toss the herbs together in a medium bowl. Add the oil and lime juice and toss to coat. Add the mango and pickled red onions and toss to combine.

2 cups torn fresh flat-leaf parsley leaves and soft stems

2 cups torn fresh cilantro leaves and soft stems

½ cup torn fresh mint leaves

1 tablespoon grapeseed or other neutral oil

Juice of 1 lime

½ cup julienned ripe but firm mango

½ cup Pickled Red Onions (page 66)

DAIRY FREE,
VEGAN,
AND
GLUTEN FREE—DELICIOUS!

THE MAIN EVENT

1. Spread the chickpeas onto a baking sheet, blot with paper towels, and leave for about 1 hour to dry (alternatively, you could dry them in a 200°F oven for about 20 minutes).

2. While the chickpeas are drying, take a large pot and pour in enough oil to come 3 inches up the sides. Place over medium heat and heat to 350°F. Add the carrots and fry until softened and caramelized, 10 to 12 minutes. Remove the carrots from the oil using tongs and place on a cutting board to cool. Turn the oil to low but do not discard. Once the carrots have completely cooled, cut them into large but bite-sized chunks (approximately 1 to 1½ inches).

3. Bring the oil up to 325°F, then use it to fry the chickpeas in batches for 6 to 7 minutes, until browned. Remove with a slotted spoon to a paper towel–lined baking sheet and season with garam masala and salt. Set aside while you finish the rest of the dish.

4. Bring the oil back up to 350°F. In the meantime, make a cornstarch slurry. Pour the club soda into a wide bowl. Whisk in the cornstarch, 1½ teaspoons garam masala, and ¾ teaspoon salt. Dredge the fried carrots and cauliflower in the slurry separately. Working in batches, fry them for about 5 minutes, until golden brown and crispy. Remove from the oil to a large bowl using a slotted spoon. Add about 1 cup of the korma sauce to the bowl, toss to coat, and season with salt. Add the fried chickpeas and toss to combine.

5. Divide the rest of the warmed cauliflower korma sauce onto the middle of individual plates. Add two-thirds of the herb salad to the vegetable mixture and toss to combine.

6. Stack the vegetable mixture on top of the korma sauce and drizzle both chutneys on top. Top with the remaining herb salad and finish with a garnish of sesame seeds.

1 (15-ounce) can chickpeas, drained and rinsed

Grapeseed or other neutral oil, for frying

2 medium carrots, peeled and root end trimmed

1½ teaspoons garam masala, plus more for dusting the chickpeas

¾ teaspoon salt, plus more for finishing the chickpeas

½ cup club soda

½ cup cornstarch

1 (2- to 2½-pound) head cauliflower, cut into bite-sized pieces

Cauliflower Korma Sauce (see previous page), warmed

1 cup Tamarind Chutney (page 63)

1 cup Coriander Chutney (page 63)

Herb Salad (see previous page), made just before serving

Sesame seeds, to garnish

One of the joys of owning a restaurant is getting to serve fresh, healthy food to all comers. The Kitchen is often cited as a pioneer in the farm-to-table movement, but we didn't set out to start a revolution. We just wanted to support our local farmers and serve our guests the most wonderful produce available. Kimbal and Chef Hugo started donating to and volunteering at local school gardens at the request of a manager at The Kitchen Upstairs (our cocktail lounge). It was through that first experience of gardening with kids that they realized growing food changes lives. It improves our nutrition security and mental health. It gets us out into nature and opens our eyes to the weather volatility created by climate change.

In 2011, Kimbal and Hugo co-founded Big Green, a 501(c)(3) nonprofit organization to help people grow their own food by starting gardens. With garden-based education; scalable, modular garden products and systems; and a community of support and collaboration, Big Green has grown into a national organization reaching hundreds of thousands of people every day.

Did you know that children who participate in gardening are twice as likely to eat their daily recommended fruits and vegetables? Big Green built a network of more than seven hundred vibrant and edible Learning Gardens in schools across the country, and the organization is now working in homes and community centers across America. Big Green also provides grants and garden materials to garden organizations nationwide and to local grassroots leaders.

OUR
BIG GREEN
COMMUNITY

If you have ever made pasta at home, you know how much fun it is—and how unpredictable the results can be, at least if you're hoping to create something approaching perfection every time. Making fresh pasta dough is as much an art as it is a science. You'll do best to start with a good recipe (we have you covered there), an open mind, and a love of experimentation. The real win here is to make pasta with your friends and family. Invite a group over (definitely include kids who have an interest in cooking), put on some great music (see my playlist on page 35), and focus on the fun of it. Our tagliatelle recipe (page 128) is the easiest one we have found to get right when cooking with your friends and family.

For those who don't like the unpredictability of working with sometimes temperamental pasta dough, we have the solution. In this chapter, you'll also find a fantastic gnocchi recipe that will turn out fluffy and satisfying every time. Made with a French pastry dough, it's unlike any gnocchi recipe you have ever tasted. It is loved by adults and kids alike—in fact, I think we'd have a riot if we took our gnocchi off the menu.

Grains &
Pasta

Fresh Pasta Dough

Makes about 1½ pounds

4 cups 00 flour, plus more for
kneading and rolling

1½ teaspoons salt

4 large eggs

4 large egg yolks (page 43 for
technique)

1 tablespoon extra-virgin olive oil

1 beaten egg, for egg wash

Semolina, for dusting

FRESH IS BEST

For this recipe you want to use the freshest eggs you can find. The eggs make all the difference in the world. Look for eggs from local farmers or natural, organic eggs from your local grocery store. Check the dates. The fresher the eggs, the better your pasta will be.

HOW TO MAKE
PASTA DOUGH

The world can probably be divided into home cooks who make their own fresh pasta and those who don't—yet. If you love pasta but have never made it yourself from scratch, this recipe may come as a revelation. We use it to make our tagliatelle (page 128) and ravioli (page 134), but that's just the beginning of the possibilities. Cut it into wider strips for lasagna or use a cookie cutter to make rounds of dough to fill and fold into tortellini. However you use this dough, the results will taste lighter and fresher than the dried stuff. For us, the best thing about making pasta is how fun it is to do with kids and friends. What's better than coming together, getting covered in flour, trying different recipes, and tasting how such simple ingredients turn into a bowl of the best pasta you've ever eaten?

1. Put the flour on a clean, dry counter with room to work. Mix in the salt. Make a mound of the flour and create a well in the center, then add the eggs, egg yolks, and oil to the well. Break up the egg yolks with a fork, mixing and slowly incorporating the flour from the edges of the well. Keep pulling flour from the edges with a bench scraper or fork and work the mixture into a shaggy dough. Keep working the dough with your hands until it comes together into a ball. Scrape up any excess dough and re-flour the work surface before continuing. Knead the dough until it has a silky, smooth texture and snaps back when stretched, 10 to 15 minutes. Add more flour if the mixture is too wet or a little water if it is too dry.

2. If you prefer to use a food processor, you can pulse the flour and salt to combine the ingredients and aerate the flour. Beat the eggs to combine, then add to the food processor and process for about 30 seconds, or until a dough is formed. Move to the counter and knead for 1 to 2 minutes.

3. Wrap the dough tightly in plastic wrap and let it rest on the counter for 1 hour or refrigerate up to overnight. Remove from the fridge about 30 minutes before using.

4. Clamp a pasta machine to a long work surface and dust the surface with flour. Sprinkle a baking sheet well with flour and put the ball of dough on top of it. Divide the dough into 6 to 8 equal-sized pieces. Working with one piece at a time (keep the other pieces covered in plastic), dust the dough lightly in flour and flatten it with your hands to form an oblong shape about ¼ inch thick.

5. Set the machine to 1 (the thickest setting) and run the pasta through, adding a little more flour if it starts to stick. Repeat once or twice. Fold this piece of dough into thirds, like folding a letter, and press it between your hands again. With the pasta machine still on the thickest setting, feed the pasta through once or twice more until smooth, getting it to fit the width of the machine. Set the machine to 2 and run the flattened dough through again. Repeat, setting the machine to progressively thinner settings, dusting with flour as needed, until you reach the second thinnest or thinnest setting. Place the pasta sheets on the baking sheet and dust with flour to avoid sticking as you fold and stack them. Cover with a very lightly dampened kitchen towel until you're ready to prepare the pasta.

The Kitchen Gnocchetti Plate

**Serves 4 as a starter or
2 as a main**

1 tablespoons grapeseed or
other neutral oil

About 48 Pâte à Choux Gnocchetti
(recipe follows)

Roasted Mushrooms
(recipe follows)

½ cup Arugula Pesto (page 52)

¾ cup heavy cream

2 tablespoons unsalted butter

Shaved ribbons of Grana Padano
cheese, for serving

Watercress sprigs, for serving

**Makes about 200 gnocchetti,
enough for 4 batches**

1 cup whole milk

3½ tablespoons unsalted butter

1¼ cups bread flour, sifted

1¼ teaspoons salt, plus more for
boiling the gnocchetti

½ teaspoon freshly ground
black pepper

¼ teaspoon freshly grated nutmeg

1¼ cups grated Parmesan cheese

3 large eggs

Grapeseed or other neutral oil

I f you need a good definition of alchemy, just look at what a skilled chef can do with butter, flour, eggs, and a splash of water. The real magic begins when those ingredients are combined to make the French pastry staple pâte à choux, a fantastically versatile dough that's used to fashion any number of delights, from churros and éclairs to cheese puffs and dumplings. Here, it's used to make Parisian-style gnocchetti—a lighter, fluffier cousin to the potato-based version from Northern Italy that's more commonly found in the U.S. These are so velvety that they practically melt in your mouth. Served with our peppery Arugula Pesto and mixed Roasted Mushrooms, this dish is rich, even unctuous, packing a ton of flavor as a shared starter or a robust vegetarian meal.

1. Heat the oil in a large nonstick skillet over medium to medium-high heat until it shimmers. Add the gnocchetti and cook until golden brown on the bottom, about 2 minutes. Flip them and heat until browned on the other side, about 2 minutes longer.

2. Meanwhile, place a large skillet over medium heat, and add the mushrooms, pesto, cream, and butter. Swirl to form a pan sauce.

3. Add the gnocchetti to the mushroom mixture and toss to combine. Divide into bowls and garnish with cheese and watercress. Serve immediately.

PÂTE À CHOUX GNOCCHETTI

1. Combine the milk and butter in a medium saucepan and bring to a simmer over medium heat. Vigorously stir in the flour all at once with a wooden spoon until a smooth dough forms. Reduce the heat to medium-low and cook, stirring vigorously, for about 5 minutes, until the starchiness of the flour has cooked out and the dough pulls away from the sides of the pot, taking care that the

mixture doesn't stick to the pot. Transfer the mixture to the bowl of an electric mixer fitted with the paddle attachment and beat on medium-low speed for 3 to 4 minutes. Add the salt, pepper, nutmeg, and cheese and mix until fully incorporated. Add the eggs one at a time and mix until they're all fully incorporated and a smooth dough is formed.

2. Spoon the gnocchetti mixture into a piping bag. You can stop at this point if you're preparing the meal components ahead of time, put the piping bag in a bowl to hold it upright, then refrigerate for up to a day.

3. When you're ready to make the gnocchetti, oil a baking sheet and set it aside.

4. Take a heavy two-handled pot, tie a piece of butcher's twine around one of the pot handles and stretch it across to the other handle, creating a taut line to cut the gnocchetti with. Fill the pot with water, salt it, and bring to a simmer over high heat.

5. Squeeze the gnocchetti mixture out and drag it across the butcher's twine to cut pieces about ½ inch long, letting them fall into the simmering water once cut. Keep doing this for 1 minute, then continue to cook the gnocchetti until they float to the surface. Give them another 2 to 3 minutes to set. Scoop out the gnocchetti using a slotted spoon or spider strainer, place on the prepared baking sheet to cool, and toss with a little more oil. Cooled gnocchetti can be stored in a container and refrigerated up to a day ahead before finishing the recipe. Freeze whatever you don't using within a day. To freeze, lay the gnocchetti out on a baking sheet in a single layer and freeze for 1 hour, or until solid, then pop them into a zip-top bag and keep in the freezer for up to 3 months.

The butcher's twine trick is both traditional and cool to pull off, but if you like you can also just cut the gnocchetti with a knife or kitchen scissors as the dough comes out of the piping bag.

ROASTED MUSHROOMS

This recipe features three of our favorite mushrooms, but you can substitute others if you'd like. Note that you'll be cooking the mushrooms in two batches so as not to overcrowd the pan, allowing them to cook all the way through and brown nicely.

Heat a large sauté pan over medium heat. Add half of the butter and heat until melted and foaming. Add half of the garlic and thyme and cook until the garlic is just softened, about 2 minutes. Add half of the mushrooms and cook until golden brown and softened, about 5 minutes. Remove the mushrooms to a bowl and repeat these steps with the remaining butter, thyme, and mushrooms. Add the first batch back to the pan, then remove the thyme and discard. Season with salt and pepper. Use immediately or store in a covered container in the refrigerator for up to 5 days.

Makes about 2 cups

2 tablespoons unsalted butter

1 tablespoon thinly sliced garlic

2 sprigs thyme

5 ounces trumpet mushrooms, cut into 1-inch pieces

5 ounces oyster mushrooms, stemmed and torn

5 ounces beech mushrooms, stemmed and torn

Salt and freshly ground black pepper to taste

Tagliatelle Bolognese

Serves 4

Salt

12 ounces Tagliatelle
   (recipe follows)

1 tablespoon extra-virgin olive oil

3 cups Bolo (recipe follows)

¼ cup heavy cream, or more
   if you like it creamier

Parmesan cheese, to top

Fennel pollen, to garnish

½ batch Fresh Pasta Dough
   (page 124)

You can make this recipe with store-bought fresh pasta if you prefer, but we put in a very strong vote for homemade. If you have a pasta maker or can lay your hands on one, you'll find that it's easier than you might think to craft your own tagliatelle—and it's deliciously rewarding, especially as a communal project. Many high-end stand mixers offer pasta-making attachments as an optional accessory, so that might be a reasonable choice for you. Our no-fail pasta recipe combines here with our beloved Bolo sauce for a rich, hearty, satisfying meal of noodles with red sauce in which every component is crafted with love. Fresh pasta cooks very quickly, so keep a close eye on it—it will need only about a minute!

1. Bring a large pot of water to a boil and salt it. Add the tagliatelle and cook until al dente, about 1 minute, then drain.

2. To prepare the sauce, heat the oil in a large sauté pan over medium-high heat. Add the prepared Bolo and cream and stir to combine, then heat to a simmer. Using tongs, transfer the pasta directly to the pan with the sauce and toss to coat. Divide among bowls and use a Microplane to grate a cloud of cheese over the top. Sprinkle with fennel pollen and serve.

TAGLIATELLE

1. Run the prepared dough through a pasta machine on the second-thinnest setting. Switch from the pasta roller to the noodle cutter and run the sheet of pasta through the cutter. Toss the noodles with a little flour to keep them from sticking and gather them into a loose basket. Set onto a floured baking sheet and cover with a very lightly dampened kitchen towel while you finish rolling and cutting the rest of the dough.

2. Freeze any pasta you're not using immediately directly on the baking sheet, then transfer to a freezer bag and store in the freezer for up to 3 months. Cook the pasta directly from the freezer without defrosting.

THE BOLO

It's no exaggeration to say that this recipe belongs in the upper pantheon of The Kitchen's classics. Ask anyone in our community—from longtime staff to dining-room regulars—what is the one dish they'd like most to cook for their families and the answer will likely be "the Bolo." Though it has varied a bit over the years, it has always returned to the ingredients here, yielding a flavor profile complex enough to be special and yet simple enough to feel like home. Enjoy it tossed with pasta, with good bread for dipping as a shared appetizer or afternoon snack, or over grits, polenta, or our Rice Middlins (page 142).

1. Trim the livers of sinew and soak in a bowl of cold water for 15 minutes, then drain and finely chop.

2. In a large saucepan, heat the oil over medium heat until it shimmers. Add the garlic, fennel seeds, and chile flakes and cook until aromatic, about 2 minutes. Add the onion, carrot, and celery and cook until the onion is softened and translucent, about 5 minutes.

3. Add the livers to the pan, then add the pork, lamb, and beef and cook until all of the meat is browned and the fat has been released. Season with salt and pepper, then add the prosciutto. Add the milk and cook, stirring, until the volume is reduced by one-quarter. Add the wine and cook until it is absorbed, then add the chicken stock and tomatoes. Wrap the bay leaf, thyme, and peppercorns in a piece of cheesecloth and tie with kitchen twine. Add to the pot and bring the sauce to a simmer. Lower the heat and cook uncovered at the lowest of simmers for 4 to 5 hours, stirring as needed to avoid sticking. The tomatoes should naturally break down during cooking; if they don't, help them along by mashing them with a wooden spoon. Taste and add more salt and/or pepper if needed. Cool any remaining sauce and store tightly covered in the refrigerator for up to 4 days or freeze for up to 3 months.

Makes about 3½ quarts

3 ounces chicken livers

¼ cup extra-virgin olive oil

3 tablespoons finely chopped garlic

1 tablespoon fennel seeds

1½ teaspoons red chile flakes

1½ cups diced yellow onion

2½ cups diced carrots

1 cup diced celery

1 pound ground pork

1 pound ground lamb

1 pound ground beef

Salt and freshly ground black pepper

6 ounces prosciutto, finely chopped

1½ cups milk

1½ cups white wine

1½ cups chicken stock

2 (28-ounce) cans whole tomatoes

1 bay leaf

3 sprigs thyme

1½ tablespoons black peppercorns

BLACK SPAGHETTI WITH SHRIMP AND SAUSAGE

THE KITCHEN
GNOCCHETTI
PLATE

TAGLIATELLE
BOLOGNESE

Black Spaghetti with Rock Shrimp and 'Nduja Sausage

Serves 4

Salt

½ (500-g/17.6-oz) package
  squid ink spaghetti

2 tablespoons grapeseed or
  other neutral oil

2 garlic cloves, sliced

12 ounces rock shrimp,
  the smallest you can find,
  peeled and deveined

7 to 8 ounces 'nduja sausage

8 ounces fennel, sliced ⅛ inch
  thick on a mandoline or
  with a sharp knife

½ cup clam juice

4 tablespoons unsalted butter,
  cut into chunks

1 tablespoon fresh lemon juice,
  or to taste

8 orange supremes
  (see below for technique)

8 grapefruit supremes
  (see below for technique)

Sliced green onion tops

4 tablespoons homemade
  breadcrumbs, or
  use store-bought

2 teaspoons fennel pollen

So many cultures from around the world find ways to marry the complementary flavors and textures of pork and shellfish, balancing the meat's mild flavor and rich mouthfeel with fresh, briny, delicately flavored seafood. This dish punches up those elements in a couple of fun ways, for a really robust, flavor-packed dish. Squid-ink pasta doesn't just bring a cool color into the mix; the ink introduces oceanic, briny notes as an undertone to the tiny, sparklingly fresh shrimp. Calabrian 'nduja sausage has the intense spice and rich flavor to tie this dish together into something that looks amazing on the plate and tastes even better.

1. Bring a large pot of water to a boil and salt it. Add the pasta and cook until al dente, following the instructions on the package. Drain, reserving some pasta cooking water.

2. Meanwhile, heat the oil in a large skillet over medium-high heat. Add the garlic and shrimp and cook until the shrimp just begin to turn pink, about 3 minutes. Reduce the heat to low and add the 'nduja, fennel, and clam juice, using a spoon to break up the 'nduja and incorporate it. As the 'nduja and shrimp cook, toss the pan to coat the shrimp and begin building the pan sauce. Keep the heat low so as not to break the sauce (i.e., let it separate).

3. Add the pasta to the pan with a little of the pasta cooking water. Toss to combine. Add the butter and continue tossing the pasta to coat and emulsify the sauce. If the sauce breaks, add a little pasta water and re-emulsify. Add more pasta water if needed to finish the sauce. Add the lemon juice and season with salt if needed.

4. Twirl the pasta into the center of 4 plates, then spoon the shrimp mixture over the pasta. Garnish with the orange and grapefruit supremes, green onions, and breadcrumbs. Wipe the plate rims clean and sprinkle the fennel pollen over the pasta and over the rest of the plate.

SUPREME CITRUS

Making supremes is a way of serving just the juicy, delicious flesh of an orange, grapefruit, or other sizable citrus fruit free from any peel, pith, or membranes. It's only a little more effort than just cutting the fruit into segments, and it really pays off. Using a very sharp knife, cut horizontal slices from the top and bottom of the fruit through the rind, just barely exposing the flesh. Set one of the now-flat ends on your cutting board. Next, slice the rind and pith off together, carefully following the curve of the fruit. Place the fruit lightly on its side and very carefully cut along the edge of one of the membranes, separating the flesh of one segment from another. Then slice along the other side of the segment until your cuts meet and you can gently remove just the segment. Set it aside and continue cutting until you've freed all of the segments. Any segments you don't use in this recipe could be added to a salad or smoothie—or you can snack on them as is.

Chicken Liver Mousse Ravioli w/ Green Tomato Marmalata

Serves 6 to 8

Salt

32 Chicken Liver Mousse Ravioli
   (recipe follows)

½ cup unsalted butter,
   cut into pieces

1 cup Green Tomato Marmalata
   (recipe follows)

Freshly ground black pepper

½ cup fresh or frozen green peas,
   blanched

Marigold flowers (optional)

Torn fresh flat-leaf parsley leaves

The Kitchen's executive chef, Michael Bertozzi, learned to make pickles at a young age, watching his mother, who hailed from Texas, put up jars of vegetables in their home kitchen. Michael loved the process and how it often created a mix of sweet, salty, and savory flavors in one bite. It was that affection for pickles that led him to come up with a sauce based on a green tomato marmalade, or *marmalata,* which cuts the richness of the chicken liver in this recipe.

1. Line a baking sheet with paper towels before you begin, so you'll have somewhere to hold the ravioli as you make them.

2. Next, bring a large pot of water to a boil and salt it. Working in batches of 4 to 6, add the ravioli to the boiling water and cook until they float to the top, about 1 minute (2 minutes if you are using frozen ravioli). As each batch is done, scoop them out with a slotted spoon and place them on the prepared baking sheet.

3. When all of the ravioli are cooked, transfer half of them to a large sauté pan (if you have two pans you can do one batch in each simultaneously). Place over medium heat and add ¼ cup of the butter. Add ½ cup of the marmalata, black pepper to taste, and a little of the pasta water and gently toss to melt the butter and coat the ravioli. Add half of the peas and swirl the pan to create an emulsified sauce. Remove from the pan and repeat with the remaining ravioli and sauce. Divide among plates and garnish with marigold flowers, if using, and parsley.

CHICKEN LIVER MOUSSE RAVIOLI
Makes about 1½ pounds

1⅓ batch Fresh Pasta Dough
  (page 124)
Chicken Liver Mousse
  (page 190)

1 egg beaten, for egg wash
Semolina, for dusting

Using a pastry wheel or cookie cutter, cut the rolled pasta dough into 3-inch squares or circles. Stuff the chilled mousse into a pastry bag, then pipe a scant 1 tablespoon into the center of each pasta piece. Brush the edges of the pasta sheet with egg wash, then fold the dough in half to create either a triangle or half-moon shape, and seal the pasta. Gently press with your fingertips to seal the edges, making sure to avoid trapped air pockets. When done, dust with semolina. Cover the ravioli on your baking sheet with plastic wrap and place in the refrigerator until you're ready to cook them. You can also freeze them on the baking sheet until solid, then transfer to zip-top freezer bags and freeze for up to 2 months before using. Cook the ravioli directly from frozen, do not defrost.

GREEN TOMATO MARMALATA
Makes about 1½ cups

2 pounds green tomatoes, diced
Rind of 1 lemon, thinly julienned
2 tablespoons fresh lemon juice,
  or to taste

1⅓ cups sugar
2 sprigs thyme
½ teaspoon salt, or to taste

In a large saucepan, combine all the ingredients and bring to a boil over medium-high heat. Reduce the heat but maintain a high simmer. Simmer for 40 to 50 minutes, until it reaches a jammy consistency. Remove and discard the thyme twigs. Transfer the hot marmalata to a food processor and process until smooth. Taste and add more lemon juice and/or salt if needed. Cool completely, then refrigerate in an airtight container until ready to use. It will keep sealed and refrigerated for up to 2 months.

DENVER

Coming Together at the Corner

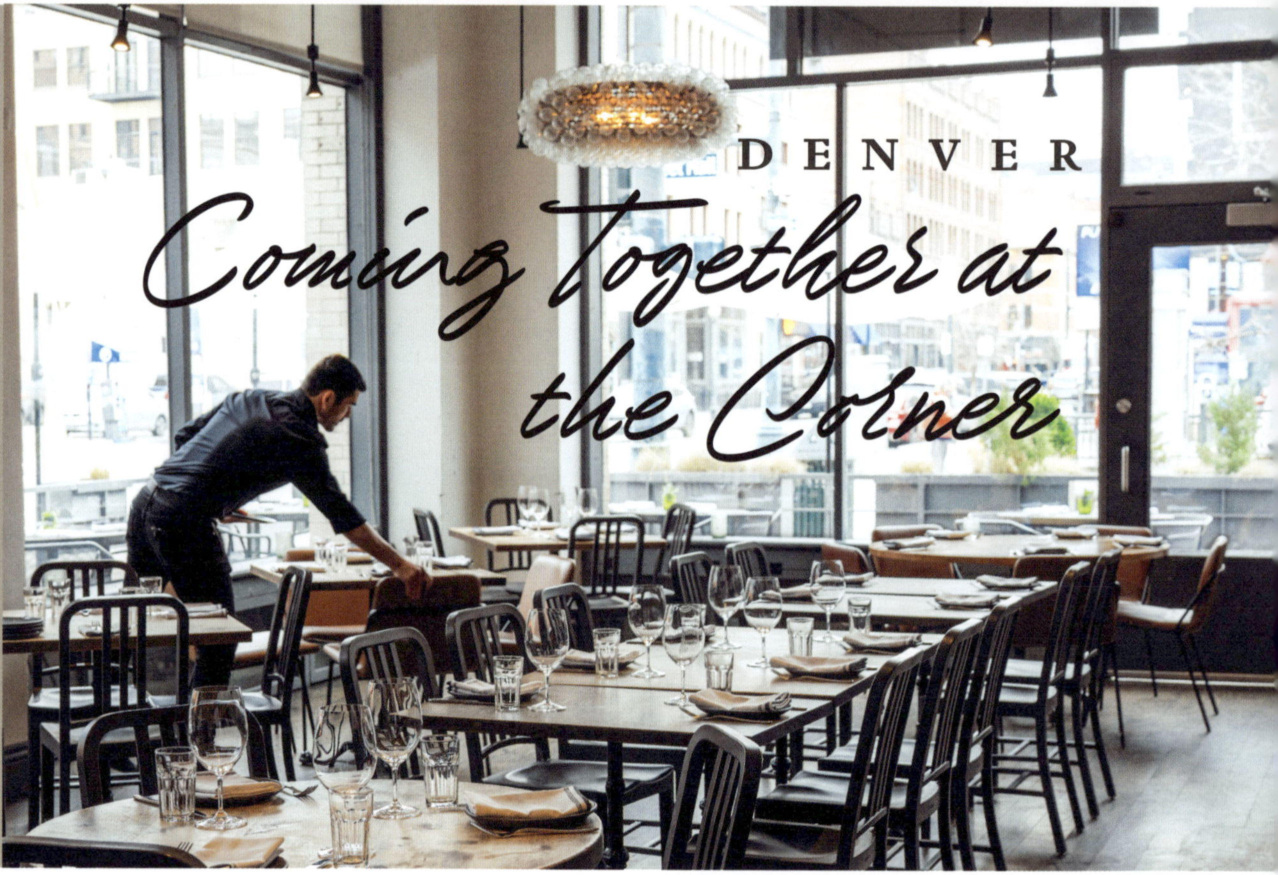

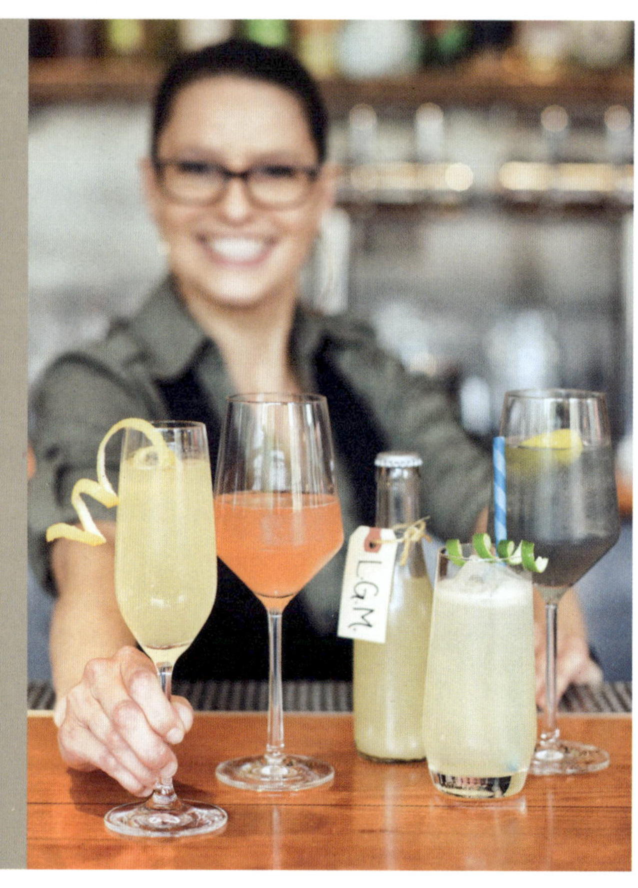

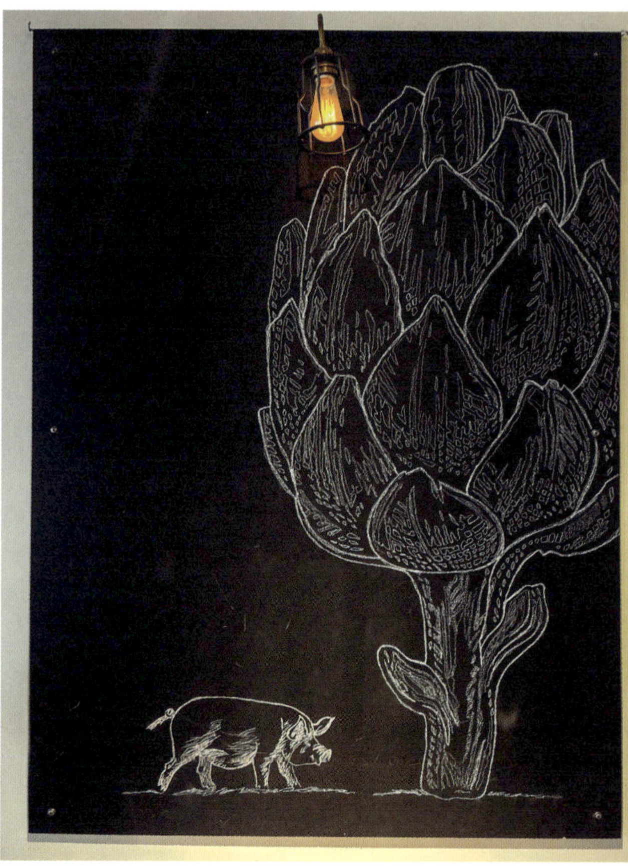

When we started looking for the right space for The Kitchen Denver, we knew it had to be within walking distance to the other cool spots our guests would want to visit downtown. We also knew we were ready to try out a bigger space than our first home in Boulder. But most of all, we wanted to find a spot with soul, a place with real history. What we didn't expect was how perfectly all the items on that wish list would come together right here in the historic Sugar Building. We're a stone's throw from Denver's gorgeous Union Station (designed by the same architects as the Sugar Building), Coors Field, and the Ball Arena (home of the Denver Nuggets).

Built in 1906 to house the Great Western Sugar Company, the Sugar Building is on the National Registry of Historic Places, for its place in Colorado history and for its form-meets-function design. By the 1980s, sugar beets were no longer the economic powerhouse they'd been before, and the building was falling into disrepair. Luckily for us, the building was lovingly renovated in the early 2000s. We opened there in 2012, in a space designed by our multitalented co-founder Chef Hugo Matheson and the Denver-based design firm Semple Brown. We wanted to give the finished space a unique, modern vibe while also respecting the building's history. The design team literally peeled away layers of paint and finish that had been applied over a hundred years, to reveal the very heart of the structure. Today, the worn plaster, original support columns, and exposed brick honor that history.

Grilled Halloumi Cheese on Roasted Garlic Naan

Serves 4

Herb Salad

½ cup julienned ripe but
firm mango

½ cup Pickled Red Onions
(page 66)

1 tablespoon fresh lime juice

1 tablespoon grapeseed or
other neutral oil

2 teaspoons agave nectar

1 cup picked fresh cilantro
leaves and soft stems

1 cup picked fresh parsley
leaves and soft stems

¼ cup roughly torn fresh
mint leaves

Salt

Naans and Toppings

4 Naans (recipe follows)

1 (8-ounce) package
halloumi cheese

Grapeseed or other neutral oil

Salt

1 cup Sweet Yogurt
(recipe follows)

½ cup Curry Mayo (page 59)

½ cup Coriander Chutney
(page 63)

½ cup Tamarind Chutney
(page 63)

This is a really fun dish to make and share. How about planning a baking Saturday where you and a group of friends make a batch of naans together and then enjoy this dish with a big meal? It's also a dream of a shared appetizer or a wonderful vegetarian main dish. Warm, fresh naan topped with tangy cheese, fresh mango and herbs, and a handful of edible flowers is basically a grilled cheese sandwich on its best day ever. Halloumi cheese is popular throughout the Mediterranean and beyond; it has a high melting point that makes it ideal for grilling, plus a briny bite that we love paired with this sandwich's acid crunch of pickled onions. If you have two pans to use in preparing this, things will go a lot more quickly. If you don't, someone you invite probably will—all the more reason to hold a gathering.

1. To make the herb salad, start by placing the mango and pickled red onions in a medium bowl. Add the lime juice, oil, and agave nectar and toss to coat. Add the cilantro, parsley, and mint. Season with salt.

2. To finish the naans and pull the dish together, heat a large cast-iron skillet or griddle over medium-high heat. Add a par-cooked naan and cook until well charred on one side, about 1 minute, then flip and cook to char the second side, about 1 minute more.

3. While the naan is cooking, cut the halloumi into 4 slices. Heat a nonstick skillet over medium-high heat. Dry the halloumi slices by blotting them with a paper towel, then brush both sides lightly with oil. Place the cheese in the pan and cook until a deep brown crust forms, 1 to 2 minutes. Flip and cook until seared on the second side (the cheese will soften but won't melt). Season with salt.

4. Place one naan on each plate and drizzle with ¼ cup sweet yogurt and 2 tablespoons curry aioli. Place the cooked halloumi on top, then drizzle 2 tablespoons

Continued

coriander chutney and 2 tablespoons tamarind chutney over it. Top with even portions of the salad and serve.

ROASTED GARLIC NAAN

Premade naans are available in many grocery stores, and if you're lucky enough to live near an Indian bakery, you might be able to purchase them hot from the oven for a special meal. We suggest you try making your own at home. As a flatbread, naan is much simpler to prepare than most leavened breads, great for time-pressed or less experienced bakers. Plus, it's so rewarding to create fresh, authentic accompaniments for your Indian-influenced meals (or for snacking on any time).

Makes 8 naans

2 cups self-rising flour, plus more if needed
1 teaspoon salt
2 cups plain Greek yogurt
¼ cup Roasted Garlic Oil (page 73)
Grapeseed oil, for oiling the bowl and brushing the naan
All-purpose flour, for rolling

1. In a large bowl, whisk together the self-rising flour and salt. Add the yogurt and roasted garlic oil and mix with a non-stick spatula until thoroughly combined. Knead a few times with your hands, adding a little more flour until the dough is smooth and no longer sticky. Oil a clean bowl, place the dough ball in the bowl and turn it over to coat it all over in oil. Cover the bowl with plastic wrap and rest it on the counter for 1 hour.

2. Lightly dust a work surface with all-purpose flour. Roll the dough into a tube shape and cut into 8 pieces, about 3 ounces each. Using lightly floured hands, form each piece into a smooth ball.

3. Preheat a cast-iron skillet or grill pan over medium-high heat.

4. Using a lightly dusted rolling pin, flatten a dough ball to about ½ inch thick, then roll it out into a ¼-inch-thick circle, adding more flour to the work surface and/or rolling pin if needed. Lift the dough, one end in each hand, and pull it in opposite directions into an oval. Immediately put the naan on the pan. Par-cook the naan for about 30 seconds on each side, until it is set with light brown spots. Repeat with the remaining naans, stacking them in a kitchen towel–lined basket. Keep the basket covered with another kitchen towel in order to keep the naans warm.

5. Cool any naans you're not enjoying right away on a wire rack, then store in a plastic bag or airtight container for up to 3 days.

SWEET YOGURT

In a small bowl, combine the jaggery and granulated sugar, then pour the boiling water on top. Whisk, then leave to dissolve and cool for 10 minutes. Stir in the yogurt.

Makes about 1 cup

2 tablespoons jaggery or light or dark brown sugar
1 teaspoon granulated sugar
2 tablespoons boiling water
1 cup plain Greek yogurt

Rye Spaetzle

The little pasta dumplings known as spaetzle (German for "little sparrows" because of their shape) are a staple of Bavarian cooking. Like the macaroni they somewhat resemble, spaetzle can be served with butter and cheese as a simple meal, or as a side dish or base for roast meat, chicken, or hearty winter vegetables. Denser than most pasta, spaetzle is simple yet versatile, with a very satisfying mouthfeel. In our recipe, we use rye and caraway for autumnal flavors that pair well with pork (such as the Double-Cut Pork Chops, page 203) or root vegetables. You could sub out corn flour for the rye, lose the caraway seeds, and add a touch of sage to serve alongside poultry. Or go Bavarian old-school with all-purpose flour for the entire batch, plus a dusting of nutmeg.

Makes about 4 cups

1 cup all-purpose flour

½ cup rye flour

¾ teaspoon caraway seeds, toasted

1 teaspoon salt, plus more for cooking the spaetzle

2 large eggs, lightly beaten

½ cup milk

Extra-virgin olive oil, for coating the baking sheet and spaetzle

1. In a large bowl, combine the all-purpose flour, rye flour, caraway seeds, and salt and whisk to incorporate. Fold in the eggs. When the eggs are fully incorporated, fold in the milk and mix thoroughly. Set the batter aside for 30 minutes to rest.

2. Coat a baking sheet with oil.

3. Bring a large pot of water to a boil and salt it. Working in two batches, pour the spaetzle mixture through the holes of a turned-upside-down large-hole colander (or a spaetzle maker if you have one) into the boiling water. Use a bench scraper or a sturdy spoon to push it through (it may get a little messy!). Cook until the spaetzle floats to the surface plus about 1 minute more. Scoop them out with a slotted spoon onto the oiled baking sheet. Repeat with the remaining spaetzle. Add a little more oil and toss to coat. The spaetzle can be stored in a covered container in the refrigerator for up to 1 day.

Rice Middlins with Poached Eggs & Kimchi

Serves 4

3 cups water

3 cups heavy cream

1½ teaspoons salt,
  plus more to taste

1 cup rice middlins

4 tablespoons unsalted butter

4 poached eggs (method follows)

4 tablespoons Black Vinegar
  Sauce (recipe follows),
  or more to taste

Beef Short Ribs (page 217)
  (optional)

½ cup packed kimchi, cut into
  julienne

1 large radish, cut into julienne

Handful of tender cilantro stems

In the American South and beyond, a creamy bowl of grits practically defines comfort food. Throughout Asia, the ultimate comfort food is the rice porridge called congee, which is also commonly topped with eggs and served with the option of adding hot sauce and picked vegetables. We wanted to create a dish that evoked the best of both worlds but at first could not find the right grain for it. Once we learned about Carolina Gold rice middlins (from Marsh Hen Mill), we knew we had, well, struck gold. Middlins are the broken grains left over from processing Carolina Gold rice, an unusually flavorful and healthy grain that was first grown in America's coastal lowlands by enslaved people who brought their agricultural knowledge and seeds from Africa. In this dish, we take that creamy, nutty rice (which has a consistency similar to risotto) and add some traditional congee toppings. Serve it as a hearty vegetarian brunch or lunch dish, or add slow-cooked pork short rib for the meat eaters.

1. In a large saucepan, combine the water, cream, and salt and bring to a boil over medium-high heat. Add the rice middlins, stir once, and return to a boil. Reduce the heat to maintain a simmer and cook for 15 to 20 minutes, stirring occasionally, until al dente (as you would with risotto). Strain the middlins, reserving the cooking liquid.

2. If you'd like, you can prepare the middlins in advance. If you do, be sure to reserve the cooking liquid, because you'll need it later. Cool the middlins spread out on a baking sheet to avoid clumping, then store them and the cooking fluid in separate covered containers in the fridge.

When ready to use, reheat them using as much of the reserved liquid as you need to get your desired consistency, then discard the rest.

3. Divide the cooked rice middlins among 4 bowls and season with salt. Add 1 tablespoon butter to each bowl and let it melt. Add as much reserved cooking liquid as needed for your desired consistency. Discard the remaining cooking liquid. Place a poached egg in the center of each bowl and drizzle the black vinegar sauce over the top. If desired, add a piece of short rib, then garnish the bowls with kimchi, radish, and cliantro and serve immediately.

POACHED EGGS

Fill a medium pan halfway with water, then add two teaspoons of vinegar and a dash of salt. Place over medium heat and bring to a simmer. Crack each egg into a teacup and gently slip the egg out into the water. Let cook for 2 to 3 minutes, then remove each egg carefully with a slotted spoon.

BLACK VINEGAR SAUCE

Combine the tamari, vinegar, and sugar in a medium bowl and whisk to dissolve the sugar. Add the Szechuan chili crunch and whisk to incorporate. Add the cilantro and scallions and whisk to combine.

Makes about ½ cup

¼ cup tamari or other soy sauce

¼ cup sherry vinegar

3 tablespoons sugar

½ tablespoon Szechuan Chili Crunch (page 63) or a store-bought brand

1 tablespoon chopped fresh cilantro

1½ tablespoons thinly sliced scallion

Jimmy Red Corn Grits with Spring Veggies & Eggs

Serves 4

Grits

4 cups water

4 tablespoons unsalted butter

Salt

1 cup Jimmy Red corn grits or
   other stone-ground grits

For Serving

2 tablespoons unsalted butter

½ cup fresh or frozen green peas,
   blanched

½ cup asparagus tips, blanched

½ cup Roasted Mushrooms
   (page 127)

Salt

4 poached eggs (page 143)

Shaved Grana Padano, to garnish

1 cup watercress, to garnish

This is like a springtime answer to our Rice Middlins (page 142). If you think about spring, particularly in our Boulder home, it's about the juxtaposition of seasons—one day it might be 75 degrees, the next day it could snow. So, this dish gives you something warm and comforting with the grits and eggs, but also the fresh, green brightness of asparagus, peas, and watercress that are coming into season. Jimmy Red corn has beautiful, ruby-red kernels. Once ground, the grits still have little flashes of red in them. If you can't find Jimmy Red, you can use any high-quality stone-ground grits.

1. In a large saucepan, combine the water, butter, and salt and bring to a simmer over medium-high heat. Whisk in the grits, bring to a simmer, then lower the heat and cook, stirring often to avoid sticking to the bottom of the pan, for 30 to 40 minutes, until the liquid is absorbed and the grits are thick and tender, adding more water if needed.

2. Meanwhile, melt the butter in a large sauté pan over medium heat. Add the peas, asparagus, and roasted mushrooms and toss to heat through. Season with salt.

3. Spoon the grits into 4 bowls. Top each with a poached egg, then the vegetables. Finish with shavings of cheese and the watercress. Serve immediately.

A COLORFUL HERITAGE

Jimmy Red corn is a heritage variety with stunning blood-red kernels and a complex flavor profile. Once beloved by moonshiners and bootleggers, Ol' Jimmy almost vanished before it could gain the culinary cachet it has today. As late as the 1980s, if you knew the right places to ask, you could find a jar of Jimmy Red hooch for sale in the Carolina islands. When the last bootlegger who'd grown it passed away in the early 2000s, the grain almost died with him. Someone saved the last two ears and passed them to celebrated local farmer and seed saver Ted Chewning, suggesting they might make good hog feed. Chewning's passion is preserving heirloom plants. He has revived many nearly extinct strains, including Jimmy Red. Little did he realize it would become a culinary darling, soon showing up in grits and flapjacks locally—as well as in boutique whiskeys produced with 100 percent Jimmy Red corn mash for a bourbon those old-time bootleggers could only dream of.

When hosting a communal meal, I always include at least one seafood dish to share. Fish is just so healthy, so delicious, and so easy to cook, as we'll show you in the pages that follow. A go-to recipe in this book is the Tiradito (page 151), which is a relatively new addition to our menu. Our version has a pretty cool backstory. Before the pandemic, we almost always had something like a tuna crudo on the menu. When the post-pandemic supply chain started looking unreliable, we had the inspiration to switch it up since you can use a wide variety of fish in tiradito.

Mentioning supply-chain issues now feels funny when we think back on the early days of the restaurant. As we were getting The Kitchen off the ground, our "supply chain" consisted of a far-flung community of individuals. We still talk about the late Ingrid Bengis. She was probably the only Fulbright Scholar and National Book Award finalist to settle on a tiny island off the coast of Maine. She was happy to spend her days diving for oysters, riding along with local fisherfolk, and FedExing just-caught local fish to chefs around the country. Over the years, our pool of purveyors has expanded, but sustainability is still one of our top priorities. That's why we follow the Monterey Sea Watch's sustainability guidelines in all our sourcing—to ensure everything we serve is not only delicious and good for you, but also good for the planet.

Seafood

Lobster Roll with Old Bay Chips

Serves 4

About 8 tablespoons
  unsalted butter, softened

4 brioche lobster rolls or large
  hamburger rolls, split open
  (in a pinch, top-cut hot dog
  buns will do)

1 pound lobster meat
  (claw and knuckle)

Hondashi Mayo (page 60)

Black sesame seeds, to garnish

Fresh cilantro leaves, to garnish

Old Bay Chips (recipe follows)

Riffing on our favorite easy-to-eat, low-fuss takeaway foods led to this spin on the classic Maine-style lobster roll you'll find sold in clam shacks and food trucks throughout New England. In place of plain mayonnaise, we spiked it with sriracha and then added Hondashi, a Japanese seafood flavoring. Use a light hand with the mayo, barely coating the fresh, chilled lobster to add just a hint of brine and heat.

Serve the lobster on a warm, buttered roll with Old Bay chips on the side and it's like a little vacation to the Cape for your taste buds. The brioche bread really matters. Make sure it's as freshly baked as possible. We make our own Old Bay chips; if you like, you can serve this with any high-quality Old Bay chips or sprinkle Old Bay seasoning over your favorite plain potato chips.

1. Spread about 1 tablespoon of butter on each bun half and toast both sides in a toaster oven or broiler, on the grill, or in a skillet until golden brown.

2. Meanwhile, in a medium bowl, toss the lobster with Hondashi mayo to coat. Stuff into the buns, garnish with black sesame seeds and cilantro, and serve with Old Bay chips.

OLD BAY CHIPS

2 pounds unpeeled
  Yukon Gold potatoes

2 tablespoons distilled
  white vinegar

Peanut or other
  neutral oil, for frying

Fine salt

Old Bay seasoning

1. Fill a large bowl with cold water. Slice the potatoes $\frac{1}{8}$ to $\frac{1}{16}$ inch thick using a mandoline, sliding the slices directly into the water. Drain, then soak again in a few more changes of water until you no longer see starch accumulating in the soaking water. Cover the potato slices with 2 quarts of fresh, cold water and add the vinegar. Stir and leave to soak for 30 minutes.

2. While the potatoes are soaking, pour enough of the oil into a large saucepan to come at least 3 inches up the sides and affix a frying thermometer to the pan. Heat over medium-high heat to 350°F.

Continued

3. Drain the potatoes and, working in batches, place the potato slices on a clean kitchen towel in a single layer. Roll up the slices in the towel to absorb as much water as possible, then transfer the slices to a clean, dry bowl and dry them individually, slice by slice, with another dry towel.

4. Next, line a baking sheet with paper towels and keep it close to the stove. Working in batches again, carefully add the potatoes to the oil. Fry each batch, stirring gently with a slotted spoon or spider until golden brown, about 5 minutes. Remove from the oil with the slotted spoon or spider, place on the paper towel–lined sheet, and sprinkle with salt and Old Bay.

5. Make sure to let the oil get back up to temperature before adding each batch of potatoes. Cool any leftover potato chips completely and store in an airtight container in a cool, dry place for up to 1 week.

ON A ROLL

Most sandwiches can be served on just about any bread, but a lobster roll is not most sandwiches. The fresh, tender claw and knuckle meat, lightly coated in mayo, belongs on a soft, white bun, lightly toasted. We already had a source for sustainably caught lobster—all we needed before we could bring the sandwich to our menu was the right bun. Chef Michael discovered the Fireking Baking Company in Massachusetts and its authentic "lobster brioche roll." Sometimes all the pieces just fall into place. Fireking was started by a New England chef who couldn't find the high-quality traditional breads he wanted locally and decided to make his own. Fireking breads are now available in selected stores nationwide. If you can't find them in your area yet, don't worry. Any soft, slightly sweet roll will do the job once it's buttered, toasted, and topped with our Hondashi-sauced lobster.

Oyster Shooters

Sometimes known as Oysters Romanoff, this is a very fancy way to do an oyster shooter. The luxurious caviar and crème fraîche paired with the clean, crisp bite of the vodka and chives is what defines this classic dish. We've had some fun mixing it up for festive gatherings, riffing on our favorite spirits. Oysters Jalisco uses tequila or mezcal instead of vodka and swaps the crème fraîche for avocado mousse (page 153). For a Japanese-inspired shooter, try sake and wasabi-flavored tabiko flying-fish roe with your oyster. However you serve them, it's an instant party.

▼

Clean and shuck the oysters, then pour about 1 teaspoon of vodka into each oyster in the shell. Add a dollop of crème fraîche, then finish each oyster with ¼ teaspoon caviar. Garnish with chives and serve immediately.

Serves 4

16 East Coast or other oysters

3 ounces vodka
(approximately ⅓ cup)

1 cup crème fraîche

4 teaspoons black caviar,
such as bowfin or paddlefish

Thinly sliced fresh chives,
to garnish

Tiradito with Aji Amarillo–Ponzu Sauce

The Kitchen's executive chef Michael Bertozzi has a Peruvian heritage, and that background shows its influence throughout our menu, but especially in this shareable dish, his own recipe based on a family favorite. Peru's national cuisine is an always engaging marriage of Latin and Asian flavors, due to the Japanese immigrants whose cuisine became intertwined with local dishes over the past century or so. Tiradito starts out with sashimi-grade raw fish; instead of being "cured" like ceviche, it's dressed in what's essentially an intense vinaigrette. The sauce really

Serves 4

Aji Amarillo–Ponzu Sauce
(recipe follows)

8 ounces sashimi-grade yellowfin
tuna or hamachi (or similar)

Maldon salt

Avocado Mousse (recipe follows)

2 teaspoons toasted sesame seeds

Fresh cilantro leaves, to garnish

Extra-virgin olive oil

Continued

leans into the acid qualities of rice vinegar and citrusy ponzu with just enough oil to balance things out. Finally, creamy avocado mousse brings back the richness and adds another level of texture to play off the crunchy toasted sesame seeds.

1. Start by ladling ¼ cup of the aji amarillo–ponzu sauce onto each of 4 chilled plates.

2. Slice the fish very thinly into about 20 pieces. Gently roll each piece of fish up tightly, taking care not to tear it. Arrange the rolled fish into the sauce and lightly season each piece with a few flakes of salt. Spoon the avocado mousse onto each piece of fish, about ⅛ teaspoon per piece of fish. (If you like, you can use a piping bag or a plastic bag with one corner snipped off for this.) Sprinkle the sesame seeds over the fish and garnish with cilantro. Using a squeeze bottle, dot about 1 teaspoon of oil around each plate into the aji amarillo–ponzu sauce and serve immediately.

AJI AMARILLO–PONZU SAUCE

Note: If you don't have a mini blender or food processor, you can add the oil to the ingredients in a jar, cover with lid, and shake until emulsified.

1. In a small bowl or jar, whisk or shake together the vinegar, ponzu, aji amarillo, and agave to combine. Add the salt and whisk until the salt dissolves.

2. Transfer to a mini blender and, with the motor running, slowly add the oil through the hole in the lid. Blend until slightly creamy and emulsified. Taste and add more salt if needed. The sauce will keep tightly covered and refrigerated for up to 3 days. It may separate a bit when stored; shake vigorously before serving to re-emulsify.

AVOCADO MOUSSE

1. Scoop the avocados' flesh into a mini blender or food processor and add the lime zest and juice. Add the cream and blend until completely smooth. Season with salt. The mousse should be eaten the day it's made, or the next day at most. You'll only be using a little for the tiradito, but you can enjoy the rest as a dip or spread.

A SLOW BURN
Latin-accented heat comes from the aji amarillo pepper, a staple of Peruvian cooking with a slow burn and a very distinct, almost fruity flavor. In the U.S., it's available only as a jarred paste. The most commonly available brand is Goya. Look for it in Latin markets or online.

153

Makes about 1 cup
2 tablespoons rice vinegar
¼ cup ponzu sauce
3 tablespoons aji amarillo paste
1½ tablespoons amber
    agave nectar
¼ teaspoon salt, or to taste
½ cup grapeseed or other
    neutral oil

Makes about 1½ cups
2 avocados
Zest and juice of 1 lime
2½ tablespoons heavy cream
½ teaspoon salt, or to taste

Fresh Mussels in Spicy Chorizo Broth

1 tablespoon grapeseed or
    other neutral oil

4 garlic cloves, thinly sliced

1 shallot, thinly sliced

Chorizo Broth (recipe follows)

4 pounds fresh mussels,
    scrubbed and beards
    removed if necessary

4 tablespoons unsalted
    butter, cubed

¼ cup chopped fresh
    flat-leaf parsley

Salt and freshly ground
    black pepper

Fennel pollen, to garnish

Lemon wedges, for serving

1 cup Saffron Aioli (page 60)

Chorizo Broth

Makes about 4 cups

1 tablespoon grapeseed or
    other neutral oil

8 ounces chorizo, sliced

1 medium yellow onion,
    roughly chopped

8 garlic cloves, roughly chopped

1 cup white wine

4 cups clam juice

1 tablespoon dried oregano,
    preferably Sicilian

1 teaspoon hot smoked paprika

2 tablespoons fresh lemon juice,
    or to taste

Salt and freshly ground
    black pepper

When Chef Michael Bertozzi first interviewed for a job at The Kitchen, he was supposed to have something like three hours to create a tasting dish that would serve as an audition of sorts. However, he and Kimbal got so absorbed in their conversations about food and time slipped away. In the end, there were only forty-five minutes left for Michael to make something that would wow the team and land him the position. He describes heading into the walk-in fridge with one of the Denver location's cooks and looking around for inspiration. Once he saw that they had fresh mussels on hand, as well as some chorizo left over from a private event's charcuterie board, he knew he was golden. Everyone agreed the dish was amazing. The sausage-and-tomato broth is so delicious, you'll want baguette slices or crostini to soak up every drop.

Heat the oil over medium heat in a large pot with a lid. Add the sliced garlic and shallot and cook until softened, about 2 minutes. Add the chorizo broth, increase the heat to medium-high, and bring to a simmer, then add the mussels and toss to combine. Cover the pot and cook, shaking the pan constantly, until the mussels open, about 6 to 10 minutes. Discard any mussels that do not open. Remove the pot from the heat, add the butter, and stir carefully to coat the mussels. Add the parsley, then season with salt and pepper if needed. Divide the mussels and broth among bowls and garnish with fennel pollen and lemon wedges. Serve with the aioli in ramekins on the side.

CHORIZO BROTH

1. Heat the oil in a medium saucepan over medium-high heat. Add the chorizo, onions, and garlic and cook until the onions are translucent and the chorizo has rendered some fat, about 10 minutes. Add the wine, raise the heat, and cook until reduced by a quarter, about 3 minutes. Add

the clam juice, oregano, and paprika and cook until reduced by one-quarter, about 5 minutes.

2. Add the lemon juice, transfer the mixture to a blender, and blend until smooth. Strain through a fine-mesh strainer, pressing on the solids to extract as much liquid as possible. Season with salt and pepper. Add more lemon juice if it's needed.

3. Discard the solids and cool the liquid. The broth will keep tightly covered and refrigerated for up to 1 week. Note that the broth will settle as it cools and the fat may rise to the top, so if you're making it in advance, return it to the blender and blend again until smooth before using.

CRAB FRIED RICE
FISH TACOS
OYSTER SHOOTERS

MUSSELS
WITH CHORIZO
BROTH

Fish "Tacos"

Serves 4

1½ pounds skinless rockfish,
  cod, or other white fish
½ teaspoon salt, plus
  more for sprinkling
1¼ cups cornstarch
½ teaspoon paprika
½ teaspoon chili powder
¾ cup cold club soda
Peanut or other neutral oil,
  for frying

To serve

12 large Bibb lettuce leaves
Jalapeño Aioli (page 60)
Fresh cilantro leaves
Pickled Red Onions (page 66)
1 watermelon radish, cut into
  julienne
Fresh lime juice

We take a lot of pride in our menu; it's crafted to offer equally delicious options to vegans, red-meat-loving carnivores, and everyone in between. The key to making it all work together at one table is our dedication to finding that little twist or surprise that makes every dish special and unique to The Kitchen. The starting point for a signature dish might be anything from a chef's Latin American heritage, our favorite street-food vendors from travels abroad, or a slightly homesick Brit's yen for proper fish and chips here in landlocked Colorado. Chef Hugo, one of our co-founders, was that Brit. He taught us how to make authentic pub-style fried fish, with extra-crispy batter coating a flaky white fish like rockfish or cod. The twist? We serve the fish with taco fixings in lettuce cups instead of tortillas. The whole presentation is so light and airy, crispy and crunchy, and fresh without ever feeling heavy. It's a great shared dish, especially for anyone with a gluten-free diet. We use rockfish, but you'd get equally delicious results with cod, hake, or even red snapper.

1. Cut the fish into 12 pieces, each about 2 ounces, and season with salt. Place the cornstarch in a large bowl and whisk in the paprika, chili powder, and ½ teaspoon salt. Gently pour the club soda into the cornstarch and mix with a fork.

2. To fry the fish, pour oil into a wide sauté pan or saucepan to come about 3 inches up the sides. Heat over medium-high to 325°F. When the oil is ready, dredge the fish in the cornstarch mixture, then shake off the excess. Using a slotted spoon, add half of the pieces of battered fish to the oil and fry, turning once with tongs, until golden brown, about 5 minutes. Remove to paper towels. Sprinkle with salt. Repeat with the remaining fish.

3. To serve, set the lettuce leaves on plates. Spread the jalapeño mayo on the bottom of each lettuce leaf, then set the fish into the lettuce. Top each piece of fish with the cilantro, pickled red onions, and radish (we use watermelon radishes, but you can sub in plain red radishes if you like). Finish with a quick drizzle of lime juice and serve immediately.

Crab Fried Rice

Chef Michael Bertozzi was born and raised in Jacksonville, Florida, catching fresh crabs with his family and enjoying "crab rice," a quintessential dish of the South's coastal low country. It's a comfort food, often thrown together with leftover rice, fresh-caught crab, maybe a little Old Bay, and a healthy dose of the local hot sauce. And this version? Michael had barely started riffing on ideas for a new crab-and-rice dish when it came to him: Thai food. He swapped the traditional Southern seasoning for Thai spices and the hot sauce for Thai Lime Nam Jim, creating a global mash-up that really sings. We use Dungeness or blue crab depending on the season—fresh is best but frozen or canned will work in a pinch.

1. Heat the oil in a large nonstick skillet over medium-high heat. Add the rice and cook to heat through. Add the nam jim and toss to coat the rice. Add the crab and cook, stirring, until just heated through.

2. Divide the fried rice among shallow bowls and top each with a sunny-side-up egg. Garnish with peanuts and cilantro.

Serves 4

1 tablespoon grapeseed or other neutral oil

4 cups cold cooked jasmine or other long-grain rice (preferably day-old)

1 cup Thai Lime Nam Jim (recipe below)

12 ounces picked crab

4 eggs, cooked sunny side up (see note, page 185)

¼ cup unsalted roasted peanuts, crushed in a food processor or with the flat of a knife

Picked fresh cilantro leaves, to garnish

THAI LIME NAM JIM

1. Use a Microplane grater to grate the zest from the limes, then squeeze the lime juice.

2. In a small bowl, stir together the lime zest and juice with the rest of the ingredients. Let the mixture sit at room temperature for at least a few minutes to let the flavors combine. The sauce will keep, covered in the refrigerator, for two weeks. Leftovers go well with any type of seafood.

Makes about 3 cups

3 limes

¼ cup finely diced ginger

¼ cup finely diced garlic

¼ cup finely diced shallots

2 bunches green onions, thinly sliced

2 Thai chiles, thinly sliced

¾ cup tamari

¼ cup mirin

⅓ cup fish sauce

1½ tablespoons rice wine vinegar

159

Grilled Oysters

When Chef Michael Bertozzi added this to the menu a few years back, Kimbal instantly named it one of The Kitchen's all-time hits and we haven't taken it off the menu since! If you've ever ordered unagi—aka grilled eel sushi—you've tasted kabayaki sauce. Also known as eel sauce, it's a light, sweet glaze that adds depth and umami without overwhelming the flavors of freshly grilled seafood. Oysters are much lower in fat than eel, so we add brown butter before grilling to balance the flavors and textures, pushing the whole package just a little bit over the top with that hint of caramelized decadence.

▼

1. Line rimmed serving plates with salt, clean and shuck the oysters, and heat a grill to high.

2. To cook, add 1 teaspoon of butter to each shell and grill until the butter melts and slightly bubbles and the oysters are warm. Remove the oysters from the grill, being mindful to avoid spilling any of the juices from the shells, to the prepared plates. Add ½ teaspoon kabayaki sauce to each shell and garnish with green onions. Serve immediately.

Note: To brown the butter, heat a sturdy, thick-bottomed saucepan over medium heat. Slice your butter so that it will melt more quickly, then add it to the pan and heat, stirring frequently until the butter is fragrant and golden brown, about 5 minutes. Keep an eye on the pan—butter can go from brown to burned very quickly. You can use plain butter in the preparation, but brown butter is quick and easy to make and really adds to the overall deliciousness of the whole package.

Serves 4

Rock salt

16 East Coast or other oysters

16 teaspoons unsalted butter, browned (or use plain unsalted butter)

8 teaspoons Kabayaki Sauce (page 62)

1 green onion, very thinly sliced

SEAFOOD FAR FROM HOME

Last time we checked, Colorado was still landlocked, which inspires some of our guests to ask how serving oysters works with our commitment to using fresh, local ingredients. We write each menu based primarily on what we can source locally, and then we think about what to add to have a well-rounded slate of offerings. For ingredients from farther away, we work with people who care as deeply about quality as we do and who can get products to us quickly. These relationships are built on trust and connection with like-minded people who form our extended community, wherever they may be.

Traditional Ceviche with Crispy Tostadas

Serves 4

Leche de Tigre

1 cup clam juice

¼ cup fresh lime juice

1 small shallot, roughly chopped

1 cup roughly chopped fresh
  cilantro leaves and tender stems

1 pound skinless halibut, cut into
  medium dice

2½ tablespoons aji amarillo paste
  (see note on page 151)

1 teaspoon salt, or to taste

½ cup torn fresh cilantro leaves,
  plus more for garnish

½ cup very thinly sliced red onion,
  plus more for garnish

Tostadas

6 corn tortillas or 12 mini tortillas

Grapeseed or other neutral oil

Salt

Often called Peru's national dish, ceviche is such a simple, clean, bright way to eat fish. Try serving it at dinner parties to whet the appetite and spark conversation. We use halibut in the restaurant, but any firm, white-fleshed fish such as grouper, rockfish, or sole would work well here. For planet-friendly zero-waste cooking, you can use scraps left over from preparing dishes like our Halibut Steak (page 170). The raw fish in ceviche is cured by immersion in an intense citrus bath known as leche de tigre, or tiger's milk. It's spiked with the round, almost mellow heat of Peruvian aji amarillo. The just-fried tostadas are a special finishing touch, though if you'd rather spend more time at the party, nobody will mind if you buy them pre-fried from a supermarket with a good Latin foods section.

1. To make the leche de tigre, combine the clam juice with ¼ cup of the fresh lime juice and the roughly chopped shallot and cilantro in a blender or food processor and blend until smooth.

2. Place the halibut in a chilled bowl and add the leche de tigre, aji amarillo, 1 teaspoon salt, and the remaining ½ cup fresh lime juice and toss to coat. Add the torn cilantro leaves and red onion and toss again. Cover and marinate in the refrigerator for at least 30 minutes or up to 2 hours. Taste and add more lime juice and/or salt if needed.

3. Make the tostadas: Preheat the oven to 425°F and line a baking sheet with parchment. Arrange the tortillas on the sheet, brush both sides lightly with oil, and sprinkle with salt. Bake for 5 to 7 minutes per side, until the tortillas are crispy like a chip and lightly browned. Remove from the oven. They will continue to crisp a little as they cool. Break each tostada in half before serving.

4. To serve, divide the ceviche among bowls and garnish each with some tostada halves. Alternatively, you could serve the ceviche in a large bowl with a spoon and let guests scoop onto the tostadas themselves.

EAT IT LIKE
CHIPS & SALSA

Salmon with White Bean Ragout

Serves 4

3 tablespoons grapeseed or
    other neutral oil

¼ cup finely diced pancetta

2 shallots, thinly sliced

2 garlic cloves, thinly sliced

1½ cups very thinly sliced fennel
    (from an 8-ounce bulb)

1 cup Simple Tomato Sauce
    (recipe follows)

2 cups Cannellini Bean Ragout
    (recipe follows)

4 tablespoons unsalted butter

¼ cup mix of finely chopped
    flat-leaf parsley, chives, and
    tarragon

4 ounces escarole,
    cut into chiffonade

Salt and freshly ground
    black pepper

Splash of fresh lemon juice

4 (7-ounce) salmon fillets

Green Olive–Lemon Salmoriglio
    (page 52)

Fresh basil leaves, to garnish

*HERE'S HOW TO
GET THE SALMON
SKIN CRISPY*

We love this dish's adaptability: If you're cooking for a group of folks with different ways of eating, you can serve the ragout component in a separate dish as a hearty, satisfying vegetarian main in its own right, alongside crusty peasant bread and a green salad. Then serve the salmon on a platter for the pescatarians at the table. The creamy beans are complemented by a simple tomato sauce and set off by the greens, with their hint of bitterness. To top it all off, a bright, salty, citrusy salmoriglio really accentuates the flavors without overwhelming them. You can use any sturdy dark leafy green in place of escarole if you like. You'll have some tomato sauce left over from this recipe—and that's a good thing. It's delicious as a base for pasta sauces, over vegetables, in a casserole, or anywhere you'd use a basic red sauce.

1. Heat a large skillet over medium heat. Add 1 tablespoon of the oil, then add the pancetta, shallots, and garlic and cook until the shallots are translucent, about 3 minutes. Add the fennel and cook until softened, about 5 minutes. Add the tomato sauce and beans and toss to combine. Add the butter, herbs, and escarole and toss to combine and wilt the escarole. Add a splash of water or stock if the mixture is too thick or dry, then season with salt and pepper and add the lemon juice. Keep warm while you cook the salmon.

2. Press the salmon fillets between paper towels to dry them on every side. Score the fish's skin with a sharp knife, being careful not to cut the flesh of the fish, then season well with salt.

3. Heat 2 large cast-iron skillets over medium-high heat and add 1 tablespoon of the remaining oil to each pan. (If you don't have two suitable skillets, it's fine to cook the fish in batches.) Once the oil shimmers, place the salmon skin side down in the pan. Lower the heat to

Continued

medium. Press the fish with the back of a metal spatula to ensure that the skin is in complete contact with the pan's surface. Cook, occasionally pressing on the fillets with your spatula, until the skin crisps and the flesh is almost fully cooked through, about 5 minutes. Flip and cook for another 30 seconds to 1 minute, until an instant-read thermometer registers 120°F for medium-rare, or to your desired doneness.

4. Divide the cannellini ragout among shallow bowls and place the salmon skin-side up on top of the beans. Finish with the salmoriglio and garnish with basil.

CANNELLINI BEAN RAGOUT

Makes about 4 cups

8 ounces dried cannellini beans

2 tablespoons extra-virgin olive oil

½ yellow onion, finely diced

2 garlic cloves, thinly sliced

½ cup chicken or vegetable stock

2 sprigs thyme

Salt

Any leftover ragout can be a hearty vegetarian lunch or dinner all by itself, or you can add precooked sausage, shredded chicken, or other proteins before reheating.

1. Soak the beans overnight in enough water to cover them by a few inches. Drain before cooking.

2. In a medium saucepan, heat the oil over medium heat. Add the onion and garlic and cook until translucent but not colored, 2 to 3 minutes. Add the drained beans and enough water to cover by 2 inches. Add the stock and thyme. Bring to a simmer, then lower the heat and cook, skimming any foam that arises, for about 1½ hours, until the beans are cooked through. Season with salt during the last half hour or so of cooking and add more water as needed to keep the beans submerged. Discard the thyme and drain. The beans can be made 3 or 4 days in advance and kept covered and refrigerated.

SIMPLE TOMATO SAUCE

Makes about 2 cups

1 tablespoon extra-virgin olive oil

½ small onion, finely chopped

1 garlic clove, finely chopped

2 tablespoons grated carrot

1 (28-ounce) can whole tomatoes

2 teaspoons fresh thyme leaves

Salt

In a medium saucepan, heat the oil over medium heat. Add the onion and garlic and cook until translucent but not colored, 2 to 3 minutes. Add the carrot and stir to coat in oil. Add the tomatoes and thyme and bring to a simmer. Lower the heat to low and simmer for 1 hour, stirring to break up the tomatoes as the sauce cooks. Season with salt. The sauce will keep tightly covered and refrigerated for up to 5 days or frozen for up to 6 months.

Scallops with Celery Root Puree

This recipe started out as a way to win a bet, and ended up as a menu favorite. It all began when Chef Michael set out to sell his wife on the joy of celery, a vegetable she had despised since childhood. However, she just happens to adore scallops, and he set himself the challenge of winning her over by taking something she absolutely loved and combining it with something she absolutely . . . didn't. Spoiler alert: It worked. Everyone in our kitchen loved the dish as well, and it's still on the menu to this day. The creamy earthiness of the celery root pairs perfectly with seared scallops. You'll have some celery root puree left over. You can cook a few more scallops and make another meal of it, stir it into mashed potatoes, or serve it cold as a dip.

Serves 4

Grapeseed or other neutral oil

12 large scallops

2 tablespoons unsalted butter

¾ cup Celery Root Puree (recipe follows)

¼ cup celery leaves, very thinly sliced

⅓ cup hazelnuts, toasted and crushed

⅓ cup Granny Smith apple, cut into julienne

Lemon and White Balsamic Vinaigrette (page 68)

2 tablespoons pomegranate arils

Kosher salt, to taste

1. Heat a large cast-iron skillet over medium-high heat and add a light coating of oil. Season the scallops with salt on one side, then add to the pan in a circle formation around the perimeter, salted side down. Gently press on each of them to make sure the entire surface is touching the hot pan. Sear the scallops until they are golden brown on the edges. Season the side facing upward with salt, then turn them over. Add the butter and cook, basting the scallops for 1 minute, or until they are cooked through. Remove from the pan to a paper towel–lined plate.

2. Meanwhile, mix the celery leaves, hazelnuts, and apple in a medium bowl. Toss with the vinaigrette and season with salt. Add the pomegranate arils (the proper name for its seeds) and gently mix with a spoon. For each serving, spread 3 tablespoons of the celery root puree over a plate, arrange 3 scallops on top of the puree, then top the scallops with salad and serve immediately.

CELERY ROOT PUREE

Makes about 3 cups

1½ cups milk

1½ cups water

1½ teaspoons salt, plus
more as needed

1 pound celery root, peeled
and cut into 1½-inch cubes

1 small russet potato, peeled
and cut into 1½-inch cubes

1 small onion, peeled and
quartered

½ cup (1 stick) unsalted butter,
chilled and cubed

⅛ teaspoon ground white pepper

Zest of ½ lemon

1. Combine the milk, water, and salt in a medium heavy-bottomed pot and bring to a simmer over medium-high heat. Add the celery root, potato, and onion and let return to a simmer. Lower the heat and simmer for 30 minutes, or until the vegetables are tender. Strain them out and discard the cooking liquid.

2. Transfer the vegetables to a blender or food processor and blend, starting on low speed and increasing to high, until you have a smooth puree. Scrape down the blender's sides and, with the motor running, add the butter cube by cube until it is fully incorporated. Add the white pepper and lemon zest, taste, and season with more salt if needed. The puree can be made up to 3 days ahead; cover and refrigerate, then reheat over low heat.

Halibut Steaks Glazed with White Ponzu Sauce

3 tablespoons grapeseed or
  other neutral oil
4 (11- to 12-ounce) bone-in halibut
  steaks (about 1 inch thick)
Salt
4 tablespoons unsalted butter
White Ponzu Sauce
  (recipe follows)
2 cups sugar snap peas,
  stems and strings removed
1 tablespoon fresh lime juice,
  or to taste
4 to 8 tablespoons Yuzu Kosho
  Mayo (page 59)
Black sesame seeds, to garnish
Microgreens, to garnish

Makes about 1 cup
½ cup white soy sauce
Juice of 1 large orange
1 tablespoon fresh lime juice
1½ tablespoons fresh lemon juice
¼ teaspoon red chile flakes
Heaping ¼ teaspoon Hondashi
1 tablespoon thinly sliced fresh
  chives

This recipe leans into a palette of Asian flavors that work magnificently with a bone-in halibut steak. We use white soy sauce, which has a lighter color and flavor and thickens up nicely to make a beautiful golden glaze with the brown butter. If you can't find cross-cut bone-in steaks, you can use fillets; just be sure to keep a close eye on them as they cook so the fish doesn't dry out.

1. In each of two large cast-iron or other heavy skillets that are at least 12 inches in diameter, heat 1 tablespoon of the oil over medium-high heat until it shimmers. Season the halibut liberally with salt on both sides, place in the pan, and sear until the edges turn golden brown, about 5 minutes. Flip the steaks and add 2 tablespoons butter to each pan. As soon as the butter starts to brown, add half of the white ponzu sauce to each pan and baste the steaks until the fish is cooked through, 3 to 5 minutes. Remove to a cutting board, pour the sauce into a sauce boat or small bowl, and let the fish rest for a couple minutes.

2. While the fish is resting, quickly wipe out one of the pans you cooked it in with paper towels. Add the remaining 1 tablespoon oil to the pan, then add the sugar snap peas, season with salt, and sear, tossing to char on both sides, for about 5 minutes. Toss with the lime juice.

3. Put each halibut steak on the center of a plate, pour the sauce over it, and arrange the snap peas at an angle to the top of the steak. Dot with the yuzu kosho mayo and top with black sesame seeds and microgreens.

WHITE PONZU SAUCE

In a jar with a lid, combine all the ingredients and shake to combine. Place in the refrigerator and let it sit overnight before using to allow the flavors to meld. It will keep tightly sealed and refrigerated for up to 2 weeks.

WHITE SOY SAUCE
MAKES A BEAUTIFUL
GOLDEN GLAZE WITH
THE BROWN
BUTTER.

Charred Bass with Salsa Verde

Like all the best showstopper recipes, this one has a story behind it. When Chef Hugo impulsively invited Kimbal and Jen to dinner after their chance meeting on the street in Boulder, this is what he served them. The dinner itself was unforgettable, even if it hadn't been the moment that launched a decades-long friendship and the start of The Kitchen. This recipe takes some effort, but it pays off with crisp skin and tender, moist flesh. Some diners love the crispy, almost burned skin; others may prefer it without. There's no wrong choice here, just personal taste. If you can't find a whole bass, you can substitute a similarly sized red snapper or branzino.

1. Remove the fish from the refrigerator about 20 minutes before you're ready to cook and pat dry with paper towels.
2. Heat a charcoal or gas grill to high heat.
3. Slice the lemon into ⅛-inch rounds, then smash the garlic cloves with the flat part of a chef's knife.
4. Brush the fish all over with oil. Season the inside of the fish liberally with salt, then season the outside. Place the lemon slices, garlic, and thyme inside the fish's cavity.
5. Place the fish onto the grill and cook for 6 to 10 minutes, until the bottom of the skin is charred and easily releases from the grill grate. Turn and grill until the flesh is white throughout, 6 to 10 minutes longer.
6. Remove the fish from the grill and allow it to rest for about 10 minutes. Gently remove and discard the herbs, lemon slices, and garlic from the body, place the fish onto a serving platter, then gently remove and discard any overly charred skin. Ladle salsa verde over it and serve.

Serves 4

1 lemon

4 garlic cloves

1 (2½- to 3-pound) whole striped bass, gutted and scaled

Grapeseed or other neutral oil, for brushing

Salt

2 sprigs thyme

Salsa Verde (page 54)

173

y very first experience cooking for my community was at the age of eleven. The community was my family, and the meal was a roast chicken and a batch of soggy french fries. It all started with my mom's boiled gem squash, a South African staple that I hated. One evening, after choking down yet another dinner featuring the horrible things, I asked my mom if I could cook the next meal. She laughed, but when she saw I was serious she agreed. The next day she took me to the grocery store, which I attacked with a passion. I found potatoes and put them in the cart while my mother and sister stood back and watched. I asked the butcher for a chicken and, as he packed it up for me, I asked him how to cook it. He said, "Put it in a hot oven for one hour."

We went straight home, and I turned on the oven. I asked my mom for help cutting the potatoes. I put the chicken in the oven and set the timer for 1 hour. I put the potatoes in the oil and turned on the heat. Nothing happened. That didn't faze me; french fries were going to be on the menu. My nine-year-old sister Tosca set the table. My older brother Elon even looked up from his book for a moment. Everyone was curious. We all sat down, and that's when something life-changing happened. I had become a cook. I've kept that chicken recipe with me ever since: Hot oven. One hour. You're done.

Poultry

Whole Roasted Chicken

This is one of Kimbal's favorite ultra-simple yet delicious dishes to prepare for friends, family, and the occasional lucky stranger (who never remains a stranger for long). Many folks in Boulder who've known him for years have a wonderful memory of enjoying this lemon, garlic, herb-infused chicken at a convivial dinner along with salad, bread, a good wine, and the kind of far-ranging conversation we all could use a little more of in our lives.

Serves 4

Whole chicken (3½ to 5 pounds)
1 lemon
1 head garlic
2 sprigs thyme
2 sprigs rosemary
1 to 2 tablespoons grapeseed oil, enough to coat the chicken
1 tablespoon salt
Additional thyme and rosemary sprigs, to garnish
Additional lemon wedges, to garnish

1. Pat the chicken dry, then place it onto a wire rack placed over a baking sheet. Refrigerate for a minimum of 4 hours or overnight. This dries the skin so it'll get super crispy once roasted.

2. Remove the chicken from the refrigerator and preheat your oven to 400°F.

3. Cut a lemon in half and remove its seeds, then trim any root ends from the garlic and halve the head horizontally. Place the lemon, herbs, and garlic into the cavity of the chicken.

4. Drizzle the oil over the chicken and then season with salt and massage the chicken thoroughly to ensure that the skin is completely covered with salt and oil. Finally, before placing the chicken into the oven, tuck the wing tips underneath its breast.

5. Place the chicken into the oven and roast for 1 hour. After an hour, check the temperature at the breast with an instant-read thermometer. Once the chicken has reached 165°F, remove it from the oven and allow it to rest for at least 15 minutes. This is a key step that allows the meat to reabsorb all of its flavorful juices, resulting in moist, tender flesh.

6. After the chicken has rested, place it on a cutting board and, using kitchen shears, cut out its backbone. Next, use a kitchen knife to split the chicken in half, cutting through the breastbone. Cut away the leg quarters with your knife, then separate the drumsticks from the thighs. If you wish, finish by removing the wings from the breast by cutting at the joint.

7. Place the 8 pieces of chicken onto a serving platter and garnish with additional thyme, rosemary sprigs, and lemon wedges and serve with a salad or vegetable side of your choice.

We love to serve this roasted chicken with The Kitchen Greek Salad (page 84), Urfa Carrots (page 97), Charred Broccolini (page 111), or Roasted Delicata Squash (page 99). If you want a sauce, the Chimichurri (page 52) or Salsa Verde (page 54) are good options.

HOW TO SERIOUSLY SEASON A CHICKEN

177

Cast Iron-Roasted Chicken with Hand-Cut Fries & Truffle Cream

Serves 4

1½ tablespoons grapeseed or
  other neutral oil

2 boneless, skin-on chicken breast
  halves (about 1½ pounds)

2 boneless, skin-on chicken thighs
  (about 12 ounces)

Salt

2 tablespoons unsalted butter,
  softened

3 garlic cloves, smashed and
  peeled

2 to 3 sprigs thyme

Black Truffle Cream (recipe below)

Chopped parsley, tarragon, and
  chives (for topping)

The Kitchen 3-Day French Fries
  (page 80), to serve

For the Black Truffle Cream

Makes about 1 cup

1½ teaspoons grapeseed or
  other neutral oil

1 medium shallot,
  roughly chopped

1½ tablespoons roughly
  chopped garlic

2½ to 3 ounces canned black
  truffle peelings, drained of
  any liquid they came in

2 tablespoons sherry vinegar

1 cup heavy cream

½ teaspoon fresh lemon juice,
  or to taste

Salt and freshly ground black
  pepper, to taste

This recipe is more elaborate than the one Kimbal cooked at the age of eleven—and now he knows the secret to making properly crispy and delicious fries—but it comes from the same impulse: the joy of serving food you love to people you love even more. For an indulgently luxe dinner, we like to serve this succulent chicken over our famous fries with a mouthwatering truffle cream sauce. For a simpler meal, the chicken pairs well with just about any side dish, so experiment at will! You can make the sauce in advance or prepare it while the oven is preheating; the fries can be soaked the day before (or defrosted if you've par-fried and frozen a batch). You can use all breasts or all thighs if you want to without any changes. We bone the chicken out ourselves; if you can't find boneless skin-on pieces, bone-in works just as well, but the plating will look a bit different.

1. Preheat the oven to 400°F.

2. Pour the oil into a large (at least 12-inch) cast-iron skillet and heat over medium-high heat until very hot.

3. Season the chicken liberally with salt and place in the pan skin-side down, pressing firmly down on it with a spatula or tongs to ensure that all parts of the skin touch the cooking surface. (At the restaurant, we use a cast-iron grill press for this process. The press is inexpensive and easy to find at specialty shops or online.)

4. Cook until the skin becomes golden brown at the edges, about 5 minutes. Flip the chicken over, place the pan in the oven, and bake for 15 to 20 minutes, until an instant-read thermometer registers 165°F in the breasts.

5. Remove the pan from the oven, return it to the stove over low heat, and add the butter. Once the butter starts to foam, add the garlic and thyme sprigs. With a large spoon, continuously baste the chicken with the foaming butter for 2 minutes to continue to crisp the skin, watching carefully so the butter doesn't burn. Remove the chicken from

the pan to a wire rack placed over a baking sheet and let it rest for 3 to 5 minutes to allow the juices to reabsorb into the meat. (If you slice it immediately, the chicken can become dry.)

6. Divide the fries among 4 plates. Lay the chicken on a cutting board skin-side down to slice. Make sure you don't mangle or accidentally remove the skin while slicing. Place the slices of chicken on top of the fries in a uniform straight line.

7. Ladle on the truffle cream and garnish with parsley, tarragon, and chives. Serve immediately.

BLACK TRUFFLE CREAM

We love to dip fries into this luxurious sauce, but it's also fantastic over scallops and other seafood. Sometimes we'll poach a couple of lobsters, remove the poached meat from the shell, and sauté it with butter and fines herbes. Once the meat is seasoned and warmed through, we carefully place it back into the shells and serve with fries, ladling black truffle cream over everything.

1. In a small saucepan, heat the oil over medium heat. Add shallots and garlic and cook until the shallots are translucent but do not take on any color, about 3 minutes.

2. Add the truffle peelings and sherry vinegar and cook until the liquid is reduced by around half, about 3 minutes.

3. Stir in the cream, bring to a simmer, and cook until the sauce is reduced by about one-quarter and is thick enough to lightly coat the back of a spoon, about 10 minutes. Lower the heat if the cream starts to bubble too vigorously. Once it's reduced, remove from the stove and cool slightly.

4. Transfer sauce to a blender or food processor and blend until smooth. Return sauce to the pot, add the lemon juice, and season with salt and pepper. Taste and adjust the lemon juice, salt, and pepper as needed.

5. You can make the sauce up to 1 week in advance. To reheat, place in a small saucepan over low heat until just hot, stirring often and watching carefully; heating the sauce too quickly will cause it to break and separate. If this does happen, blend it again to re-emulsify. It will keep tightly sealed and refrigerated for up to 1 week.

Halal Cart Chicken Wrap

Serves 4

For the marinated chicken:

½ cup extra-virgin olive oil

2 tablespoons finely chopped
   fresh oregano

1 tablespoon fresh lemon juice

1 tablespoon minced fresh garlic

1 tablespoon minced fresh ginger

1 tablespoon salt

1½ teaspoons paprika

1 teaspoon freshly ground
   black pepper

1 teaspoon onion powder

1 teaspoon ground cumin

½ teaspoon garlic powder

½ teaspoon chili powder

1 teaspoon ground turmeric

¾ teaspoon cayenne pepper

¾ teaspoon ground coriander

4 (5-ounce) boneless skinless
   chicken breasts

To serve:

Salt

4 pita breads

1 cup Tzatziki (recipe follows)

½ cup thinly sliced English
   cucumbers

½ cup thinly sliced plum tomatoes

½ cup thinly sliced red onion

2 teaspoons fresh lemon juice

2 teaspoons extra-virgin olive oil

Freshly ground black pepper

½ to 1 cup Halal Hot Sauce (recipe
   follows)

1 cup arugula

Have you ever tasted a dish out somewhere and yearned to re-create it at home? The process of figuring it out can be tricky but also so satisfying because in the end you come up with a recipe that is all your own. That's what happened here. Chef Michael, while working his last job as a chef in Atlanta, had become obsessed with the local halal chicken cart that parked on the street near his restaurant. Its specialty: wraps filled with marinated, perfectly juicy chicken and a blazing hot sauce that played off a second topping of a cooling, mysteriously named "white sauce." New Yorkers may be nodding in recognition, but most of the country has yet to discover this handheld marvel. Our version adds some fresh veggies, and pulls in a Greek tzatziki in place of the white sauce. To complete the experience, serve with The Kitchen Fries (page 80)—fresh, hot, and salty, like the street food of your dreams.

1. Combine all the ingredients for the marinade, except the chicken, in a large bowl and whisk to combine. Add the chicken and toss to coat. Cover and refrigerate for at least 6 hours, or overnight.

2. Once the chicken is ready, heat a grill pan—with ridges if you have one—over medium-high heat. Remove the chicken from the marinade and season with salt, then add it to the pan and cook until the meat is cooked through and charred in spots, about 4 minutes on each side. Remove the chicken to a cutting board to rest.

3. While the chicken is resting, grill the pitas in the same pan you used for the chicken for about 2 minutes per side, working in batches as necessary, until they begin to char just a little. Remove the pitas from the heat and slather tzatziki generously onto one side of each.

4. Combine the cucumber, tomatoes, and onion in a medium salad bowl. Add the lemon juice and oil and toss to coat. Season with salt and pepper.

5. Cut the chicken into ½-inch slices and arrange them on top of the tzatziki-dressed pitas. Pour on the hot sauce and then add the dressed vegetables. Place the arugula in the empty salad bowl and toss with the oil and lemon juice that remain in the bowl. Place on top of the vegetables. Wrap the sandwiches halfway with foil and serve.

HALAL HOT SAUCE

Alter the ratio of hot sauce to tzatziki according to how hot your friends and family like it. If you like, you can substitute grapeseed or other neutral oil for the roasted garlic oil.

1. Combine the Fresno chiles, Thai chiles, onions, lemon juice, hot sauce, cumin, vinegar, and salt in a blender and blend thoroughly. With the motor running, slowly drizzle in the roasted garlic oil until emulsified. Taste and add more salt if needed. Place in a jar or squeeze bottle. The hot sauce will keep tightly covered and refrigerated for up to 1 week.

TZATZIKI

A cooling counter to the blistering Halal Hot Sauce in this sandwich, tzatziki also shines on its own as a dip for pita or vegetables or spread on crackers and topped with a dot of hot sauce.

1. In a large bowl, whisk together all the ingredients. If you have time, cover and let it rest overnight in the refrigerator to develop the flavors. It will keep tightly covered and refrigerated for up to 4 days.

Halal Hot Sauce
Makes about 1 cup

30 Fresno or other red chiles, stemmed, seeded, and deveined

10 Thai chiles, stemmed

2 medium yellow onions, roughly chopped

¼ cup fresh lemon juice

2 tablespoons Texas Pete or Tabasco hot sauce

1 tablespoon ground cumin

2 tablespoons champagne vinegar

2 teaspoons salt, or to taste

¼ cup Roasted Garlic Oil (page 73)

Tzatziki

¼ English cucumber, peeled, cut in half, seeded, and grated

1 cup crème fraîche or Greek yogurt

2 garlic cloves, grated with a Microplane

2 tablespoons finely chopped fresh dill

1 tablespoon fresh lemon juice, or to taste

½ teaspoon salt

Pinch of freshly ground black pepper

Southern Fried Chicken Sandwich

Serves 4

1 quart warm water

3 tablespoons salt

4 (5-ounce) boneless, skinless
chicken breast halves

1¼ cups buttermilk

⅓ cup Frank's RedHot Sauce

Dredging mix

1 cup all-purpose flour

2 teaspoons garlic powder

2 teaspoons onion powder

1 teaspoon salt

¾ teaspoon smoked hot paprika

¾ teaspoon mustard powder

¾ teaspoon freshly ground black
pepper

For frying and serving

Peanut or other neutral oil

6 tablespoons mayonnaise

4 potato buns, preferably Martin's

12 to 16 dill pickle slices

This is a winner that we started serving as a takeout dish during the pandemic, when everyone craved comfort food. It was so good that we kept it on the lunch menu. Now we can't take it off or there would be a mutiny. This sandwich is just perfection on a bun—and a nice soft potato bun, at that. Crispy fried chicken is one of life's great joys, and we prepare it Southern style—brined in buttermilk spiked with Frank's RedHot, a vinegar-based hot sauce.

1. Begin by brining the chicken: Pour the warm water into a large bowl, add the salt, and stir to dissolve. Cool completely, then add the chicken, cover, and brine in the refrigerator for at least 12 hours or up to 24 hours. Drain, then pat off excess brine with paper towels.

2. Pour the buttermilk and hot sauce into a shallow container and whisk to combine. Add the brined chicken, cover, and refrigerate for at least 2 hours or up to 6 hours.

3. While your chicken is soaking, make the dredging mix by putting the flour in a shallow bowl, adding all of the seasonings, and whisking to combine.

4. Once the chicken has soaked for at least 2 hours, remove it from the buttermilk soak and pat dry with paper towels. One at a time, coat the chicken pieces completely in the dredging mix.

5. To fry, pour enough oil into a wide sauté pan to come about 1 inch up the sides. Heat over medium-high until a pinch of flour tossed into the oil sizzles. Working in batches if necessary to avoid crowding the pan, add the chicken breasts to the oil and panfry for about 5 minutes on each side, until the chicken registers 165°F on an instant-read thermometer. Using tongs, remove from the oil to a paper towel–lined plate.

While the chicken is frying, heat a large cast-iron skillet over medium-high heat. Spread ½ tablespoon of mayonnaise over each top bun half and toast in the skillet, mayo side down, until nicely browned. Spread the remaining mayonnaise over the bun's bottom halves. Place the pickles on the top bun and the fried chicken on the bottom one. Close the sandwiches, wrap each one in sandwich paper, cut in half, and serve.

Chilaquiles with Chicken

Serves 4

3 cups Salsa Roja (page 58)

4 ounces tortilla chips

4 cups (about 1 pound) shredded
Roasted Chicken (page 177), or
other leftover roast chicken

8 eggs, cooked sunny side up
(see page 185 for technique)

½ cup Lime Crema (recipe follows)

½ cup Pickled Red Onions
(page 66)

1 large red radish, cut into julienne

½ cup grated cotija or
Parmesan cheese

¼ cup toasted pumpkin seeds

Torn fresh cilantro leaves

A classic Mexican breakfast dish, chilaquiles is often baked like a casserole, with tortilla chips there to soak up the sauce. We wanted to come up with a version that's just as delicious but with a little more crunch to it. Here, the salsa roja softens the chips a bit and ties the ingredients together while still letting them retain some snap and texture. Done right, it's like the best nachos ever. Once you add the sunny-side-up eggs and a bright, tangy dash of lime crema, you have an irresistible brunch dish to share. To get the timing right, you'll want to start the lime crema two days ahead—or, in a pinch, you can mix a bit of lime juice into sour cream before serving for a similar effect. If you don't already have a stash of our pickled red onions in the fridge, know that those will need about 12 hours overnight to pickle. Plan a Sunday brunch with friends and you'll be able to prep on the preceding Saturday.

Place 1 cup of the salsa roja in a saucepan over low heat, and keep warm while you prepare the chilaquiles. Pour the remaining 2 cups of the salsa into a large skillet set over medium heat. Once the salsa is simmering, toss the chips with the salsa in the skillet and sauté the chips for a few minutes. Toss the chicken with the chips and salsa in the skillet, and cook just until the chicken is heated through. Divide the chicken mixture among 4 serving plates or shallow bowls. Pour ¼ cup of the remaining salsa roja over each serving, then place the sunny-side-up eggs on top. Finish with the lime crema, pickled onion, radishes, cheese, pumpkin seeds, and cilantro and serve immediately.

LIME CREMA

Note that the crema must be started at room temperature; it won't thicken in a cold environment. Once it's ready, you can pop it into the fridge to cool and keep fresh.

1. In a small jar, whisk the yogurt into the cream. Cover loosely and leave at room temperature for 36 to 48 hours, until the mixture is set (check by slightly tipping the jar).

2. Whisk in the lime juice and salt. Taste and add more lime-juice and/or salt if needed. Cover and refrigerate until cold before using. The lime crema will keep tightly covered and refrigerated for up to 2 weeks.

Makes 1 cup

1 tablespoon plain whole-milk yogurt

1 cup heavy cream

2½ teaspoons fresh lime juice, or to taste

⅛ teaspoon salt, or to taste

STAY ON THE SUNNY SIDE

If you've eaten at The Kitchen for years, you may recall that this dish has evolved over time. One of its first incarnations was as an omurice omelet, a shout-out to the Japanese comfort food classic often made from leftover fried rice and scrambled eggs. The presentation shown in the photo on page 187 is how we're currently serving it—the sunny-side-up eggs look like a perfect taste of morning, are easier for the home cook than an omelet and, most important, taste just as delicious.

To cook perfect sunny-side-up eggs, start by turning on your oven to broil. Then heat 2 tablespoons of grapeseed or other neutral oil in a large ovenproof skillet over medium heat. Carefully break 2 eggs into the skillet, season with salt, and cook until the whites are opaque but still a little runny on top. Place in the oven on the top rack. Broil for 15 to 30 seconds and you're done. Repeat with the remaining eggs required.

ROMAN CHICKEN SALAD
CHICKEN LIVER MOUSSE PÂTÉ

CHILAQUILES

Roman Chicken Salad

Serves 4

For the marinated chicken

1 cup extra-virgin olive oil

¼ cup orange juice

2 tablespoons honey

3 garlic cloves, grated
   on a Microplane

¼ cup ground fennel seeds

¼ cup ground coriander

2 tablespoons ground anise seeds

2 teaspoons salt

1 teaspoon freshly ground
   black pepper

¼ teaspoon red chile flakes

1½ pounds boneless skinless
   chicken breast

For the vegetables

½ small head cauliflower,
   cut into bite-size florets

½ small head broccoli,
   cut into bite-size florets

2 tablespoons extra-virgin
   olive oil

Salt

For the grains

1 cup freekeh

2½ cups water

½ teaspoon salt

This salad is kind of a modern cousin to the classic chicken Caesar. The dressing is inspired by a Caesar dressing, but with our miso vinaigrette as its base. Instead of the traditional anchovies, it's the miso that provides that salinity and the umami, balanced by the lemon juice. In this preparation, you get an interesting contrast on the plate between the tender caramelized vegetables, pleasantly chewy grains, and the warm spiced chicken. Freekeh, also called farik, is a wheat-based grain much like farro (which can serve as a substitute if you like).

1. To marinate the chicken, combine all the marinade ingredients, except the chicken, in a blender and blend until smooth. Place the chicken in a bowl or zip-top bag, then add the marinade, making sure the chicken is evenly coated. Marinate in the refrigerator for at least 8 hours or up to 24 hours.

2. To roast the cauliflower and broccoli, preheat the oven to 425°F and line 2 baking sheets with parchment paper. Place the broccoli and cauliflower florets on separate baking sheets. Toss each with 1 tablespoon olive oil and season with salt. Roast for about 20 minutes, until softened and nicely browned. Remove from the oven and cool.

3. While the cauliflower and broccoli are roasting, prepare the freekeh. In a medium saucepan, combine the freekeh, water, and salt. Bring to a simmer over medium heat, then lower the heat, cover, and cook for about 20 minutes, until all the liquid has been absorbed. Fluff the freekeh, then transfer to a baking sheet in an even layer to cool.

For Serving

Salt

2 tablespoons grapeseed or other neutral oil

Miso Sauce (page 62)

1 tablespoon fresh lemon juice, plus more if needed

1 tablespoon extra-virgin olive oil, plus more if needed

1 cup thinly sliced kale leaves

1 cup thinly sliced radicchio

Grana Padano cheese, for serving

4. To cook the chicken, remove it from the marinade, letting excess drip off. Season with salt.

5. Heat the grapeseed oil in a large skillet or grill pan (cast iron is a good choice) over medium-high heat until the oil is shimmering. Add the chicken and cook for 5 to 7 minutes without moving it, until it easily releases. Flip and cook for another 5 to 7 minutes, until it reaches an internal temperature of 165°F. Remove the chicken from the pan and place on a cutting board to rest for about 5 minutes.

6. While the chicken is resting, spread the miso sauce on the bottom of a large bowl and whisk in the lemon juice and olive oil to create a vinaigrette. Add the freekeh, kale, radicchio, broccoli, and cauliflower to the bowl and toss to thoroughly coat. Taste and add salt if needed.

7. Cut the chicken into bite-sized cubes and gently toss with the dressed salad. Divide the salad among bowls and liberally grate cheese on top. Serve immediately.

Chicken Liver Mousse with Cognac & Apple Brandy

Makes about 3 cups

1 pound chicken livers

3 ounces (4 strips) bacon, diced

1 yellow onion, finely chopped

2 shallots, finely chopped

1 cup cognac

¼ cup apple brandy

4 large eggs

1½ teaspoons salt

½ teaspoon Instacure #1

1 teaspoon freshly ground
   black pepper

1 cup clarified butter

This lighter, more spreadable take on pâté is the secret to our melt-in-your-mouth mousse-filled fresh ravioli (page 134). Silky and spiked with cognac, it will be the life of the party when presented with crostini or crackers and maybe our Green Tomato Marmalata (page 134) or another bold agrodolce on the side. Serve it to your guests or bring as your contribution to a festive communal dinner. If you are making this recipe specifically for the ravioli, note that it yields enough for three batches. If you're not making that many ravioli, the mousse will keep tightly covered and refrigerated for up to 1 week, or in the freezer for up to 2 months. Or, just an idea here, but why not use any leftovers as inspiration to throw a fabulous party?

1. Trim the livers and soak them in a bowl of cold water for 15 minutes, then drain.

2. Meanwhile, in a medium skillet, combine the bacon, onion, and shallots. Cook over medium heat until the fat is rendered from the bacon, about 10 minutes. Add the cognac and brandy and bring to a simmer. Cook for 2 minutes, stirring occasionally. Turn off the heat and let rest for 10 minutes.

3. Strain the mixture through a fine-mesh strainer, using a spatula to press down and extract most of the liquid; this should yield about ½ cup. Discard the solids.

4. In a blender, combine the liquid from the onions and bacon with the livers, eggs, salt, Instacure, and pepper and blend until smooth. Slowly add the clarified butter through the hole in the lid and continue to blend to incorporate. Working quickly, pass the puree through a fine-mesh sieve into a waiting bowl. Transfer to a saucepan and cook on the lowest heat setting, whisking constantly so as not to curdle the egg until thickened and smooth, about 10 minutes. Be sure to keep it under a simmer. If the liquid starts to curdle, remove it from the heat and use an immersion blender on it until it's smooth again. Once it has thickened, transfer to a container, cool completely, and refrigerate until ready to use.

PINK POWER

Instacure #1, which this recipe calls for, is generally used for any type of cured meat that will be cooked further, such as bacon or smoked sausages. In this recipe, we use it not to cure the livers, but to keep the mousse from taking on a gray color. This is purely aesthetic—the mousse will taste just as good without Instacure, but with it, the lovely fresh color is preserved.

Crispy-Skinned Duck Cassoulet

Cassoulet has been a staple of French peasant cuisine since medieval times, and it's one of Kimbal's favorite dishes to share at a cozy winter gathering. Add a simple green salad and a bottle of red wine, and you're golden. Every cassoulet begins with a tender, slow-cooked bean ragout. What else goes into the pot depends on seasonal availability, personal taste, and the chef's creativity. In this country, you'll most often see it prepared using pork loin and sausage; in France, traditional regional variations include goose, partridge, and mutton. In a delicious break from tradition, we sear the duck with its skin on, so you get that wonderful crispy skin for luxurious richness, together with the vinegar-forward gastrique to cut through the fat. This recipe takes some time and attention to detail, but it more than pays off in flavor and presentation.

SEE HOW TO RENDER THE FAT

TO PREPARE THE DUCK LEGS

1. Start by combining all of the cure seasonings in a small bowl. Next, rinse the duck legs and pat them dry. Using a sharp knife, score the legs about an inch from the top, making sure to cut through the tendons completely to the bone, exposing the bottom of the legs. Place the legs in a nonreactive container large enough to arrange them in a single layer, then pour the cure mixture over to coat. Cover with plastic wrap and let sit in the refrigerator for 12 to 24 hours.

2. Preheat the oven to 300°F.

3. Remove the duck legs from the cure and rinse them thoroughly. Pat dry with paper towels and place them in an 8-quart Dutch oven. Coat the legs completely with duck fat, put the cover on the pan, and bake for 90 minutes, or until the duck meat can be easily pulled from the bone with a fork. Take the pot out of the oven, remove the lid, and let sit for 1 hour. Reserve 1 tablespoon duck fat for the gastrique. Remove the duck legs to a plate and let them

Continued

Serves 10 to 12

Duck Legs

2 tablespoons salt

2 tablespoons sugar

1 teaspoon freshly ground black pepper

1 star anise pod, toasted and ground

1 teaspoon juniper berries, toasted and ground

½ teaspoon crushed red pepper

2 pounds duck legs (4 legs)

3 to 4 cups duck fat

cool until they can be handled comfortably. (Once cooled, you can cover tightly and refrigerate them for up to 1 month.) Remove the meat from the legs, discard the bones, and reserve the duck for the next step.

192

Cassoulet

1 pound flageolet beans, soaked overnight in water to cover by a couple of inches
4 tablespoons unsalted butter
4 ounces slab bacon, cut into medium dice
6 garlic cloves, peeled
8 ounces Toulouse sausage, sliced into ¼-inch coins
2 medium yellow onions, finely chopped
2 medium carrots, finely chopped
2 ribs celery, finely chopped
1 tablespoon herbes de Provence
¼ cup white wine
2 fresh or dried bay leaves
1½ quarts chicken stock, warmed, plus more if needed
Salt and freshly ground black pepper
4 ounces breadcrumbs

Duck Breasts and Garnishes

4 duck breasts
1 tablespoon grapeseed or other neutral oil
Salt and freshly ground black pepper
Fresh flat-leaf parsley leaves
Roughly chopped fresh chives
Fresh tarragon leaves

TO MAKE THE CASSOULET

1. While the duck legs are in the oven, drain the beans and cover with fresh water. Bring to a boil, then reduce the heat and simmer for about 45 minutes, until cooked through but very al dente. Drain.

2. Preheat the oven to 325°F.

3. Heat the 8-quart Dutch oven over medium-low heat. Add 2 tablespoons of the butter and swirl around the pan, being careful not to brown the butter. Add the bacon and cook, stirring often to render out the fat, for about 10 minutes, until the bacon is crisp and golden. Using a slotted spoon, remove the bacon to a plate and set aside.

4. Add the garlic and cook until golden and soft, about

5 minutes, watching the heat so it doesn't burn. Remove the garlic and all but 1 tablespoon of the fat from the Dutch oven to a small blender and blend until smooth.

5. Raise the heat to medium, add the sausage to the pan, and cook, stirring often, until the edges start to crisp, about 10 minutes. Add the onions, carrots, celery, herbes de Provence, and a liberal pinch of salt. Cook the vegetables for about 10 minutes, until softened without taking on color. Add the white wine and reduce by half, about 5 minutes, then stir in the garlic puree.

6. Add the cooked beans, bay leaves, reserved duck confit meat, reserved cooked bacon, and warm chicken stock. Season with salt and pepper. Bring the mixture to a simmer, cover, and place in the oven. Bake for 90 minutes, or until the beans are soft but not falling apart and the liquid has reduced by one-quarter.

7. While the cassoulet is cooking, melt the remaining 2 tablespoons of butter in a large skillet over low heat and toast the breadcrumbs until golden brown, about 10 minutes. Remove to a plate and reserve.

TO PREPARE THE GASTRIQUE

Put the red wine, red wine vinegar, honey, and mustard in a small saucepan and whisk to combine. Add the herbs and bring to a simmer over medium heat. Lower the heat to medium-low and cook, stirring often, until the sauce is reduced and thick enough to coat the back of a spoon, about 30 minutes. Remove from the heat and discard the herbs. Whisk in the reserved duck fat and season with salt. Set aside for serving. If the gastrique thickens too much while cooling, it can be thinned with hot water to reach your desired consistency.

TO COOK THE DUCK BREASTS AND ASSEMBLE THE FINAL DISH

1. Once the cassoulet is done, remove it from the oven and let it rest, covered, on the stovetop. If it is on the dry side, add a little stock.

2. Heat a heavy bottomed sauté pan large enough to cook the duck breasts in a single layer over medium-low heat (use two pans if necessary). Season the duck breasts liberally with salt and pepper. Add the oil to the pan and swirl to coat. Place the duck breasts in the pan skin-side down and cook without moving the duck until the skin is golden and crisp, about 8 minutes. Flip the duck over and continue to cook, basting the top of the duck with rendered fat from the pan for an additional 3 to 4 minutes, until just cooked to a beautiful pink, taking care not to overcook it. Remove the duck from the pan to a cutting board and allow to rest for 5 minutes.

3. Ladle about 1 cup of the cassoulet into deep serving bowls, making sure every serving includes both sausage and beans. Drizzle about 1 tablespoon of the gastrique on top. Slice the rested duck breast on a bias and arrange the slices skin-side up over the cassoulet. Garnish with the toasted breadcrumbs and finish with parsley, chives, and tarragon.

Red Wine Gastrique

½ cup red wine	1 sprig tarragon
½ cup red wine vinegar	1 small sprig whole
½ cup honey	rosemary
2 teaspoons Dijon	1 tablespoon reserved
mustard	duck fat
2 sprigs thyme	Salt

193

Kimbal's Soft-Scrambled Eggs

2 large eggs
Salt and freshly ground black
    pepper
1½ teaspoons butter
Bread for toast

GET THE GOOEYNESS YOU WANT

One touchstone we return to again and again at The Kitchen is the joy of taking a seemingly humble ingredient and making it the star of the show. Kimbal's scrambled eggs provide a deliciously rewarding and easy to prepare example of how this ethos plays out. You can eat them for breakfast every day, but why stop there? Whip some up for a simple lunch or a late-night snack. Or take them uptown as an appetizer served on bruschetta topped with Parmesan cheese and herbs. One fun thing about these "daddy eggs," as Kimbal's kids have been known to call them, is the timing. Put your bread in the toaster, then start cooking the eggs; when the toast pops up, your eggs are ready. It takes about as long to cook in the pan as it takes your bread to toast. When you get good at it, this makes for a fast, delicious, and easy eggs-and-toast breakfast for you and your family.

▼

1. Crack the eggs into a bowl. Sprinkle a pinch of salt over each egg yolk, then grind some pepper over the eggs. Whisk vigorously with a fork for about 20 seconds, until most of the whites are dissolved. Let the eggs sit in the bowl for about 1 minute while the salt dissolves the rest of the whites.

2. In that minute, take two slices of bread and pop them into the toaster—that will be your timer! When the toast pops up, the eggs are ready.

3. Pour your egg mixture into a small nonstick skillet and add the butter. Turn the stove to medium-high heat and let the whisked eggs sit over the heat for 30 seconds to 1 minute until the egg just starts to cook around the edges, then start stirring. (If you're fast, you should be able to grab a plate, knife, and fork while you're waiting.)

4. Slowly stir the mixture for about 30 seconds, until it starts to come together. Turn the heat down to low and finish cooking until the eggs are cooked to your preference. You can keep them really gooey (Kimbal's daughter likes them really gooey) or cook them a bit longer, but don't overcook—the soft in soft-scrambled is there for a reason.

5. Ding! The toast should be ready by now. Time to eat!

Turkish Eggs

Recently we wanted to give our brunch menu a refresh, but we wanted to go beyond the expected eggs Benedict and its variations. While brainstorming, Chef Michael thought back to his college days, when his roommate, who was Turkish, would invite him to share family meals back at home. It was there that Michael learned about how in many Mediterranean countries eggs are served at breakfast along with some form of yogurt, bread, and loads of fresh herbs. And that became the inspiration behind this interpretation, which has now become a fan favorite.

1. Prepare the Za'atar Spice: In a small pan set over medium-low heat, toast the cumin and coriander seeds, stirring occasionally. Be careful that the seeds do not burn; remove them from the pan as soon as they become fragrant and start to turn golden. Let the seeds cool, and then coarsely grind them in a spice grinder or with a mortar and pestle. In a bowl, combine the ground seeds with the other spices and salt. You can make the Za'atar Spice in advance; it will keep, covered at room temperature, for at least a month.

2. Poach the eggs (see page 143 for the technique). Keep them warm while you prepare the rest of the recipe.

3. Pick the leaves from the mint, cilantro, and dill. Tear the leaves in halves (or thirds if they are large) and toss together in a bowl.

4. Brush both sides of the naans with the melted butter, and sprinkle about 2 teaspoons of the Za'atar Spice on one side of each naan. In a large skillet set over medium heat, toast the naans for a few minutes, flipping halfway, until they are warmed through and slightly crispy. Lay the naans, spiced side up, on a cutting board, and cut each into quarters.

5. In the bottom of each serving plate, smear a generous ¼ cup of the labneh in a wide circle and top it with 2 poached eggs. Ladle about ¼ cup of the urfa marinade over the two eggs. Sprinkle each serving with a teaspoon of sesame seeds and Maldon salt to taste, then top off with about ¼ cup of the fresh herb mixture. Serve with the naan in a basket to pass at the table.

Serves 4

For the Za'atar Spice:

1 tablespoon whole cumin seeds

1 tablespoon whole coriander seeds

1 tablespoon dried oregano

1 tablespoon toasted sesame seeds

1½ tablespoons sumac

1 teaspoon Maldon salt

½ teaspoon ground Aleppo chile

8 large eggs

1 bunch mint

1 bunch cilantro

A few sprigs dill

4 Naans (page 140), par-cooked

4 tablespoons melted butter

1½ cups labneh (page 91)

1 cup Urfa Marinade (page 97)

3 tablespoons Za'atar Spice (recipe precedes)

4 teaspoons toasted sesame seeds

Maldon salt, to taste

love a good steak. One thing I learned in culinary school is that traditional French cooking methods don't really teach you what to *do* with a good steak (besides cover it in rich sauces that will mask its flavor).

I don't think I appreciated just how good a simply prepared steak could be before I moved to Boulder, which has a rich history in cattle ranching. Sustainability is hugely important in everything The Kitchen does. When we were just starting up, we knew we wanted to stay away from anything like factory-farmed meat. I met with local farmers to educate myself about sustainable beef production, which is how I met Colorado rancher Roger Koberstein. Roger has been delivering two whole cows a week to our kitchens for ages, and he's become a real friend. One other very important takeaway from my ranching research? In 2017, I was visiting Texas farmers and ranchers to learn more about their operations. The midday sun was brutal, and I asked to borrow a farmer's hat. Only later did I learn that that was like asking to borrow his dog—you just don't do it. So, I bought my own hat on a trip to Austin and decided it looked damn good. It still does, and I'm still wearing it.

Meat

Pulled Pork

On The Kitchen's menu from day one, this was a Chef Hugo classic. We used to serve it over simple roast vegetables for dinner, or on a toasted ciabatta bun with salsa verde (page 54) for lunch. This is a versatile centerpiece dish to prepare for a big communal meal—anything from a backyard picnic-style dinner to a fancy sit-down meal. The spices and aromatic veggies give it a lot more depth (think Italian-style pot roast) than traditional pulled pork recipes do. You can serve it with any of the classic Southern sides, including cornbread, biscuits, collard greens, and coleslaw. To dress it up a bit more, try crusty bread, fresh veggies (our Broccolini with Miso on page 111 is a favorite), and maybe an apple-forward slaw.

1. Combine the cumin seeds, coriander seeds, fennel seeds, and mustard seeds in a spice grinder and grind to a powder. Transfer to a bowl and stir in the salt. Put the pork shoulder on a sheet pan, pack the spice mixture onto it, cover loosely with plastic wrap, and cure in the refrigerator for 24 hours.

2. Preheat the oven to 250°F and take the pork out of the refrigerator.

3. Heat the oil in a large sauté pan over medium heat. Add the apples, carrots, onions, celery, chiles, thyme, and bay leaf and cook until softened without adding any color, about 10 minutes. Add the wine and apple juice, increase the heat, and cook until most of the liquid has evaporated, still without adding color to the ingredients, about 10 minutes. Transfer the vegetable mixture to a roasting pan.

Continued

Serves 12 to 18

1 tablespoon cumin seeds

2 tablespoons coriander seeds

2 tablespoons fennel seeds

1 tablespoon mustard seeds

¼ cup salt

1 (8- to 10-pound) bone-in pork shoulder

2 tablespoons grapeseed or other neutral oil

2 large apples, cored and chopped

2 large carrots, trimmed and chopped

2 onions, chopped

4 ribs celery, chopped

2 Fresno chiles, chopped

6 sprigs thyme

1 bay leaf

½ cup white wine

½ cup apple juice

THE RIGHT WAY TO STORE HOT FOOD

201

4. Heat the largest pan you have (we like a 12-inch cast-iron skillet) over medium-high heat. Place the pork into the pan and brown on all sides, about 5 minutes per side. Place the pork on top of the vegetable mixture and put the pan in the oven. Roast for 8 to 10 hours (about 1 hour per pound), until it registers 180°F in the center and you can feel that the meat is soft throughout as you slide the thermometer in.

5. Remove the meat to a cutting board. Strain the juices from the pan, pressing on the solids to express as much liquid as possible, then discard the solids. Let the pork cool until it can be handled, then shred it with two large forks. Transfer the shredded meat to a platter and add the strained juices back to the meat to moisten it to your liking. Serve with the accompaniments of your choice. Any leftovers can be stored tightly covered in the fridge for up to 4 days, or frozen for up to 6 months. You can prepare the pork a couple of days before you plan to serve it. Refrigerate the cooked pork in a tightly covered container and reheat to serve.

Double-Cut Pork Chop with Bourbon Apple Glaze

Serves 8

2 cups apple juice

¼ cup kosher salt, plus more as needed

2 sprigs thyme

1½ teaspoons black peppercorns, crushed

2 cups water

4 (1-pound) double-cut bone-in pork chops, about 2 inches thick

Grapeseed or other neutral oil

2 tablespoons unsalted butter

2 cups prepared Rye Spaetzle (page 141)

4 spring onions, root ends trimmed and cut in half lengthwise

Bourbon Apple Glaze (recipe follows), warmed

Maldon salt, to finish

This is a long-time favorite, especially when crisp fall evenings roll around and we all crave hearty seasonal fare. A double-cut chop comes from the loin, which is a little leaner, so you really want that bone-in cut to help keep the meat from drying out. Once you've brined the meat and given it a quick sear, you're ready to slow-roast it to perfection. The Bourbon Apple Glaze doubles down on how well apples pair with pork, and our Rye Spaetzle (page 141) is a traditional companion dish that's a lot of fun to make. Note that the chops need 48 hours for brining, so plan accordingly. If you don't have two cast-iron skillets, you could sear the chops in batches, putting the first two chops on a baking sheet while you prepare the other two.

1. Combine the apple juice, kosher salt, thyme, and peppercorns with the water in a medium saucepan. Place over medium heat and simmer until the salt dissolves, about 5 minutes. Remove from heat and let cool completely. Put the pork chops in a heavy-duty zip-top bag and pour the brine over them. Seal the bag, place it in a bowl for stability, and brine in the refrigerator for 48 hours.

2. When ready to cook, remove the pork chops and discard the brine. Pat dry with paper towels and let come to room temperature, about 30 minutes.

3. Preheat the oven to 350°F and heat 2 large cast-iron skillets on the stove over medium-high heat until they're almost smoking. Rub the pork chops with a thin layer of oil and sear until well browned, about 5 minutes, then flip and cook until browned on the other side, about 5 minutes more. Transfer the pans to the oven and cook for about 20 minutes, or until the internal temperature reaches 150°F in the thickest part of the chop.

Continued

IT'S LIKE A REFINED
BBQ SAUCE

4. While the pork chops are in the oven, heat the butter in a large nonstick skillet over medium heat until it starts to brown. Add the spaetzle and cook until heated through and nicely browned, about 3 minutes. Season with kosher salt and spoon onto 4 serving plates to cover one half of the plate.

5. Brush the spring onions with a thin coating of oil, then season with kosher salt, add to the pan, and cook, turning a couple times, for about 2 minutes, until they are browned in spots and can be easily pierced with a knife. (If you have an extra pan, you can cook the spaetzle and spring onions at the same time.)

6. Lay the spring onion next to the spaetzle on the plates. Cut the pork off the bone into thin slices and fan them out on each plate alongside the spaetzle and onions. Place the bone at the top of the plate. Ladle the bourbon apple glaze over the pork and finish with a sprinkle of Maldon salt. Serve immediately.

BOURBON APPLE GLAZE

Makes about 1½ cups

½ cup bourbon
1¼ cups apple cider vinegar
¼ cup boiled apple cider
   (available online) or
   fresh apple cider
1 cup honey
Salt and freshly ground
   black pepper

Pour the bourbon into a medium saucepan and set over medium heat. Light a long match and quickly place it above the alcohol to ignite. Do not leave your workstation while it's burning and be sure to have a lid for the pan handy in case the flames flare up too high and need to be quickly extinguished. Otherwise, leave the pan untouched until the flames subside. Add the vinegar, cider, and honey and cook, swirling the pan occasionally, for about 15 minutes, until the sauce has thickened to the consistency of thin maple syrup. Remove from the heat and add a good pinch of salt and pepper. The sauce will keep tightly covered and refrigerated for up to 2 weeks.

Fennel-Stuffed Pork with Apricot-Chamomile Chutney

Serves 4

4 tablespoons grapeseed or
    other neutral oil

1 small onion, very thinly sliced

½ small fennel bulb, cored and
    very thinly sliced

2 garlic cloves, minced

1½ teaspoons fennel seeds

¾ teaspoon red chile flakes

1 tablespoon fresh lemon juice,
    or to taste

Salt and freshly ground
    black pepper

1 (1½-pound) pork tenderloin

2 shallots, very thinly sliced

2 garlic cloves, very thinly sliced

2 bunches Swiss chard,
    stems removed and leaves cut
    into 1-inch ribbons

Apricot Chamomile Chutney
    (recipe follows)

In traditional Italian cooking, porchetta originally referred to a boned, stuffed suckling pig. Over the years, it's come to describe a pork tenderloin wrapped in pork belly and rolled around a stuffing, which is how we prepare it at the restaurant. You don't need an elaborate preparation to experience what's wonderful about this dish. You can simply take a good pork tenderloin, create a pocket in it, and fill it with tasty sautéed vegetables and spices. If apricots are in season, we make a fresh apricot chutney as an accompaniment. Apricots are one of the fruits that are commonly served with pork, and the Indian-influenced spices are an unexpected delight.

1. Preheat the oven to 400°F.

2. Heat 2 tablespoons of oil in a medium sauté pan over medium heat. Add the sliced onion and fennel and cook until softened, about 5 minutes. Add the minced garlic and cook for another minute. Add the fennel seeds and red chile flakes and cook for 1 minute more. Turn off the heat, add the lemon juice, and season with salt and pepper. Remove from the heat and let cool completely.

3. While the mixture is cooling, remove the silverskin—a white fibrous outer layer that covers the tenderloin—then pat the meat dry with paper towels. Cut a pocket in the tenderloin lengthwise from the thick end to just before the shape starts tapering down to the thinner end, and about three-quarters of the way through to the other side. Use your fingers to open the pocket you've just made, place the stuffing inside, and roll it up like a log. Using butcher's twine, tie up the tenderloin along the pocket in 1-inch intervals to keep it closed while cooking. Season the outside of the tenderloin well with salt.

4. Heat 1 tablespoon of oil in a wide skillet over medium-high heat. Add the tenderloin and cook for about 3 minutes on each side, until lightly browned.

5. Transfer to a wire rack set over a roasting pan, place in the oven, and roast for 35 to 45 minutes, until the thickest part of the tenderloin registers 145°F on an instant-read thermometer. Remove to a cutting board and let rest for 10 minutes.

6. While the tenderloin is resting, heat the final tablespoon of oil in a large skillet over medium heat. Add the shallots and garlic and cook until softened without taking on any color, 2 to 3 minutes. Add the chard and toss with tongs; pull it from the heat as it just begins to wilt. Season with salt.

7. Cut the pork into 1-inch-thick slices. Divide the chard among 4 plates and top with the pork. Spoon the chutney over the pork and serve.

APRICOT CHAMOMILE CHUTNEY

The soothing, almost perfumed quality of chamomile here interacts subtly with delicate spices and sweet apricots for a mild yet complex chutney that complements pork, lamb, and poultry

1. Heat the oil in a small saucepan over medium heat. Add the onion and cook until softened, 3 to 5 minutes. Add the apricots, water, honey, lemon zest and juice, chamomile, cardamom, and star anise. Bring to a simmer and cook, mashing it a little with a spoon, until almost all the liquid is absorbed and the mixture is thick and syrupy, about an hour. Remove the cardamom and star anise with a spoon. Cool completely. The chutney can be kept tightly covered and refrigerated for up to 1 month.

Makes about 1½ cups

- 1 tablespoon grapeseed or other neutral oil
- 1 small yellow onion, finely chopped
- 1 cup dried apricots, chopped
- 1 cup water
- ¼ cup honey
- Zest and juice of 1 lemon
- 1 tablespoon dried chamomile flowers
- 3 cardamom pods
- 2 star anise pods

Seven-Spice Lamb Arayes

Serves 4

Lamb filling

1 pound ground lamb

1 cup minced yellow onion

½ cup finely chopped fresh
   flat-leaf parsley

2 garlic cloves

¼ cup Baharat Seven Spice
   (recipe follows), or use
   store-bought

1 teaspoon sweet paprika

1½ teaspoons salt

To serve

4 small pita breads (with pockets)

2 tablespoons sunflower oil

2 cups Labneh (page 91)

4 tablespoons extra-virgin
   olive oil

Paprika

Maldon salt

Fresh dill fronds, to garnish

Zest of ½ lemon, to garnish

rayes is a beloved Lebanese street food we've brought to our menu in recent years, to universally glowing reviews from the people who matter most—our guests. Particularly memorable was the reaction from our COO Sam Hallak who grew up in a family that operated Arabic restaurants. He tried it and told us, "This tastes like my childhood!" Hearing that made Chef Michael smile; he knew then he'd hit on the right formula. The meat filling here is like an amped-up lamb burger. It gets melded with a toasty pita after you cook it in a pan, similar to how you'd make a grilled cheese. Then you get to swipe the sandwich with homemade labneh. If you've never made labneh, not to worry. You really just strain Greek yogurt to get a thicker, richer consistency that takes everything you love about yogurt up a notch. Baharat is a Lebanese spice blend used throughout the Middle East. Make your own with our recipe or find it in well-stocked grocery stores or online.

1. In a large bowl, combine the lamb, onion, and parsley. Using a Microplane, grate the garlic into the mixture. Add the Baharat spice blend, paprika, and salt and use your hands to thoroughly combine to a homogenous mixture (be mindful to not overwork the meat, which will make the texture dense when cooked). The lamb will keep covered and refrigerated for up to 3 days before cooking or frozen for up to 1 month.

2. To fill the arayes, start by slicing the pitas in half and carefully breaking open the pockets. Divide the meat into 8 equal portions and carefully pack a portion of the mixture into each pita half. Slice each packed pita half down the middle. You will end up with 16 small arayes. Smooth the edges with your fingers so the meat isn't overflowing.

Continued

3. To cook the arayes, heat two large cast-iron skillets over medium-high heat (or cook in two batches). Add 1 tablespoon of the oil to each. Once it's heated, place the arayes in the skillet and sear on all sides, turning carefully with tongs, until the pita is golden brown and slightly crispy and the lamb is cooked through (160°F on an instant-read thermometer). Lower the heat if the meat is browning too quickly before it is cooked through. Remove the arayes from the pan to rest while you plate the dishes.

4. To serve, spoon ½ cup labneh over each of 4 plates. Press and swirl it into an even layer with a spoon, drizzle with 1 tablespoon of olive oil, and dust with paprika. Sprinkle the labneh with a pinch of Maldon salt, then top with fresh dill and a big pinch of lemon zest. Place the cooked arayes over the labneh and serve immediately.

BAHARAT SEVEN SPICE

1. Preheat the oven to 350°F.

2. Place all of the spices except the cinnamon in a skillet and toast for 3 to 5 minutes, until the spices are aromatic and the coriander and cumin seeds darken in color.

3. Transfer to a spice grinder, cool to room temperature, and grind to a powder. The spice mixture will keep in a covered container for up to 3 months.

Makes about ¼ cup

1 tablespoon cumin seeds

1 tablespoon coriander seeds

1 whole nutmeg, crushed with a meat mallet or metal measuring cup

1 tablespoon whole allspice

1 tablespoon black peppercorns

1½ teaspoons whole cloves

1 tablespoon ground cinnamon

THE LITTLE CHILE SMUGGLER

One thing you'll notice throughout this book is that we call for chile paste in a number of Peruvian-influenced marinades and sauces. That's because most of the fresh peppers used in Peru are not available in the U.S.—although as produce markets extend their offerings, Chef Michael holds out hope that these precious commodities may eventually become common. But don't ask him whether he's considered a glamorous career as a chile smuggler! When he was little, on a family trip to Peru, his mother mentioned to her mother-in-law how hard it was in the States to find the peppers that her husband so loved. Michael's grandmother had what seemed like a sensible solution, picking some peppers from her garden and setting them out to dry so that the family could have seeds to plant back home. Little Michael proudly carried them in his bag on the plane. But after they landed in Miami, an "ag dog"—trained to sniff out smuggled or forgotten agricultural products—darted up to him in the line for Customs. Mortified, he discovered that the peppers hadn't fully dried, and wouldn't be allowed into the country. His father, also embarrassed, apologized, and the family got off with a warning. And resigned themselves to aji paste for the time being.

Peruvian Lamb Sirloin over Hominy with Salsa Verde

This dish is something of a play on Peruvian cuisine, with a lamb sirloin soaked in anticucho marinade, which is traditionally used for grilled beef heart skewers (anticucho literally means "meat skewers"). We serve the meat over a hominy dish that's almost like a succotash made with giant kernels of corn. It's a fantastic dish for early summer, when you're craving corn but it's not quite in season.

▼

1. In a large bowl, mix all the marinade ingredients and whisk to combine. Place the lamb in a heavy-duty zip-top bag and pour in the marinade. Seal the bag and turn a few times, making sure the marinade fully covers the lamb. Refrigerate for at least 8 hours or up to 24 hours.

2. Remove the lamb from the refrigerator 30 minutes to 1 hour before cooking.

3. Preheat a grill to medium-high or 2 large cast-iron skillets over high heat until smoking. Remove the lamb from the marinade. Add the lamb and cook until well browned on the bottom, about 2 minutes. Flip the steaks and cook for about 2 more minutes, until they reach an internal temperature of 130°F for medium-rare. Remove to a cutting board to rest.

4. While the lamb is resting, heat the oil in a large sauté pan over medium heat. Add the garlic and shallot and cook until translucent, about 2 minutes. Add the coriander and cumin and cook for 1 more minute. Stir in the aji amarillo, then add the hominy, peppers, and green onions and cook to heat through and wilt the green onions. Season with salt. Stir in the butter until melted and combined. Turn off the heat and stir in the lime juice. Taste and add more salt and/or lime juice if needed. Stir in the cilantro.

5. Slather the lamb with the salsa verde, then cut into ¼-inch slices.

6. Spoon the hominy mixture into the center of shallow bowls or large rimmed plates. Arrange the sliced lamb around the hominy, garnish with cilantro, and serve.

Serves 4

Anticucho Marinade

½ cup aji panca paste (see note on page 219)

½ cup grapeseed or other neutral oil

¼ cup red wine vinegar

3 garlic cloves, grated on a Microplane

1 tablespoon roughly chopped fresh oregano

1 tablespoon salt

1 teaspoon ground cumin

4 (5- to 6-ounce) boneless lamb sirloin steaks (¾ inch to 1 inch thick)

1 tablespoon grapeseed or other neutral oil

2 garlic cloves, thinly sliced

1 shallot, thinly sliced

1 teaspoon ground coriander

½ teaspoon ground cumin

2 tablespoons aji amarillo paste (see note on page 153)

2 cups cooked hominy

1 cup roasted red bell peppers, sliced

2 green onions, chopped

Salt

¼ cup unsalted butter

1 tablespoon fresh lime juice. or to taste

¼ cup chopped fresh cilantro, plus more to garnish

Salsa Verde (page 54)

PERUVIAN LAMB
SIRLOIN OVER
HOMINY

STEAK
TARTARE WITH
CHICHARRONS
PORTER-
HOUSE STEAK
WITH GARLIC
PUREE

Porterhouse Steak w/ Black Garlic Puree & Mushrooms

Serves 4

1 (36- to 42-ounce) bone-in
   porterhouse steak
Kosher salt and freshly
   cracked pepper
1 tablespoon grapeseed or
   other neutral oil
Black Garlic Puree (page 72)
4 tablespoons unsalted butter
Roasted Mushrooms (page 127)

If you're having a group over for dinner and want to showcase a big, beautiful cut of meat, this is the recipe for you. It's a simple plating, and that's all you need. The great thing about a porterhouse is that it includes both the New York strip and the fillet, so there's something for everyone who loves a good steak. The New York side is slightly firmer; the fillet is more tender. For a big piece of meat like this, tempering before cooking and resting after are absolutely essential. Tempering means letting the steak come up to room temperature—in this case, for about an hour before you cook it—to ensure it cooks through evenly, even close to the bone. Letting the meat rest before carving allows the juices to reabsorb into the meat.

1. Remove the steak from the refrigerator and pat dry with paper towels. Season liberally on both sides with salt and pepper and bring to room temperature for about an hour.

2. While the steak is getting ready, preheat the oven to 400°F.

3. Heat a large cast-iron skillet on high flame until very hot, about 5 minutes. Add the oil and spread it over the pan to coat. Add the steak and sear until a hard crust forms, about 5 minutes. Flip the steak and transfer the pan to the oven. Roast until an instant-read thermometer inserted in the thickest part registers 120°F for medium-rare, about 12 to 15 minutes.

4. Transfer the steak to a cutting board to rest for 10 minutes.

5. After it's rested properly, brush the steak with a light coating of black garlic puree and return it to the hot pan. Add the butter to baste the steak and let it sit in the pan for about 2 minutes to form a crust. Return it to the cutting board and cut along the bone to remove the large strip section. Turn the steak around and cut the tenderloin section off the bone. Cut each steak crosswise into ¼-inch-thick slices. For an impressive presentation, nestle the slices back in formation inside the bone. Top with the mushrooms and serve.

Steak Tartare with Chicharrons

Serves 4

1 pound eye of round, fillet, or flank steak (preferably wagyu beef)

¼ cup very finely chopped green onions

½ cup Szechuan Chili Crisp (page 63), or to taste

½ cup Chinese black vinegar

¼ cup tamari or soy sauce, or to taste

4 teaspoons toasted sesame seeds

Salt to taste

4 large egg yolks (page 43 for technique) (optional)

About 24 pieces warmed chicharrons (see note below)

Micro-cilantro, to finish

One day Chef Michael fell in love with a Szechuan chili crisp sauce he sampled at a Chinese dumpling truck. He became determined to re-create that sauce at the restaurant and find a new way to showcase it. The result was this recipe, a reimagined Steak Tartare. Steak Tartare is usually served with bread, but to make it accessible for our gluten-free friends, we had the inspiration to use chicharrons, or fried pork rinds, as an accompaniment. At the restaurant we top the tartare with egg yolk jam, but you can just put an egg yolk atop each serving if you like.

1. Trim the steak of any visible pieces of fat (the steak is lean, so there shouldn't be much). Freeze the steak for 20 minutes in order to make cutting it easier.

2. In a chilled bowl, combine the green onions, chili crisp, vinegar, tamari, sesame seeds, and salt. Stir to combine.

3. Cut the steak into ⅛-inch cubes, add to the liquid mixture, and gently fold in to coat the cubes evenly. Taste and add more vinegar, salt, and/or chili crisp if needed.

4. Press approximately a quarter of the tartare into the center of a shallow bowl and shape into a circle. Repeat with 3 more bowls to use up all the tartare. Create a small divot on top of each mound of tartare and top each with an egg yolk.

5. Place the chicharrons around the edge of the bowl for dipping. Pull the tenderest leaves from the cilantro and sprinkle them on top of the tartare. Repeat with the remaining 3 bowls. Serve immediately.

CHICHARRONS AT HOME

Store-bought chicharrons, heated in the oven, will serve you well in this recipe. But if you want to take that extra step that pushes the dish from fantastic to mind-blowing, try deep-frying them up fresh like we do at the restaurant. We use high-quality dehydrated rinds (generally called pellets), which really streamlines the process. Sure, you could go really old-school and cut your own strips of fresh pig skin for frying, but that is not easy to find unless you have a friendly local butcher or live in farming country. It's okay though—the pellets give you excellent results. They have a long shelf life, and with the popularity of gluten-free and keto diets, you can now find them in small batches online

Beef Short Ribs w/ Taleggio Cream & Tomato Jam

T his dish may well remind you of the best of French peasant fare, those traditional preparations in which the humblest of cuts are slow-cooked with vegetables and herbs until they're fork-tender and infused with flavor. In this recipe, the transformation happens when you take this inexpensive cut and, with a little time and patience, are rewarded with a soft and buttery main dish that tastes something like a pot roast, but with a steak-like tooth to it. You can cut the meat with a fork, but it won't be falling apart when you do. We serve it a few different ways, including over the Rice Middlins (page 142) and in this stand-alone entrée.

1. Preheat the oven to 325°F.

2. While the oven is preheating, heat 1 tablespoon of the oil over medium heat in a large Dutch oven or other oven-safe pot with a lid. Add the onion, carrots, and celery and cook, stirring often, until softened, about 5 minutes. Add the tomato paste and cook, stirring, for 2 more minutes. Pour in the wine and cook until most of the liquid has evaporated, scraping the bottom of the pan to release any browned bits. Add the beef stock, season with salt and pepper, and reduce to a simmer.

3. Next, heat the remaining 1 tablespoon of oil in a wide skillet over medium-high heat. Season the ribs with salt and pepper, add to the skillet, and brown on all sides, about 5 minutes per side. Transfer the ribs to the pot with the vegetables and stock, cover, and bake for 3 hours, or until the ribs are very tender but not falling apart.

4. To serve, spoon the Taleggio cream over the serving plates and drag it to create a "yin" shape. Spoon the tomato jam alongside the Taleggio cream to complete a yin-yang symbol. Place the short ribs on top and garnish with shallots and microgreens.

Continued

Serves 4

2 tablespoons grapeseed or
   other neutral oil

1 large onion, finely chopped

2 large carrots, finely chopped

4 stalks celery, finely chopped

1 tablespoon tomato paste

1 cup dry red wine

About 4 cups beef stock

Salt and freshly ground
   black pepper

4 large beef short ribs

Taleggio Cream (recipe follows)

1 cup Tomato Jam (Page 56)

Fried shallots, to garnish

Microgreens, to garnish

A SAFETY TIP
FOR HOT POTS

TALEGGIO CREAM

Makes about 1 cup

8 ounces Taleggio cheese

½ cup heavy cream

Salt

1. Cut the rind off the cheese and discard, then cut the cheese into ½-inch pieces. Put in a heatproof bowl and let come to room temperature, about 20 minutes.

2. While the cheese is warming, heat the cream in a small saucepan over medium heat until it comes to a simmer. Immediately remove from the heat and pour over the cheese. Cover the bowl with plastic wrap right away and let stand for 20 minutes. Remove the plastic wrap and, using an immersion blender, blend until smooth. Taste and season with salt if needed. Any sauce that's left over will keep tightly covered and refrigerated for up to 1 week.

Grilled Ranch Steak with Romesco & Catalan Spinach

Serves 4

For the marinade

½ cup aji panca paste
   (see note below)

½ cup grapeseed or other
   neutral oil

¼ cup red wine vinegar

2 garlic cloves, grated
   through a Microplane

1 tablespoon roughly
   chopped fresh oregano

1 tablespoon salt

1 teaspoon ground cumin

Once we started working directly with local ranchers, one unexpected benefit was being able to buy an entire cow for the restaurant and get expert butchering and cooking advice. That led to our whole kitchen crew getting an education in some of the less familiar cuts and how to do right by them. Ranch steak is a shoulder cut known for being flavorful but not always tender. That's where the marinade comes in. Give the steak time to marinate at least overnight and it will cook up beautifully with the subtle touch of herbs, spices, and aji panca, a mild Peruvian pepper. You can also use a hanger, flat iron, or Denver steak with equally delicious results. To give the presentation a kind of Spanish vibe, we pair it with the smoky, nutty romesco sauce used throughout Catalonia. For a finishing touch, the steak is plated with Catalan-stye greens. The leaves should be just slightly wilted; studded with pine nuts and currants, it's like a Spanish take on a warm spinach salad.

▼

1. Combine the marinade ingredients in a large bowl and whisk to combine. Put the steaks in a heavy-duty zip-top bag, add the marinade, and gently massage the bag to

make sure the steaks are well coated. Seal the bag and marinate for at least 8 hours or up to 24 hours in the fridge. Bring steaks up to room temperature before grilling.

2. To cook the steaks, heat a charcoal or gas grill to high (you can also use 2 large skillets over medium-high heat). Season the steak with salt and pepper and sear for 3 minutes per side, or until desired doneness (130°F for medium-rare or 140°F for medium).

3. Meanwhile, heat a tablespoon of oil in a large skillet over medium heat. Add the garlic and shallots and cook until softened without taking on any color, 2 to 3 minutes. Add the pine nuts and currants and cook for another 2 minutes, until the pine nuts are lightly browned. Add the spinach and toss with tongs; pull it from the heat as it just begins to wilt. Add the sherry vinegar syrup and season with salt.

4. To serve, spread romesco over each of 4 serving plates, then top it with the spinach, making sure not to carry over any of the spinach water from the cooking pan.

5. Slice the steak against the grain and fan it next to the spinach. Finish with a sprinkling of Maldon salt and herbs and serve immediately.

SHERRY VINEGAR SYRUP

Makes ½ cup

1 cup sherry vinegar

1 cup light brown sugar

In a small saucepan, combine the vinegar and brown sugar and bring to a boil over medium heat, stirring frequently until the sugar dissolves. Reduce the heat and simmer until reduced by half, about 15 minutes. Cool completely. The syrup will keep tightly covered in a cool, dark place for up to 2 months.

4 (8- to 10-ounce) ranch steaks

1 tablespoon grapeseed or other neutral oil

2 garlic cloves, very thinly sliced

2 shallots, very thinly sliced

¼ cup pine nuts, toasted

2 tablespoons currants

6 ounces (4 cups packed) fresh spinach leaves

1 tablespoon Sherry Vinegar Syrup (recipe follows)

Kosher salt

Romesco (page 56)

Maldon salt, to finish

Fines herbes or fresh flat-leaf parsley leaves, to garnish

Aji panca, a mild chile, is an essential ingredient in Peruvian cooking. It's used more for the berry-like flavor it brings than for heat. Look for it in Latin markets or online.

DON'T BE STINGY WITH THE COMEBACK SAUCE.

The Kitchen Burger

We switch up our burgers every so often, but we always return to this riff on a quintessential American cheeseburger that checks all the boxes for preparation and flavor. We love Tillamook cheddar; if you can't find it locally, any high-quality cheddar will work here. For your beef, look for a "steakhouse grind," with an 80/20 ratio of lean to fat to get that nice, juicy patty with a solid seared crust. Shocking the onions in ice water may sound odd if you've never heard of it, but it's one of those kitchen hacks that really pays off in terms of mellowing their sharpness while also making them super-crispy. Be sure to dip your fries into the Comeback Sauce as well as spreading it on your burger!

1. Fill a bowl with ice water and add the onion slices to shock them; let them sit in the ice water while you prepare the burgers.

2. Season each burger patty on one side with 1 teaspoon of the Montreal steak seasoning. Heat an extra-large cast-iron skillet over medium-high heat (or use 2 smaller skillets). Place the patties on the skillet seasoned-side down and sear until a solid crust forms, 3 to 4 minutes. Flip the patties and cook for 1 minute more, then add 1 slice of cheese to each and let it melt.

3. While the patties are cooking, butter the buns and toast them in a toaster oven until golden brown. Add 1 tablespoon of Comeback Sauce to each side of the buns.

4. Remove the onion slices to a paper towel–lined plate to absorb excess water. Place an onion slice on the bottom bun and top with the patty. Follow with 2 lettuce leaves, then 2 slices tomatoes and 4 pickle chips on top of each patty. Finish with the top bun. Serve immediately, with fries and the extra comeback sauce for dipping.

Serves 4

4 (⅛-inch) slices yellow onion
4 (6-ounce) burger patties
4 teaspoons Montreal
   steak seasoning
4 slices cheddar cheese,
   such as Tillamook
4 brioche buns, split
4 tablespoons unsalted
   butter, softened
8 tablespoons Comeback Sauce
   (page 59), plus extra
   for serving
8 Bibb lettuce leaves
8 (⅛-inch) slices tomato
16 pickle chips
Kitchen Fries (page 80)

221

Ranchero Steak w/ Roasted Potatoes & Eggs

Serves 4

1½ pounds Yukon gold potatoes, cut into ½-inch cubes

1 large onion, chopped

1 large red bell pepper, chopped

2 shallots, chopped

2 garlic cloves, minced

3 tablespoons grapeseed or other neutral oil

Salt and freshly ground black pepper

4 (8-ounce) picanha, hanger, or flat iron steaks

8 large eggs, cooked sunny side up (page 185)

Ranchero Sauce (recipe follows)

When it comes to cooking a simple, delicious weekend brunch or easy dinner for the family, steak and eggs is one of Kimbal's go-to dishes. Cooking for friends and loved ones is a beautiful way to start the day, and creating something simple, familiar, and delicious for them is almost like a moving meditation. What makes this dish so delicious is more about the process than the specific cut of meat. And the timing is so easy; you sear your steak and then, while it's resting, you cook your eggs sunny side up (or why not scrambled, see page 194). It works out so that the eggs are ready to serve just as the steak has finished resting. The spicy ranchero is a shout-out to huevos rancheros, the popular Mexican egg dish, and it works equally well with steak. We use a picanha steak, a slightly less common cut from the cow's rump that has a little more fat than the standard rump steak. You could also use a hanger or flat iron cut—or get a little fancier with a rib eye if you want.

▼

1. Preheat the oven to 375°F and line a baking sheet with parchment paper.

2. In a large bowl, combine the potatoes, onion, bell pepper, shallots, and garlic. Toss with the oil and season with salt and pepper. Spread out over the prepared baking sheet and roast for about 45 minutes, stirring once or twice, until everything is browned and the potatoes can be easily pierced with a fork.

3. Meanwhile, heat 2 large skillets over medium-high heat. Season the steak with salt and pepper and sear for 3 minutes per side, or until it reaches your desired doneness (medium-rare is 130°F; medium is 140°F). Let rest for about 10 minutes, while you prepare the eggs, then serve with ranchero sauce. To make sure the eggs don't under- or overcook, you may want to make them two at a time.

RANCHERO SAUCE
Makes about 4 cups

1 tablespoon extra-virgin olive oil
1 medium yellow onion, roughly
   chopped
4 garlic cloves, roughly chopped
1 tablespoon dried oregano
1 teaspoon ground cumin
2 poblano chiles, roasted, peeled,
   seeded, and roughly chopped
2 jalapeño chiles, roasted, peeled,
   seeded, and roughly chopped
1 (28-ounce) can whole San
   Marzano tomatoes
1 cup chicken stock
3 tablespoons fresh lime juice, or
   to taste
1 tablespoon red wine vinegar
¼ cup chopped fresh cilantro
1½ teaspoons salt, or to taste

223

Heat the oil in a medium saucepan over medium heat. Add the onion and garlic and cook for about 5 minutes, until they have softened. Add the oregano and cumin and cook for 1 more minute. Add the remaining ingredients, bring to a simmer, and cook until reduced by one-quarter, about 20 minutes. Transfer to a blender and blend until smooth or with a little texture remaining, as you like. Taste and add more salt and/or lime juice if needed. The ranchero sauce will keep, tightly covered and refrigerated, for up to a week.

Grilled Kansas City Strip Steak with Chimichurri

A Kansas City cut is similar to a New York strip, but trimmed a bit differently so that it has a little more fat. If your butcher can't cut you a Kansas City steak, you can substitute a New York strip. To complement the rich grilled meat, we take a little side trip to Argentina, a country that knows its way around a steak, for a vinegary, chile-spiked chimichurri. The sauce rounds out the meat's richness, but remember: As long as you start with a good cut of meat and treat it right, the results will be excellent. Grilling is traditional for this cut of meat, but it will also be delicious prepared on the stovetop in a cast-iron pan, as described on page 214.

Serves 2 or 3

1 (18-ounce) bone-in
   Kansas City strip steak
Kosher salt and freshly ground
   black pepper
2 tablespoons grapeseed or
   other neutral oil (if cooking
   on the stovetop)
2 tablespoons unsalted butter
   (if cooking on the stovetop)
Chimichurri (page 54)
Fresh flat-leaf parsley leaves,
   to garnish
Maldon salt, to finish

1. Remove the steak from the refrigerator 1 hour before cooking to allow it to come to room temperature. Season liberally on both sides with salt and pepper.

2. To cook on a gas or charcoal grill, begin by heating the grill to high. Place the steak onto the grill grates and sear for 3 minutes, then turn 45 degrees and cook for another 3 minutes. Flip the steak over and repeat the process. Pull from the grill when the internal temperature, measured with a meat thermometer, is 130°F for medium-rare (140°F for medium), and let it rest on a cutting board for about 5 minutes. To cook in a pan, start by preheating the oven to 400°F. Place a large cast-iron pan in the oven to heat up for 15 minutes. Remove the pan from the oven and place onto the stovetop over medium-high heat. Slick the pan with the oil. Place the steak into the heated pan and sear one side for 5 minutes. Flip the steak over and sear the other side for 3 minutes, or until a meat thermometer registers 130°F for medium rare (140°F for medium). Baste the steak with the melted butter and drippings over low heat for 1 minute, then let it rest on a cutting board for about 5 minutes.

3. Cut the steak from the bone and cut into ¼-inch slices. Plate the meat shingled beside the bone, slather with chimichurri, and top with parsley and Maldon salt.

THE RIGHT
AMOUNT OF SALT

irst and foremost, dessert should be fun. It's pure enjoyment, created to delight whether you're looking for a little something sweet after dinner at The Kitchen or a glorious array of shared plates for the table. We aim to have something for every kind of dessert person and for every season. Many of our favorites, like the Chèvre Cheesecake (page 269), stay on the menu year-round. We mix things up and keep it fresh by adapting sauces, toppings, and other elements to show off the best, most delicious produce we can find.

One thing we had to learn when we opened The Kitchen Boulder was how to adapt to baking at our altitude in the Rocky Mountain foothills. When you live some 5,000 feet above sea level, you realize that most recipes for baked goods will need some tweaks to get the best results. In this chapter, we supply the information you need to create wonderful desserts and other baked goods no matter where you live. In fact, we begin this chapter by breaking down some of the science behind these guidelines.

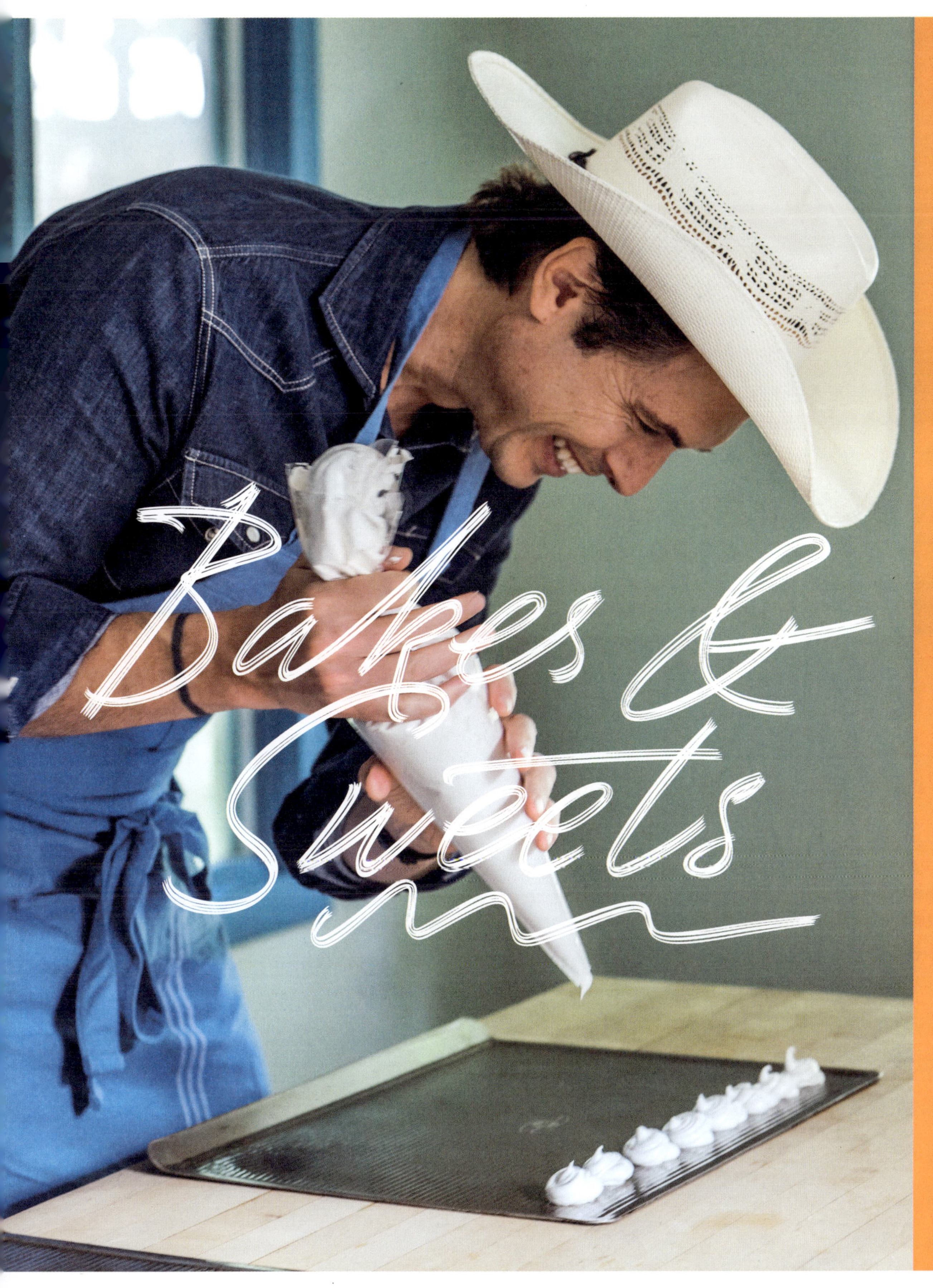
Bakes &
Sweets

High Altitude Basics

I n creating our pastry program 5,000 feet above sea level in the Colorado Rockies, we had to make several adjustments most restaurants don't deal with. That's because the higher the altitude, the lower the air pressure. This can have a range of effects that may need to be corrected for. Cookies like to rise and then collapse, spreading into thin pools. Cakes like to fall at the center. Certain custards set at higher temperatures; others need extra fat to set properly. Liquids evaporate more quickly, which can dry out your pastries. Finally, the gases produced by leavening agents like baking powder and baking soda expand and react more quickly when the pressure is lower, creating tunnels and holes in some batters and doughs, which leads to instability. Temperature, humidity, and low air pressure all affect the delicate structures of pastry. It can be hard to figure out the right adjustments but certainly not impossible. Many of the recipes that follow are designed to work without any changes. For those that are more sensitive to these factors, we've given our suggested alterations right in the ingredients list. For a big-picture look at how and why this all works, here's a quick rundown!

Baking powder or baking soda or a combination of the two	3,000–5,000 ft.	5,000–6,500 ft.	6,500–8,000 ft.
1 teaspoon	⁷⁄₈	½	¼
1½ teaspoons	1¼	¾	½
2 teaspoons	1½	1	¾
2½ teaspoons	1¾	1¼	1
3 teaspoons	2	1¼	1
3½ teaspoons	2½	1½	1
4 teaspoons	2½	1½	1

* You'll often get better results if you increase the temperature of your oven by 10 to 15 degrees and decrease the baking time by 5 to 6 minutes per 30 minutes of "sea level" bake time. The shorter time spent in a hotter oven prevents the final product from losing moisture and rising too quickly.
* Decrease the sugar in a recipe by 1 to 3 tablespoons per every cup. Sugar has extra moisture, which can evaporate too quickly at high altitudes and cause cakes to collapse.

* The most successful way to help prevent dry cakes and cookies is to increase the liquid in your recipe by adding another egg.
* Adding an extra 1 or 2 tablespoons of flour per cup in your recipe will help retain structure and ensure a much more even rise overall.
* Because of how quickly the gases produced by leavening agents expand, you may want to decrease the baking powder or baking soda in your recipe by 15% to 25%. The table here is one we swear by and use every day when adapting recipes that were written for locations around sea level.

A NOTE ON MEASUREMENTS

You may have heard the phrase "baking is chemistry" in cookbooks or on food blogs. In truth, all cooking is chemistry to some degree: mixing, heating, marinating, and otherwise modifying ingredients is both art and science. That said, much of baking could almost be mistaken for alchemy—take these items, in exactly these measures, heat for precisely this long, and the magic occurs. Creating wonderful baked goods isn't more difficult than other kinds of cooking, but it can require more precision.

For this reason, many American pastry chefs have adopted the practice of weighing rather than measuring ingredients by volume. Weighing is standard practice for home chefs in Europe and throughout the rest of the world. That generally means metric weights and measures, and U.S. chefs keen on precision generally tend to use metrics. If you use a kitchen scale at all, it probably has both ounces and pounds as well as metric measurements, which means you don't have to worry about any conversions.

In this chapter, our focus is on amazing recipes that anyone should feel confident cooking. If you don't have a food scale, we suggest that you consider adding one to your countertop. If you don't, every recipe in this chapter still has the information you need to get wonderful results because we've taken a hybrid approach to handling measurements, geared to the way many of us cook.

Dry ingredients are the most finicky, particularly flour, which varies so much in density. For example, though most types of flour weigh about 120 grams per cup, the exact same cup filled with rye flour weighs in at 106 grams, whole wheat pastry flour at 96 grams, and gluten-free all-purpose flour at 156. For that reason, we've provided measurements in both volume (cups, tablespoons, etc.) as well as grams where it would matter most. The ingredients that benefit most from precise measurements are flour, sugar, ground nuts, and cocoa powder.

Our basic guideline is to look at our recipes the way any of our friends, family, and guests would when heading to the grocery store excited to make something new. For flour, we gently recommend weighing it in grams. However, some recipes are more forgiving when it comes to having a little more or less of the liquid ingredients. If you're interested in learning more, or just want to go down a rabbit hole of food nerdery, look up the King Arthur Baking Company's Ingredient Weight Chart. It is the gold standard, giving cup measurements, ounces, and grams for everything from agave syrup to zucchini.

Sourdough Focaccia

Kimbal grew up eating focaccia made daily by his best friend's Italian grandmother. It literally doesn't get any better than that. But he's spent two decades with our chefs at The Kitchen and we've gotten pretty close.

Focaccia is so versatile when it comes to toppings and modifications. We keep it pretty simple in the restaurant, just rosemary and salt, but you can have fun playing with add-ins and toppings to match whatever you're serving for dinner. In the summer, you can top it with chopped cherry tomatoes. In the winter, think about kalamata olives and thyme. Cheese lovers, try crumbled feta or goat cheese, or grated Parmesan with a healthy dose of cracked black pepper. One note: The olive oil is an essential part of the bread's flavor, so choose one that you love.

Makes 1 sheet of focaccia

2 cups plus 1 tablespoon (480 grams) warm water

¾ cup (150 grams) ripe sourdough starter (recipe follows)

4¾ cups (600 grams) all-purpose flour

2 tablespoons (28 grams) kosher salt

¼ to ½ cup high-quality olive oil

Maldon salt, to sprinkle

Fresh rosemary leaves, chopped, for topping

1. Put the water, starter, and about half of the flour into a medium bowl and mix until fully incorporated. Cover with plastic wrap and allow to sit for 30 minutes at room temperature. In cold weather, do your best to find a warm spot for the bowl; this will help the dough rise properly.

2. After 30 minutes, add in the rest of the flour and the kosher salt. Stir well with a rubber spatula or your hands, until the dough comes together in a sticky, shaggy mess. It won't look pretty yet, and that's okay. Cover again with plastic wrap and allow the dough to rest for 1 hour at room temperature.

3. After an hour, stretch the dough away from each side of the bowl, then fold it back together. Cover and allow to rest for another hour at room temperature.

4. Repeat the stretching and folding process 2 more times, letting it sit for 1 hour between each round. After the final set of folding, cover the bowl well and place it in the fridge overnight.

5. The next day, generously spread about ¼ cup olive oil onto a 9 x 13-inch pan.

Continued

6. Dump the dough onto a baking sheet and gently stretch it as much as it will let you. Don't push it more or it will tear. The dough may feel tight and cold at first, but as it sits and rises, you'll be able to gradually and gently spread it out further.

7. Cover the pan with oiled plastic wrap and allow the dough to rise for 2 to 3 hours. The timing is highly dependent on your home's temperature—the colder it is, the longer it will take to proof. If you want to speed things up a bit, you can turn on the oven for 5 to 8 minutes and then immediately turn it off and place your dough in it to rise. After 30 minutes, stretch the dough out further if you were previously unable to get it to fill the pan.

8. Preheat the oven to 475°F. Pro tip: Open your windows and keep an eye on your smoke alarm. This is essentially bread fried in olive oil, and it can get a little smoky.

9. Once properly proofed, the dough will feel almost spongelike. It will be fluffy and jiggly, and when you press your fingers lightly into the dough, you should be able to feel how airy it is.

10. Drizzle olive oil around the edges and under the dough. Pour more oil on top and press your fingers into the dough to create dimples. Sprinkle liberally with Maldon salt and chopped rosemary, or the toppings of your choosing. Bake for 30 to 40 minutes, until the focaccia is a deep golden brown. Allow to cool for 10 to 15 minutes and then carefully remove from the baking sheet onto a cooling rack to cool

completely. This step will keep your bottom crust crisp, so don't skip it!

SOURDOUGH STARTER

Remember during the pandemic when everyone was making sourdough and trading sourdough starters? If you never jumped on that delicious, tangy bandwagon, now's the time! And speaking of time, making your own sourdough requires some advance planning, since it takes about 10 days for a starter to come into full fruition, so you might want to get it going now. This recipe has two stages, which may sound complicated, but don't worry: We'll talk you through it.

First stage:

1. In a small mixing bowl, mix together ⅓ cup plus 1 tablespoon (50 grams) whole wheat, spelt, or rye flour; ⅓ cup plus 1 tablespoon (50 grams) all-purpose flour; and ¼ cup plus 3 tablespoons warm water. Stir until it resembles a thick batter. Cover the bowl with a kitchen towel or plastic wrap, or transfer to a container with a matching lid. Let the starter sit out at room temperature for at least 3 days.

It will slowly begin to activate and bubble up; check in on it every day to see what's happening.

2. For this next step, weighing the starter will be far more accurate than using a measuring cup because, due to several factors, starters can vary in density. Once the starter begins to bubble, separate out 50 grams (about 3 tablespoons) and discard the rest. Now, feed the starter another 50 grams whole wheat, spelt, or rye flour; 50 grams all-purpose flour; and ¼ cup plus 3 tablespoons warm water. Mix until the starter is cohesive and batter-like. Congratulations! You have now successfully started a starter! Think of it like a new pet. It needs to be fed every day, with the same ratios of flour and water as above, at the same time, for the next 7 days. This ripening stage creates a starter that will successfully rise and fall at a predictable pace—essential to making sourdough bread successfully. After this point, you can continue to feed the starter and keep it going indefinitely; just keep it in the fridge and feed it at least once a week.

3. After 1 week, you're ready for the second stage.

Second stage:

60 grams (about 4 tablespoons) sourdough starter

1 cup (120 grams) either all-purpose or bread flour

½ cup plus 1 tablespoon (120 grams) water

1. For the flour to be added in this stage, you can make a half-and-half mix of all purpose and whole wheat, spelt, or rye flour, which will mostly make the starter taste more robust. We prefer a more neutral sourdough flavor as it makes for a more consistent and versatile starter, so we use either all-purpose or bread flour.

2. In a small bowl, mix everything together until combined, then allow to rise for 6 to 12 hours. Why the range? It all depends on the strength of your starter, the temperature of your home, and how consistently you are feeding or using your starter. Check it after 6 hours; you're looking for a texture that's fluffy and bubbly, with a fruity, yeasty aroma. When ready, it will also float when dropped in water.

235

Flaky Pie Dough

2½ cups (300 grams) all-purpose
flour

1 teaspoon (5 grams) granulated
sugar

½ teaspoon kosher salt

1 cup (2 sticks) unsalted butter,
cut into ½-inch cubes and
chilled

½ to 1 cup ice water

Kimbal's training in fine French baking led him to challenge The Kitchen's pastry chef Natalie to show him how he could make an excellent pie dough at home without the many hours required by other techniques. Chef Natalie won the challenge. Her technique is simple and easy, and the results are fantastic. This recipe will make 1 full galette (page 275) or 1 (9-inch) quiche (page 240) or pie.

1. In the bowl of an electric mixer fitted with the paddle attachment, mix the flour, sugar, and salt. Once they're fully combined, add the butter cubes and toss with your hands to thoroughly coat each cube with flour. Mix on low speed until the butter begins to flatten into ¼-inch flakes.

2. Once the butter has broken down, feel the dough's temperature. If it's still cold, continue to the next step. If it has warmed a bit, refrigerate it for 15 to 20 minutes.

3. Remove the bowl from the machine and, using your hands, press any particularly large butter pieces into the flour to further incorporate. You want the butter to be in flakes, not clumps.

4. Make a well at the bottom of the bowl and slowly add about 3 tablespoons of water. Using your hands, toss the flour into the water to incorporate. It is crucial not to stir or knead the dough at this point! Rather, your goal is to lightly lift and toss the water and flour together to keep your hands from warming the dough any further, and to avoid overmixing or overworking. As the ingredients incorporate, continue to create that well in the center, adding a bit of ice water and tossing (you will probably not use all of your water, and that's okay). As soon as the dough begins to hold together, set aside the clumps as they begin to form, while you continue to toss the remaining flour until it starts clumping together as well. This will avoid overmixing. The dough should be neither overly sticky nor so dry that it can't hold together. Wrap the dough in plastic wrap and lightly roll into a disk. Chill in the refrigerator for 30 minutes.

5. Once the dough is chilled, roll it into a rough rectangle about ½ inch thick. Bring the top side toward the center, then bring the bottom over to meet it, forming a classic three-fold shape. Wrap in plastic wrap and chill again for at least 20 minutes or up to 1 hour. The dough will keep, tightly wrapped, in the fridge for up to 2 days and in the freezer for up to 1 month.

As you sit in our Chicago dining room, with its abundant natural light and expansive views of the Chicago River, you'll likely feel a palpable sense of history. The Kitchen Chicago is located on the main floor of the landmark Reid Murdoch building, gateway to the vibrant River North neighborhood. The stunning red-brick Arts and Crafts structure was built in 1914 to serve as the office and warehouse for the Reid Murdoch grocery company. One cool bit of synchronicity is that Reid and Murdoch got their start selling provisions to immigrants heading west to the Rockies and beyond. And now we're returning the favor, bringing Colorado's culinary inspirations to the Windy City.

Looking over the past 100 years, this location has gone through some surprising incarnations. In 1915, a scant year after it was constructed, the building briefly became a makeshift hospital, after a major shipwreck on the Chicago River. In the 1950s, the city of Chicago used it to house traffic courts and city attorneys' offices. In fact, one or two early reviews of The Kitchen Chicago noted that longtime Chicagoans may be particularly delighted to sip champagne and share a daily oyster special in the space where they once went to argue about parking tickets.

Deep-Dish Quiche with Mushrooms and Leeks

Serves 8 to 10

4 teaspoons grapeseed or other neutral oil

1 cup sliced button mushrooms (about 4 ounces)

2 cups sliced halved leek whites (2 large leeks)

2 cups (454 grams) heavy cream

½ cup (113 grams) cream cheese, at room temperature

4 large eggs (200 grams) plus 4 large egg yolks (72 grams) (page 43)

1½ teaspoons (7 grams) kosher salt

½ teaspoon freshly ground black pepper

Cooking spray

Flaky Pie Dough (page 236) or storebought roll-out crust (see note above)

2 cups shredded Parmesan cheese

This is another one of those classics that's been on our menu for years. We've varied the ingredients from time to time and found that this mushroom-leek version is a crowd-pleasing keeper. It's a brunch favorite, so much so that sometimes guests will order a whole quiche to take home for a special celebration. The main thing that sets our quiche apart from others is its wonderful, creamy mouthfeel, which comes courtesy of adding cream cheese as well as the more standard heavy cream. It also has a satisfying density that makes it easy to slice and serve. Our Flaky Pie Dough recipe will allow you to make this a deep-dish quiche the way we serve it at the restaurant. If you'd rather use a storebought pie crust, this recipe will yield enough filling to make two regular-height (not deep-dish) quiches.

1. Preheat the oven to 425°F.

2. In a medium skillet, heat 2 teaspoons of the oil over medium heat. Add the mushrooms and cook until they're browned and softened but still hold their shape, about 5 minutes. Remove from the pan to a plate to cool. Add the remaining 2 teaspoons of oil to the pan, then add the leeks and cook until softened but not browned, about 5 minutes. Remove to the plate with the mushrooms and let them cool completely.

3. While the vegetables are cooling, make the custard. Combine the heavy cream and cream cheese in a blender and blend until smooth.

4. Add the blended mixture to a large bowl and whisk it together with the eggs and egg yolks until smooth, then whisk in the salt and pepper.

Continued

5. To bake, spray a 9-inch springform pan (or a false-bottom tart pan) with cooking spray, making sure to coat the edges well. Cut two pieces of parchment paper to the diameter of your pan's base. Set one aside for later and place the other on your pan's base. Spray with cooking spray.

6. If you're using homemade pie dough, roll the dough into a ¼-inch-thick circle that's about 14 inches wide. Lightly fold the rolled-out dough into a semicircle and set it over the pan. Gently place the pie dough onto the bottom base of the pan, folding its edges up. Next, press the dough up and around the edges of the pan, making sure it's well set into the base of the pan. Cut any excess dough from the top, leaving about 1 inch of overhang. Gently pinch and crimp that overhang around the pan.

7. Next, whether you are using homemade dough or a storebought crust, prick the bottom of the crust liberally all over with a fork (this is called docking, and it helps to release steam while baking). Cover with plastic wrap and place in the freezer for at least 30 minutes, until the dough is thoroughly chilled.

8. Remove the dough from the freezer and remove the plastic wrap. Place a piece of parchment paper on top of the chilled dough and fill the pan with dry beans or pie weights. Bake for 20 to 25 minutes, until the crust is lightly golden around the edges.

9. Gently remove the parchment and beans and bake again for another 5 to 8 minutes, until the crust is no longer visually wet and is lightly golden in the center. If the dough puffs up, this is not a bad thing—it means that you're making a flaky crust. Gently press down on any bubbles to help release excess steam. Allow the crust to cool completely before proceeding.

10. Lower the oven temperature to 325°F.

11. Once the crust has cooled, place half of the mushrooms and leeks on the bottom and sprinkle with 1 cup Parmesan cheese. Layer the rest of the veggies on top of the Parmesan, then sprinkle the remaining 1 cup Parmesan on top.

12. Pour the custard over the filling; you should have about 1 inch of space between the top of the crust and that of the custard.

13. Place the quiche on a baking sheet and carefully transfer it to the oven. Bake for 60 to 75 minutes, until the quiche is set. There should be just a bit of jiggle remaining in the center, and the internal temperature should read 170°F according to an instant-read thermometer. If at any point the top begins to brown too quickly, gently cover it with foil. Remove the quiche from the oven and let it cool completely at room temperature before serving.

HOW TO PRE-BAKE THE CRUST

Savory Crullers with Whipped Allium Butter

These crullers take a little bit of work, but for a special occasion it's so worth it. We created them as an unusual and delightful alternative to traditional restaurant bread service..You might be surprised to learn that they start with the same dough as our gnocchetti (page 126)—pâte à choux, that wonderfully versatile French pastry dough. The result is something that looks and eats like a doughnut: crisply fried on the outside, soft and tender inside, with a savory hit from the shower of cheese on top. One of the many things we love about this preparation is that you can make the dough ahead of time, pipe it out, and then freeze it until you're ready to fry up a batch of crullers. The finished product is really beautiful, and definitely not something you see every day.

Makes about 12 crullers

7 tablespoons (100 grams) unsalted butter

½ cup (126 grams) milk

½ cup (113 grams) water

½ teaspoon (2 grams) kosher salt

1 cup (120 grams) all-purpose flour

4 eggs

Oil, for frying

Block of Parmesan cheese, for topping

Whipped Allium Butter, to serve (recipe follows)

243

1. Put the butter, milk, water, and salt in a medium pot and bring to a simmer over medium heat. Add the flour and stir vigorously for about 2 minutes, until it forms a smooth, cohesive ball. Transfer it to a stand mixer fitted with the paddle attachment and mix on medium speed for 3 minutes. Add the eggs one at a time, beating after each one until it's incorporated before adding the next. Scrape the sides of the bowl and the paddle once or twice if needed, then mix again until the pâte à choux batter is smooth and cohesive. Transfer it into a piping bag with a star tip, place the bag in a bowl to hold it upright, and refrigerate for at least 2 hours or up to 8 hours.

2. Line a baking sheet with parchment paper, then pipe the chilled batter into 3-inch-diameter rings on the parchment, to create cruller forms. Freeze the forms for at least 3 hours, until solid. When you're ready to use them, remove from the freezer and thaw for 15 minutes.

3. While the crullers are thawing, fill a pot with enough oil to come 2 to 3 inches up the sides and heat over medium heat to 350°F. Working in batches, add the crullers to the pot and fry until puffed and golden on the bottom, then flip and continue to cook until they're golden all around, 8 to 10 minutes total.

4. Use tongs or a slotted spoon to remove the crullers from the oil to a platter. While the crullers are still piping hot, use a Microplane to grate the cheese over them. Serve immediately with the whipped allium butter on the side.

Continued

Makes about 12 (1-ounce) scoops

1 cup (2 sticks) unsalted
   butter, softened
1 shallot, minced
¼ cup garlic cloves, minced
¼ cup finely chopped
   fresh parsley
¼ cup thinly sliced fresh chives
½ teaspoon salt

WHIPPED ALLIUM BUTTER

Some guests eat the crullers just like doughnuts; others cut them in half and eat them like a dinner roll, with butter melting into each bite. We serve these with our Whipped Allium Butter. "Allium" is the scientific name for anything in the onion and garlic family, and this butter gets its deliciousness from three members of that family.

Combine all the ingredients in a stand mixer and mix until incorporated, scraping the sides as needed. Using a 1-ounce scoop, scoop the batter onto a parchment paper–lined baking sheet and refrigerate until solid. If you don't have a 1-ounce scoop, place the batter on a sheet of plastic wrap, roll it into a log, and refrigerate until solid, then cut the log into slices to serve.

EAT LIKE A DOUGHNUT...
OR A ROLL!

Sticky Toffee Pudding

Makes about 10 to 12 portions

1 cup plus ⅓ cup (320 grams)
orange juice

2 cups dates, pitted
(approximately 20 dates)

1¾ teaspoons baking powder
(1 teaspoon at high altitude)

¼ teaspoon kosher salt

3 cups (340 grams) all-purpose
flour (3 cups plus 1 tablespoon,
or 350 grams at high altitude)

1 cup (213 grams) packed light
or dark brown sugar (195 grams,
just under a cup, at high altitude)

½ cup (100 grams) white sugar

¾ cup (1½ sticks) room
temperature unsalted butter

2 teaspoons vanilla bean paste
or 1 tablespoon plus 1 teaspoon
vanilla extract

4 eggs (5 eggs at high altitude)

Pecan Caramel (recipe follows)

Vanilla ice cream, to serve

This may be the most traditional recipe in this book—a sweet date cake served with vanilla ice cream and a swirl of caramel. It's a well-loved British recipe and one of Kimbal's favorites, which is why it's been on our menu since Day One. Our one little tweak to the traditional ingredients is the pecan caramel. In the U.K., the pecans are baked into the cake, but we wanted to do something a little different so that guests with nut allergies wouldn't have to miss out on all the deliciousness. Simply leave the pecans out of the caramel if you like. It will still taste amazing.

1. Preheat the oven to 350°F.

2. Bring the orange juice and dates to a boil in a medium pot and cook, stirring a few times, until about half of the juice has evaporated and the dates are soft and mushy. Remove the pot from the heat, drain, and allow to cool.

3. In a medium bowl, mix the baking powder, salt, and all-purpose flour and set aside. Next, in the bowl of a stand mixer fitted with a paddle attachment, beat together the brown and white sugars with the butter until light and fluffy. Add in the vanilla and beat until combined. Add the eggs one at a time, mixing after each, until fully incorporated. Add in the flour mixture a little bit at a time, mixing until it is just combined.

4. Once the dates are cool, mash with a potato masher.

5. Gently fold together the batter and the mashed dates until you have a homogenous mixture. Line a 9 x 13-inch baking pan with parchment paper and pour in the batter. (At the restaurant we usually bake the pudding in individual ramekins, but at home, baking it in a large batch in a pan is easier.) Bake for 30 to 45 minutes, until the cake has risen and lightly springs back when you press its center.

Continued

SWIMMING IN
CARAMEL

6. Using a sharp knife, cut into squares about 3 by 3 inches in size. Serve each square of cake drenched with caramel, topped with a scoop of vanilla ice cream, and then drizzled again with caramel to finish.

7. The cake will keep, tightly wrapped, for 2 to 3 days at room temperature, or up to 1 month in the freezer. To enjoy leftover cake, spoon some caramel over a piece and gently reheat it in the oven or toaster oven at 300°F, until the caramel is lightly bubbling. Top with ice cream and a drizzle more of caramel.

PECAN CARAMEL

1. Preheat the oven to 350°F.

2. Toast the pecans for 5 to 7 minutes until golden brown and fragrant. Immediately transfer the toasted nuts to a heatproof bowl and set aside.

3. In a medium pot, cook the corn syrup just until it starts to lightly simmer, then slowly add the sugar, stirring well to combine. Continue to cook until the mixture is deep amber in color and beginning to caramelize, swirling the pan to ensure that it browns evenly.

4. Add in the butter and heavy cream, stirring well to emulsify, then add the salt and vanilla.

Makes about 2 cups

1 cup (4 ounces or 110 grams) chopped pecans

½ cup plus 1 tablespoon corn syrup

1¼ cups (250 grams) sugar

2 tablespoons (¼ stick) unsalted butter

1 cup plus 2 tablespoons heavy cream

½ teaspoon kosher salt

1 teaspoon vanilla paste or extract

248

WE'D LIKE TO MAKE A TOAST!

Toasted nuts add flavor and crunch to everything from sauces to salads (and are a healthy snack all by themselves as well).

Start by preheating your oven to 350°F. Line a sheet pan with parchment paper or aluminum foil and spread the nuts on it in an evenly spaced single layer. Before you go further, make sure you have a heatproof bowl or plate ready for them as soon as they come out of the oven—otherwise, they'll keep cooking on the hot pan instead of cooling. Nuts can go from golden-brown perfection to burned and bitter in a matter of seconds, so timing matters.

Generally speaking, nuts that are softer to the tooth—like pecans, pistachios, pine nuts, and walnuts—will take about 6 to 8 minutes to toast. For harder nuts such as almonds, macadamias, and hazelnuts, it will be more like 8 to 10 minutes. Check on them at the estimated halfway point and give the pan a good shake to ensure even browning. Once your nuts are perfectly toasted, remove them from the oven immediately and transfer to your bowl or plate to cool. They're best the day you make them, but they can be stored unrefrigerated in a tightly sealed container or zip-top bag for about 1 week, or in the freezer for 1 month.

Classic Vanilla Meringues

Meringue is a key ingredient in our Eton Mess recipe (page 250), but it's also so versatile and easy to make that mastering this technique opens up a world of options. You can use meringue as a topping to turn fresh fruit into a fancy dessert or to dress up a pudding or cake. Shape them into individual shells to hold custard or fruit. Or serve them on their own any time you'd serve cookies—as a light, crisp sweet to enjoy anytime.

Makes about 120 small meringues

6 large egg whites

1¾ cup (350 grams) granulated sugar

1½ teaspoons vanilla extract or 1 teaspoon vanilla paste

1. Preheat the oven to 200°F.
2. Start by separating the egg whites into a clean, dry stainless steel bowl that will fit nicely over a small saucepan. Be sure your whites are free of even a speck of shell or yolk (see page 43 for how to accomplish this). Once you've separated the eggs, mix in the sugar.
3. Next, fill the saucepan halfway full of water and bring to a boil. Once the water is boiling, set the bowl with the egg white mixture over it like a double boiler, then reduce the heat to medium so that it remains at a consistent simmer.
4. Whisk the egg white mixture over the heat, stirring constantly but not vigorously, until the mixture comes to 165°F.
5. As soon as the egg white mixture reaches 165°F, remove from the heat and carefully transfer to the bowl of a stand mixer fitted with a whisk attachment. Whip on high speed until the meringue is glossy and very fluffy and the mixing bowl is no longer hot to the touch, about 5 to 8 minutes.
6. Next, pour in the vanilla extract or paste and whip on high speed until just combined.
7. Transfer the meringue to a piping bag. You don't really need a piping tip for this step, but if you'd like to get fancy, choose one of your liking. If you don't have a piping bag, you can use instead a large zip-top bag with one bottom corner snipped off.
8. Line a baking sheet with parchment paper. Pipe the meringue into little mounds about the size of a quarter, or larger if you like—this is definitely a choose-your-own-adventure dessert.
9. Continue to pipe until all the meringue batter is used up. They won't spread in the oven, so you can position the individual pieces quite close together.
10. Bake for 1½ to 2 hours, until the meringues are dry to the touch. Turn off the oven but don't remove the pan until the meringues are fully cooled. Meringues will last for up to 2 weeks (less when it's humid out) in a tightly covered container stored in a cool, dry place.

Eton Mess with Fresh Strawberries

Serves 6 to 8

1 cup heavy cream, well chilled

2 tablespoons sugar

1 teaspoon vanilla bean paste or
   2 teaspoons vanilla extract

About 30 small Classic Vanilla
   Meringues (page 249)

1 pound fresh strawberries,
   hulled and sliced

Thanks to Chef Hugo, one of the restaurant's co-founders and a British immigrant, we've had some version of Eton Mess, a popular British dessert, on the menu for years. It is an easy crowd-pleaser when you cook for your community. Make the meringues ahead of time. Then, to serve, all you need to do is whip the cream and put it all together.

▼

1. Pour the cream into the bowl of a stand mixer fitted with the whisk attachment. Whip on low speed until the cream begins to thicken. Once the cream has thickened slightly, pour in the sugar. Bring up the speed to medium and continue to whip until the cream begins to show soft peaks.

2. Add the vanilla paste or extract, whip again to combine, and continue to whip until it forms medium peaks, being careful to not over-whip. Keep the cream chilled until you're ready to assemble your final product.

3. Crumble the meringues, and fold them into the whipped cream along with most of the strawberries (reserve a handful for serving). Dollop out servings into individual bowls or small plates, and add a few more sliced strawberries on top for a perfect Eton mess!

WANT TO MAKE A MESS?

A GLORIOUS MESS

There are a few stories as to how this dish got its name. As early as 1836, it was served at Britain's Eton College, a rather posh boys-only boarding school founded in 1440 by Henry IV. (A college in Britain is what Americans would call a high school.) It's a relatively fast and easy dessert to put on the table from premade ingredients, and if you're throwing it together for a bunch of hungry teenage boys, presentation is less important than deliciousness, which is almost certainly why it's been light-heartedly termed a mess. We prefer the origin story in which a hurried, harried Eton chef accidentally dropped a Pavlova (a meringue-based dessert) and instead of throwing it away, he mixed all the pieces together and pretended he'd done it on purpose. The first etymology is probably the true one, but as fans of fortuitous accidents, we choose to believe the second one.

TAHINI MOUSSE CAKE
APPLE GALETTE
VANILLA BEAN CRÉMEUX

SPICED-PEAR BAKLAVA
POT AU CHOCOLAT

Crémeux Two Ways

Serves 4 to 6

¼ cup water, for proofing gelatin

1 packet (7 grams) powdered gelatin or 1 sheet silver-strength sheet gelatin

5½ ounces (157 grams) 60% to 70% dark chocolate, preferably Valrhona, broken into pieces

¾ cup (175 grams) whole milk

¾ cup plus 1 tablespoon (175 grams) heavy cream

2 tablespoons (34 grams) granulated sugar

5 egg yolks (85 grams)

Crémeux translates to "creamy" in French, and this dessert certainly lives up to its name. It's essentially a fancy pudding that starts with a crème anglaise; what you do next is what takes it into either dark chocolate or milky vanilla territory. Both versions need to chill overnight before serving, so plan accordingly. To serve, choose among several seasonal fruit toppings (see pages 74–77 for inspiration). For a gluten-free nod to German chocolate cake, try topping the dark chocolate with cherry compote. We generally only serve one or the other at any given time, paired with seasonal fruit, but for anyone who loves this kind of creamy dessert, serving both could be an impressive dish for a celebration.

1. Pour the water into a small bowl, then sprinkle the gelatin over the water. Allow to hydrate for at least 5 minutes.

2. Break the chocolate into pieces and set aside in a medium bowl. As soon as your gelatin has hydrated, add it in.

3. Make a crème anglaise. In a small saucepan, heat the milk and heavy cream together until just simmering. While the milk and cream are heating, whisk together the sugar and egg yolks. Once the milk and cream mixture reaches a simmer, carefully and gently pour it into the bowl with the egg yolks and sugar, whisking constantly to prevent curdling. Once they are fully combined, pour into the small saucepan and cook over low heat, whisking constantly, until the mixture reaches 170°F.

4. Pour the crème through a strainer over the bowl of chocolate and gelatin. Whisk well to emulsify, or blend with an immersion blender. It will be quite liquid, which is as it should be at this stage. Place a piece of plastic wrap directly on top of the crémeux and place in the refrigerator to set overnight.

VARIATION: VANILLA BEAN CRÉMEUX

Follow the preparation instructions above, but substitute 6¼ ounces (175 grams) white chocolate for the dark chocolate and stir 2 tablespoons vanilla paste into the crème anglaise in the last step when combining it with the chocolate and gelatin.

Pot au Chocolat

Rich and decadent, this is a chocolate lover's dream. It's been a menu staple since the early days without variation because, really, it's hard to improve on perfection. We love to pair it with crème anglaise for an extra touch of luxury. If you prefer, you can serve it with vanilla ice cream or whipped cream instead, and it will still be amazing.

1. Preheat the oven to 350°F

2. To create a DIY double boiler, find a heat-safe bowl that sits nicely on top of a medium saucepan. Fill the pan half-full of water and bring to a boil.

3. Once the water is boiling, place the butter and chocolate in the bowl and set atop the pan to melt. Once they're fully melted, remove from heat, stir well to combine, and set aside.

4. In a stand mixer fitted with a whisk attachment, whip the eggs with the sugar and salt on low speed until it forms a homogeneous mixture. Bring the speed up to medium and continue to whip until the mixture is thick and pale yellow, about 5 to 7 minutes. Stir in the vanilla and coffee.

5. Turn the speed back down to low and gently pour the melted chocolate mixture into the whipped egg mixture. Continue to mix until just combined, using a rubber spatula to scrape the edges and bottom of the bowl to ensure even mixing.

6. Pour the mixture into six 8-ounce ramekins, leaving room for serving them topped with a generous helping of crème anglaise. Place the ramekins on a baking sheet. Sprinkle with Maldon salt and bake for 7 to 10 minutes, until the tops are set and the center has a little jiggle to it.

7. We serve pot au chocolat hot, topped with the Crème Anglaise. It's also delicious cold. Pot au chocolat can be made up to a day in advance and reheated in the ramekin at 350°F for 5 minutes.

Continued

Serves 6

¾ cup (1½ sticks) unsalted butter

8 ounces (227 grams) 70% chocolate roughly chopped into ½-inch pieces

4 whole eggs

½ cup (100 grams) sugar

Pinch of kosher salt

1 tablespoon vanilla bean paste or 2 tablespoons vanilla extract

1 tablespoon brewed coffee

Maldon salt, to top

Vanilla Crème Anglaise, to serve (recipe follows)

255

1¼ cups (284 grams) heavy cream

1 cup (245 grams) whole milk

5 egg yolks (85 grams) (add 1 extra
egg yolk at high altitude)

½ cup (100 grams) sugar

Pinch of kosher salt

1½ teaspoons vanilla bean paste
or 3 teaspoons vanilla extract

VANILLA CRÈME ANGLAISE

1. In a small pot, gently heat the heavy cream and whole milk.

2. While the pan is heating, place the egg yolks, sugar, salt, and vanilla in a medium bowl and whisk well to combine.

3. Once the milk and cream mixture is just beginning to steam, pour it carefully and slowly into the egg yolk mixture, whisking constantly to prevent the eggs from scrambling. Putting a kitchen towel on the counter beneath the bowl will help keep it from slipping and sliding as you whisk.

4. Once all of the milk and cream have been incorporated, return the mixture to the pot and continue to cook on low heat, whisking constantly but not vigorously, until the mixture reaches 170°F, about 5 minutes. Strain through a small mesh strainer into a container to store. Allow it to cool completely, then place in the fridge to chill until ready to serve. It will keep tightly covered and refrigerated for up to 5 days. Reheat in a double boiler or small pan over low heat, stirring constantly to ensure the eggs don't curdle.

SHE SAID YES

Longtimers at the restaurant like to tell the story of an unusual engagement that took place around 2005. One afternoon, a man reserved a table and asked if he could propose to his girlfriend that night. The girlfriend showed up right on time at 6 p.m. and we seated her. The guy was supposed to be there at 6 as well, but he didn't show up. We brought her a glass of champagne, which bought a little time. She sat and sipped, but still no sign of the guy. Five minutes passed, then ten, and she was getting pretty annoyed. A server asked nervously, "Another glass of champagne?" We wanted to do anything to keep her there. And then just at the moment when we feared she was going to give up and walk out, we heard the deep rumble of a tuba, then the crash of cymbals. All of a sudden, there was an entire marching band parading into the dining room from the back of the restaurant. When they reached the young lady, they stopped and encircled the table—leaving just enough room for our missing guy to emerge from the fray. He dropped to one knee and popped the question. We still don't actually know how he pulled the whole thing off. But the important thing is that she said yes, and all was forgiven.

Spiced-Pear Baklava with Star Anise Syrup

his baklava is a show-stopper of a dessert to bring to serve at a dinner party. It's one of those treats that most of us have only seen in European or Middle Eastern bakeries and never even considered baking at home. In fact, so long as you use store-bought phyllo dough and plan a couple of days ahead, it's a remarkably chill dish to put together. You can assemble everything and then keep it in the fridge overnight to bake when it's convenient the next day—giving you more time for the party. For this funky, flavorful twist, Pastry Chef Natalie replaced the traditional, almost achingly sweet rosewater syrup that drenches a finished baklava with her own housemade syrup that's complex and spicy, weaving together notes of star anise, citrus, ginger, and vanilla. Pears add some body and substance to the dish and provide a counterpoint to the pastry's delicate texture. If your phyllo is a little wider than your pan, you can trim it, but we prefer to fold and tuck the excess into the corners, which results in extra-crispy corners. (In-the-know guests ask for a corner piece when ordering.) Note that the star anise syrup should be made at least a day—and as much as a week—ahead, as it needs to be completely chilled before use.

Makes 24 pieces

1¼ cups (188 grams) shelled
   unsalted pistachios

3 tablespoons (36 grams)
   granulated sugar

½ teaspoon ground cardamom

Zest of 1 small lemon

Pinch of kosher salt

1 to 1½ cups melted clarified
   or unsalted butter

1 (16-ounce) pack of frozen
   phyllo dough, thawed

Pear Filling (recipe follows)

Star Anise Syrup (recipe follows)

1. Preheat the oven to 375°F.

2. Grind the pistachios in a food processor until they are coarse and about the size of mini chocolate chips. Mix the sugar, cardamom, lemon zest, and salt together. Toss together with the pistachios and set aside.

3. Line a 9 x 13-inch casserole, baking dish, or brownie pan with parchment paper. Using a pastry brush, lightly brush the parchment and sides of the pan with clarified butter.

4. Begin by fitting a layer of phyllo into the pan, then brush it with just enough melted butter to coat the top. Fit another layer on top and brush again. Repeat 4 more times, until you have 6 layers. Keep a damp towel over the phyllo to keep the dough from drying out as you work.

5. After brushing the sixth layer with butter, top it with a generous helping (about ¾ of a cup) of the pistachio filling. Begin the layering process again, laying down

Continued

phyllo and brushing it with butter for another 6 sheets, then top with another ¾ cup of filling.

6. Repeat this process once more. This time, dust lightly with the pistachio mixture and carefully add the pear filling, using an offset spatula to gently spread it over the phyllo in an even layer. Cover the pear filling with a sheet of phyllo, brush it with butter, and repeat until you've used up all the phyllo (different brands will have a different number of sheets—just use them all).

7. Brush the top layer with butter and then, using a sharp knife, cut the baklava lengthwise into 4 rows, each about 3 inches wide. Then cut crosswise another 3 rows, one every 3 inches. Then cut the squares diagonally, to create triangles.

You should have 12 sets of 2 triangles.

8. If you're preparing your baklava ahead of time, cover the pan with plastic wrap and refrigerate until you're ready to bake it.

9. Bake until the top layer of phyllo is a deep golden brown and very flaky, 50 to 60 minutes. Remove from the oven and pour the syrup over it immediately.

10. Allow to cool completely before separating the triangles. Once the pan has fully cooled, wrap it in plastic wrap or transfer the triangles to a sealed container and refrigerate. Eat it chilled, at room temperature, or reheated at 350°F for 5 minutes if you prefer it warm. If you're not eating it right away, first of all we're amazed at your willpower, and second, it will keep for up to 3 days in the fridge.

PEAR FILLING

¼ cup (53 grams) packed light or dark brown sugar

1 tablespoon (12 grams) granulated sugar

Zest of 1 lemon

¾ teaspoons cardamom

Pinch of kosher salt

1½ teaspoons cornstarch

3 to 4 pears, peeled and diced into pea-sized cubes (you can substitute for apples)

1½ teaspoons fresh lemon juice

½ teaspoon vanilla bean paste or 1 teaspoon vanilla extract

In a medium-sized bowl, mix together the sugars, lemon zest, cardamom, salt, and cornstarch. Toss in the pears and lemon juice and gently mix with a wooden spoon until combined. Transfer to a medium pot and cook over medium-low heat for 8 to 10 minutes, just until the pears begin to soften. Stir in the vanilla, then transfer to a container and allow to cool completely prior to using. The pear filling will keep for 3 days in the fridge in a tightly sealed container.

STAR ANISE SYRUP

1⅓ cups (268 grams) granulated sugar

Zest of 1 lemon

Zest of 1 orange

2½ tablespoons honey

2 tablespoons fresh lemon juice

2 tablespoons orange juice

5 whole cardamom pods

5 whole star anise

1-inch piece of ginger, thinly sliced

1½ teaspoons vanilla bean paste or 1 tablespoon vanilla extract

¾ cup water

1. In a small saucepan, mix together the sugar and the lemon and orange zests. Add in the rest of the ingredients and cook over medium heat until simmering, then lower the heat and simmer for 10 minutes.

2. Remove from the stove and pour into a heat-safe container, allow to cool completely, and then strain. Since the syrup needs to be completely chilled before you pour it over the baklava, we recommend making it at least a day, and up to a week, before you'll need it and storing it in the fridge.

Tahini Mousse Cake with Cornflake Rocher

Eating a slice of this showstopper cake is like a roller coaster ride that swerves back and forth from sweet to savory notes, keeping you coming back for more thrills. The layers of sesame come through not just in the mousse filling but also in the tahini-spiked frosting and the crunchy bits of cornflake-enhanced rocher topping. Once you've experienced the cake in all its glory, you might wonder about a simplified version for occasions when you have less time but still want to wow your guests. The good news is that it will still be amazing if you make just the cake and buttercream, assemble as below, and shave a little chocolate on the top. Voilà! Note that the mousse needs to be made one day ahead, so plan accordingly. The cake and rocher can be made a day ahead as well.

2¼ cups (280 grams) all-purpose flour

1½ teaspoons (7 grams) kosher salt

¾ teaspoon baking powder

1¾ teaspoons baking soda

3 tablespoons (32 grams) black cocoa powder (also called ultra-dutched)

3 tablespoons (32 grams) cocoa powder

1½ cup plus ⅓ cup (378 grams) granulated sugar

1 cup (198 grams) grapeseed or other neutral oil

3 eggs

1 cup (220 grams) good-quality brewed coffee

1 cup (245 grams) whole milk

1 tablespoon vanilla extract

BLACK COCOA CAKE

1. Preheat the oven to 350°F.

2. Lightly grease three 8-inch cake pans and line with parchment. Set aside.

3. In a large bowl, sift together the flour, salt, baking powder, baking soda, and both cocoa powders. Then whisk in the sugar and set aside.

4. In a smaller bowl, whisk together the oil and eggs, then set aside.

5. In a small saucepan, gently heat the coffee and milk until just steaming. Remove from heat and gently pour the coffee-milk mixture into the eggs mixture and whisk well to combine.

6. Pour this wet mixture into the flour mixture, gently folding with a rubber spatula until no streaks remain. Divide the batter one scoop at a time between the 3 pans until all of the batter is used up. (We like to use a ladle or a large cookie scoop to make sure it's evenly divided.)

7. Bake for 25 to 30 minutes, until the cake is set and a cake tester comes out clean. You can also test it by gently

pressing the center of the cake. If it springs back lightly, it's ready. Allow to cool completely prior to unmolding. If you're not using it immediately, wrap in plastic wrap and refrigerate.

CORNFLAKE ROCHER

1. Preheat the oven to 350°F. Line a 9 x 13-inch pan with parchment and set aside.

2. Lightly toast the almonds on a small sheet pan until they are golden brown, about 10 minutes.

3. Toast the sesame seeds on a separate sheet pan until golden, about 5 minutes. Allow to cool before continuing. Next, in a medium bowl, toss together the cornflakes, almonds, both sesame seeds, and salt.

4. In a double boiler (or in a stainless steel bowl set over a saucepan half-filled with simmering water), melt the chocolate until smooth, then pour it over the cornflake mixture and mix well with a rubber spatula to ensure that all of the cornflakes are coated in chocolate.

5. Pour the rocher mixture onto the parchment-lined pan and gently spread it out evenly. Refrigerate until fully set, 10 to 20 minutes. Once set, chop into rough chunks. Any excess rocher can be stored tightly sealed and refrigerated for 4 days. Leftovers can be used as an ice-cream topping or a tasty snack.

CHOCOLATE TAHINI MOUSSE

1. Bloom (hydrate) the gelatin. If you're using powdered gelatin, measure a tablespoon of water into a small bowl, then sprinkle the gelatin over it and allow to set for at least 5 minutes. If you're using sheet gelatin, submerge it in cold water until soft, about 5 minutes. Gently squeeze out the excess water and keep the bloomed gelatin in a separate bowl.

2. In a medium bowl, mix together the chocolate, vanilla, salt, and tahini and set aside. Stir in the hydrated gelatin.

3. Make a crème anglaise. In a small saucepan, heat the milk and ¼ cup plus 1½ teaspoons heavy cream until just simmering.

4. While the milk and cream are heating, whisk together the egg yolks and sugar in a medium bowl.

Continued

¼ cup (50 grams) sliced almonds

2 tablespoons sesame seeds

1 tablespoon black sesame seeds

½ cup (60 grams) cornflakes

¼ teaspoon kosher salt

5 ounces (140 grams) 40% milk chocolate, chopped

½ teaspoon powdered gelatin or 1 sheet of silver-strength sheet gelatin (available online)

1½ cups (212 grams) roughly chopped (½- to 1-inch pieces) 40% milk chocolate (we like Valrhona Jivara)

¾ teaspoon vanilla bean paste or 1½ teaspoons vanilla extract

¼ teaspoon kosher salt

½ cup plus 3 tablespoons (163 grams) tahini

¼ cup (57 grams) whole milk

¼ cup plus 1½ teaspoons (64 grams) heavy cream, for the crème anglaise

1⅓ cups (300 grams) heavy cream, to be whipped

3 egg yolks (50 grams)

¼ cup (50 grams) sugar

5. Once the milk mixture is steaming, carefully pour it into the egg yolk mixture, whisking constantly to help prevent the mixture from curdling.

6. Once fully combined, pour the crème back into the small saucepan, set on low heat, and cook, whisking constantly, until the mixture reaches 170°F.

7. Pour the crème through a strainer over the chocolate mixture. Stir well to emulsify or blend with an immersion blender. Set the mixture aside to cool.

8. Pour 1⅓ cups heavy cream into the bowl of a stand mixer fitted with whisk attachment. Start whipping it slowly, then gradually increase the speed as the cream thickens. Whip until the cream makes medium stiff peaks, thick enough to hold the peak shape on a rubber spatula but not so thick that it looks like cottage cheese.

9. With a rubber spatula, gently fold ½ cup of the whipped cream into the chocolate crème. Once combined, continue adding the whipped cream a cup at a time, gently folding until the white streaks disappear. Continue to add and fold until you've added all of the whipped cream.

10. Gently pour this mousse into a medium bowl or a large storage container. Place a piece of plastic wrap directly on top of the mousse to prevent a skin from forming. Refrigerate overnight.

11. Pull out about an hour before assembling the cake so that it's a spreadable consistency. Leftover mousse will keep tightly sealed and refrigerated for up to 4 days. It's delicious by itself, and even better topped with a dollop of whipped cream.

CHOCOLATE TAHINI BUTTERCREAM

1. Have a clean stand mixer, fitted with the whisk attachment, at the ready.

2. In a medium heat-safe bowl, whisk together the egg whites and sugar. Create a DIY double boiler by placing the bowl atop a small pot filled halfway with water.

3. Bring the water to a boil over high heat. Place the bowl with the egg white mixture over the boiling water and reduce the heat to medium-high.

4. Whisk the egg white mixture over the double boiler, stirring constantly (it doesn't need to be vigorously) until the mixture comes to 165°F.

5. Immediately transfer the mixture to the stand mixer, pouring it into the bowl carefully. Whip on high speed until the mixture is glossy, super-fluffy, and the bowl is no longer hot to the touch, 5 to 8 minutes.

6. Reduce the mixer speed to medium and add the cubed butter a few pieces at a time, waiting until it fully incorporates before adding the next few pieces. The buttercream will start to look curdled and separated at first, but don't let this discourage you; keep going. Things will look worse before the buttercream suddenly comes together into a glossy, fluffy marshmallow dream.

7. Once all of the butter has been incorporated, bring the mixer up to high speed for about 15 seconds to be sure it's completely whipped in and smooth.

8. Reduce the mixer speed to low and add in the melted chocolate and tahini. Whip until just incorporated, scraping the bowl as needed.

9. Transfer half of the buttercream into a piping bag and half to a bowl. (You can also make the buttercream ahead of time and refrigerate, tightly covered, for up to 1 week.)

6 large egg whites (210 grams)

2 cups (400 grams) sugar

2 cups (4 sticks) unsalted butter, cubed, at room temperature

12 ounces 40% milk chocolate, melted and cooled

½ cup (145 grams) tahini

VERY VANILLA

Throughout this chapter, you'll see options for using either vanilla extract or vanilla bean paste. The paste is pricier than your basic bottle of extract, but it's so, so worth it for its intense, undiluted flavor. Vanilla extract is made with alcohol, which can affect both taste and consistency even in small amounts. Vanilla bean paste is available in specialty stores or online. Give it a try and you'll see why we love it so much.

BROWN SUGAR MERINGUE

1. Have a clean stand mixer, fitted with the whisk attachment, at the ready.

2. In a medium heat-safe bowl, whisk together the egg whites and sugar. Create a DIY double boiler by placing the bowl atop a similarly sized pot filled halfway with water.

6 egg whites (210 grams)

1¾ cups (350 grams) packed light or dark brown sugar

2 teaspoons vanilla bean paste or 3 teaspoons vanilla extract

3. Bring the water to a boil over high heat. Place the bowl with the egg white mixture over the boiling water and reduce the heat to medium high.

4. Whisk the egg white mixture over the double boiler, stirring constantly but not vigorously until the mixture comes to 165°F. Add in the vanilla and whip until incorporated.

TO ASSEMBLE:

1. The keys to successful cake building are to take your time and to let it chill as you build. This is not something to rush; it's a process. Give yourself plenty of time to properly assemble this magnificent dessert. Put on some tunes or a podcast you love and enjoy the ride.

2. Start by placing a 9-inch cardboard cake board on top of a cake stand (or use a large round platter). Place one of the cake layers on the cake board.

3. Pipe a 2-inch-wide border of buttercream around the edges of the cake. Think of this as a fence of buttercream that will keep your filling from escaping around the sides of the cake.

4. Next, scoop about ¾ to 1 cup of the chocolate tahini mousse into the center of the cake. Lightly and gently spread it with an offset spatula or butter knife until it meets up with the buttercream fence.

5. Place another layer of cake directly on top of the filled one. Repeat the same process of piping a 2-inch-wide border of buttercream then filling the center with mousse.

6. Place the final layer of cake on top, then carefully transfer the cake to the fridge and let it chill for 20 minutes.

7. Once chilled, pull the cake out and gently spread a thin layer of buttercream on the sides to cover the exposed crevices that separate each cake layer. A long cake scraper works well, as does a bench scraper or offset spatula, to help spread the buttercream evenly as you go.

8. Gently spread a thin layer of buttercream on the top of the cake. It doesn't need to be perfect by any means; this is your crumb coat, a base layer of buttercream that will ensure a smoother final product. Chill the cake again for 20 minutes.

9. Decide how heavily you'd like to frost your cake. If you're feeling frisky, layer the cake with dollops of buttercream and smooth it out evenly. For a more naked-style cake, spread a thin layer of buttercream instead.

10. On the top of the cake, dollop a generous amount of the brown sugar meringue and spread in a swirling motion. If you have a kitchen torch, torch the meringue until toasty and golden. If you don't have a torch, it will still be delicious. Or you can omit the brown sugar meringue entirely.

11. Generously sprinkle a heavy amount of the chocolate rocher all over the top of the cake. If you have a set of piping tips, bust them out and pipe whatever you please with the leftover buttercream. There is no wrong way to decorate a cake.

12. Slice, serve, and enjoy. Leftover cake will keep covered in the fridge for up to 3 days.

5. Immediately transfer the mixture to the stand mixer, pouring it into the bowl carefully. Whip on high speed until the meringue is glossy, super-fluffy, and the bowl is no longer hot to the touch, about 5 to 8 minutes. Add the vanilla and whip until just incorporated.

Chocolate Chunk Cookies

Makes about 2 dozen cookies

1 cup plus 1½ teaspoons
(130 grams) all-purpose
flour (increase to 144 grams,
approximately 2 more
tablespoons, at high altitude)

1 cup (120 grams) bread flour

¾ teaspoon baking soda (reduce
to ½ teaspoon at high altitude)

½ teaspoon (2 grams) kosher salt

¾ cup (1½ sticks) unsalted butter,
melted and cooled

1 cup (216 grams) packed light
or dark brown sugar

½ cup (100 grams)
granulated sugar

1 egg plus 1 egg yolk (add a
second yolk at high altitude)

1 tablespoon vanilla extract
or paste

5 ounces (140 grams)
dark chocolate

Maldon salt, for sprinkling

Pastry chef Natalie Morales's prescription for making any day better? Have a cookie. Maybe even two. Natalie came onboard to help us review and refresh our pastry program, and even before she fully had her head around high-altitude baking, she was doing her part to ensure that everybody eats dessert more often. She loves to take a familiar recipe and play with it—whether that means reimagining it entirely or, as in these life-changing cookies, just making it perfect. Chocolate chips are replaced with hand-chopped dark chocolate, the top sprinkled with robust flakes of Maldon salt. Guaranteed to make your day.

1. Preheat the oven to 350°F.
2. Mix the flours, baking soda, and salt in a medium-sized bowl and set aside.
3. In the bowl of a stand mixer, beat the melted butter with both sugars on low speed until they are well combined. Increase the speed to high and mix for an additional 5 to 8 minutes, until the mixture is lighter in color and slightly fluffier; it should look like wet sand.
4. Scrape down the sides of the bowl with a rubber spatula. Then, with the mixer on low speed, add in the egg. Wait until it is fully incorporated before adding the extra yolk (or 2 yolks, at high altitude). Scrape the bowl as needed to help with even mixing.
5. Once the mixture is well combined, add the vanilla.
6. Begin adding in the flour mixture slowly, a bit at a time, and continue mixing until it's just incorporated. Chop the chocolate into ¼-inch-square pieces (you should end up with about ¾ cup). Set aside enough chunks to top the cookies; fold the rest of the chocolate into the dough.

Continued

7. Scoop the dough onto a parchment-lined 9 x 13-inch tray, leaving about 3 inches between the cookies. You should be able to fit 6 to 8 cookies per tray. In the restaurant we use a 1-ounce cookie scoop to get the perfect size every time, but you can also use a rounded soup spoon or tablespoon measure for a similar effect.

8. Place one small piece of the reserved chocolate on top of each cookie, then sprinkle with a generous pinch of Maldon salt.

9. Bake for about 10 to 12 minutes, until the cookies' edges are golden brown and the centers are fully set.

10. Cool on the baking sheet for 5 minutes and then serve, warm and melty from the oven, or transfer them to a wire rack to cool completely. Store finished cookies in an airtight container for up to 3 days—but you'll probably finish them before that.

YOUR ANYTIME COOKIE

Pastry Chef Natalie has a little trick for ensuring she always has fresh cookies on demand: Freezing the dough. Unbaked cookie dough can be frozen for up to a month. To freeze, chill pre-scooped dough in the fridge or freezer on a small sheet pan until firm, then transfer to a freezer-safe bag or tightly sealed container before placing in the freezer. To bake straight from the freezer, transfer as many scoops as you like to a baking sheet and bake for 14 to 16 minutes at 350°F. You'll wonder how you ever lived without fresh cookies on demand whenever you like—whether a full batch for guests or just a single cookie for yourself to enjoy with a cup of coffee and a good book. There's just about no better way to turn around a bad day or make a good day into a fantastic one.

Chèvre Cheesecake

We added this cheesecake to our dessert menu fairly recently, and it's been a big hit—so much so that we serve it year-round, changing the toppings with the seasons to reflect what's freshest and most delicious at any given time (pages 74–77).

Goat cheese is rarely used in sweets, and we think that's a crying shame because its creamy texture is so satisfying, and its distinctively tangy flavor adds dimensions of depth to a familiar dish. To really make it a one-of-a-kind take on the familiar recipe, we came up with this salty, nutty Marcona almond base to replace the expected graham-cracker crust. The custard can be made up to a day in advance.

1. Preheat the oven to 300°F.
2. Mix the lemon zest into the sugar until it is moist and fragrant, then add in the vanilla and salt, and set aside.
3. In a food processor, pulse the chèvre and cream cheese together until just combined. (It won't look perfectly smooth yet, and that's okay. You don't want to overprocess it.) You can also use a stand mixer with a paddle attachment, but a food processor will result in the most mouth-wateringly smooth and creamy cheesecake of your dreams.
4. Add in the lemon-vanilla sugar and pulse no more than 2 or 3 times to combine. Use a rubber spatula to scrape the sides after each pulse.
5. Drizzle in the heavy cream a little bit at a time, pulsing as you go and scraping down the sides after each pulse. Continue to pulse in the cream until it is just combined and the mixture is smooth and shiny. The key things here are to avoid overmixing and to be meticulous in scraping and catching any bits of unmixed filling.
6. Add in the eggs one at a time, pulsing no more than 2 or 3 times to mix in each one. This is the point at which it's really easy to overmix the custard, which you want to avoid at all costs. Scrape the sides after you add each egg to

Continued

Makes 1 (9-inch cake)

Zest of 1 lemon

1½ cups (300 grams) sugar

1 teaspoon vanilla bean paste or
    2 teaspoons vanilla extract

¼ teaspoon kosher salt

10 ounces (280 grams)
    soft goat cheese (chèvre)

10 ounces (280 grams)
    cream cheese

1 cup (227 grams) heavy cream

4 eggs

Marcona Almond Crust
    (recipe follows)

269 ◀

The goat cheese and cream cheese must be at room temperature before you start, so be sure to remove them from the fridge at least 1 hour in advance.

help minimize the amount of processing needed to gently mix them in.

7. Once the custard's ingredients are just combined, pour it into a pitcher or a second bowl to check for any visible lumps or other inconsistencies. If you do see any, stir gently by hand to incorporate.

8. To bake, pour the custard into the prepared and cooled crust. Next, make a water bath by placing the pan of cheesecake into a second, deeper pan, making sure it's wide enough for the cake pan to fit with room all around. You can use a roasting pan, casserole dish, or even an aluminum roasting pan from the grocery store. As long as the cake fits, you're solid. Pour hot water into the outer pan to about an inch deep.

9. Bake for 90 minutes, until the cake is set and smooth but still has a very slight jiggle in its center. The top should not look wet, and when you lightly touch the center, your finger should come back clean. If it still looks wet and very wobbly, continue to bake in 10-minute increments until it is properly set. Overbaking is a bigger worry, so if you know or suspect that your oven tends to run hot, bake at 290°F.

10. Once the cake has set, turn off the oven and let the cake sit inside for 10 minutes, then open the oven door and let it sit for another 15 minutes.

11. Carefully remove the cake from the oven and let it sit in its bath for another 15 minutes, then gently lift the cake pan out of its bath.

12. Allow to cool fully to room temperature, then wrap in plastic wrap and chill overnight.

13. The next day, carefully remove the cake from its pan. If using a false-bottomed pan, gently press the bottom upwards to loosen. Cut the cake into 10 slices and embellish with whatever topping you please (see a range of options starting on page 74).

MARCONA ALMOND CRUST

½ cup (65 grams or 2⅓ ounces) Marcona almonds	¼ teaspoon kosher salt
¾ cup (90 grams) all-purpose flour	¼ cup (50 grams) packed light or dark brown sugar
¼ cup (30 grams) whole wheat flour	⅓ cup (¾ of a stick) unsalted butter, melted

1. Preheat the oven to 325°F.

2. Pulse the almonds in a food processor, or chop by hand, into rough pieces about the size of a pea.

3. In a medium-sized bowl, mix both flours, salt, and brown sugar, then add in the almonds. Pour the melted butter over the mixture and mix well with a rubber spatula until the dough comes together.

4. Spray the bottom of a 9-inch false-bottom or springform pan with cooking spray, then line with parchment cut to fit the bottom.

5. Pour the dough into the pan and press it down to flatten and cover the bottom of the pan evenly. You can use the flat bottom of a glass or a measuring cup to help smooth it out.

6. Chill the crust for at least 30 minutes or freeze overnight.

7 Bake for 15 to 20 minutes, until the crust is a light golden brown and looks slightly puffed up.

8. Allow to cool completely before proceeding, then wrap the pan in two layers of aluminum foil, trying to avoid any major creases along the edges. This will prevent water from getting trapped while baking the cheesecake.

Dulce de Leche Semifreddo

**Makes about 4 cups,
for 4 to 6 servings**

1¾ cups plus 2 tablespoons (425
grams) heavy cream

¼ cup (50 grams) crème fraîche or
sour cream

1 whole egg

5 large egg yolks (90 grams) (see
page 43 for how to separate)

1¾ cup (150 grams)
granulated sugar

1 tablespoon corn syrup

1 tablespoon vanilla bean paste or
2 tablespoons vanilla extract

Pinch of kosher salt

½ cup dulce de leche

f you don't have an ice-cream maker, don't worry—neither does The Kitchen! So, when it's hot outside and our guests want to cool down with something amazing, this semifreddo—literally, "half frozen" in Italian—is our go-to. In fact, if you ask around, you'd have a challenge finding anyone who noticed or cared that it's not regular ice cream. Dulce de leche's creamy texture just rockets this already-creamy treat into the stratosphere. We originally served this as an accompaniment to our Spiced-Pear Baklava (page 257); soon guests were asking for additional scoops for the table to share, so we knew we had a winner.

1. In a stand mixer fitted with the whisk attachment, whip the heavy cream with the crème fraîche on medium speed until it forms stiff yet still fluffy peaks. Transfer to another bowl and place it in the fridge to keep it chilled. You don't need to wash the mixer bowl and whisk yet—you'll need them shortly.

2. This is another method that relies on a DIY double boiler, a medium bowl that sits comfortably atop a similarly sized saucepan. Make a sabayon, also known as zabaglione, by combining the egg, egg yolks, sugar, corn syrup, and vanilla. Whisk well to combine.

3. Fill the saucepan half-full of water and bring to a boil. Lower the heat to medium, place a bowl over the pan, and cook the egg mixture, whisking constantly for 5 to 7 minutes, until its temperature reaches 170°F.

4. Carefully pour the sabayon into the stand mixer's bowl and whip on high speed until the bowl is cool to the touch and the mixture is pale, fluffy, and makes ribbons when you lift the whisk. Add in the dulce de leche and whip on high speed until well combined.

5. Remove the whipped cream mixture from the fridge and add about ¼ cup to the bowl with the sabayon. You can measure it or just eyeball it. Begin to gently fold the cream into the sabayon until no streaks remain. Continue adding the cream ½ cup or so at a time, gently folding each increment into the mixture until no streaks remain before adding the next. Keep on this way until you've used up the entire batch of whipped cream.

6. Pour into a container and cover with parchment or plastic wrap, freeze overnight until set, then scoop and serve at will.

Apple Galette

The beautiful thing about a galette is that it delivers all the deliciousness of a pie for way less effort. You can use any fruit, but we're just so taken with this "lazy apple pie" that it's become a menu staple. To save time. you can prepare the filling and the pie dough up to 2 days in advance, so that you only need to fill the pastry and bake.

▼

1. In a medium bowl, combine both sugars with the cornstarch, spices, salt, and lemon zest and set aside.

2. In a second bowl, toss the apples with the lemon juice, then add in the sugar mixture and toss well to evenly coat the apples. Add the apple mixture to a medium saucepan over medium-low heat and cook, stirring with a rubber spatula every few minutes to prevent the mixture from sticking, until the apples have just started to soften and the juices have thickened, about 6 to 8 minutes. If your apples are extra juicy, they may release so much juice that the mixture doesn't thicken in this amount of time. In that case, drain off any excess liquid once the apples have cooked.

3. Stir in the boiled cider and butter and continue cooking until the butter has completely melted and the ingredients are fully incorporated. Remove from the heat and allow to cool completely before using.

4. Roll out the dough to a thickness of ¼ inch. Using a small knife, cut the dough into a 9-inch-diameter circle. (Save those scraps for later use; pie dough freezes like a dream and can be used in any number of sweet or savory recipes.)

Continued

Serves 8 to 10

¾ cup (160 grams) packed light or dark brown sugar

¼ cup (50 grams) granulated sugar, plus more for sprinkling

2 tablespoons (20 grams) cornstarch

¾ teaspoon ground cinnamon

¼ teaspoon ground nutmeg

¼ teaspoon ground cardamom

Pinch of kosher salt

Zest and juice of 1 lemon

4 to 5 Honeycrisp apples, unpeeled, cored and sliced into ¼-inch-thick slices (600 grams)

3 tablespoons boiled apple cider syrup (available online if you can't find it locally)

2 tablespoons unsalted butter

Flaky Pie Dough (page 236) or storebought roll-out crust

1 egg, for egg wash

275

5. Transfer the pie dough to a parchment-lined sheet pan. Carefully pour the apple filling onto the center of the pastry circle, gently spreading it to form an even layer. Be sure to leave a solid 2 to 3 inches of free space all around the edges.

6. Now fold those edges of dough up and over the filling, all the way around, creating a barrier to prevent the filling from spilling out when baked. Freeze the galette for at least 30 minutes before baking, or overnight.

7. When you're ready to bake the galette, preheat the oven to 400°F.

8. Whisk the egg to form an egg wash. Pull the galette from the freezer and brush the exposed pie dough with egg wash. Sprinkle generously with sugar.

9. Bake for 30 to 45 minutes until the galette has puffed up a bit. The crust should be a deep golden brown, the filling lightly bubbling. Baking time can vary by oven, so go by how it looks, and don't be afraid to go longer if it's not done yet.

10. Remove from the oven and let it cool before serving.

Chef Michael Bertozzi and Kimbal Musk with a fresh delivery of carrots.

ALL ABOUT THE APPLES

For this galette, we use Honeycrisp because, of all the varieties out there, it's the best for retaining maximum flavor and texture when cooked. Because this galette is like an open-face pie, you want an apple that will hold its shape for a beautiful presentation. (This is why we also leave the apples unpeeled here, so you get that pop of red color.) If you can't lay your hands on Honeycrisps, you can substitute Granny Smith, SugarBee, or Braeburn apples and your galette will still be amazing. The boiled apple cider syrup that's mixed in with the apples helps amp up their flavor. It's an old-time pantry staple (used as a more affordable sweetener when sugar was hard to come by), and it adds a subtle tang to balance everything out.

"What's the secret to your success?" can be a tough question. But for us, the answer is simple. It's the amazing people who have been part of The Kitchen team over the decades. The restaurant industry tends to change often—new places open, old favorites close, staff and chefs move around. All of this action can be exciting, but it also reminds us to treasure the people who've been a part of The Kitchen for many years. This is equally true of long-time current employees and of those who've moved on to new adventures elsewhere.

The employee who's been with us the longest, practically from Day One, is Jaime. Jaime has worked with steadfast dedication behind the scenes, providing all kinds of support for the kitchen in Boulder. From his perspective, what makes The Kitchen such a rewarding place to work is the general culture of respect, hard work, and of course the Bolo (page 129). Another long-time team-member, Jason Hein, general manager at our Boulder location, has been here long enough to see the restaurant evolve from its early days as a pioneer of hyper-local, farm-to-table cooking to its current incarnations in four cities. He's amazed at how throughout it all, the restaurant has never lost its essence: a love of real food, grown by real people. As he says, "There's a care and there's a soul that transmits from the farmers' hands into the produce, into the truck, into the fridge, onto the cutting board, and onto the dish that is served. And that's something special for me." It is for all of us. This book could never have happened without the love and support of our staff—as well as our guests—who've become part of our story.

The Secret of Our Success

Gratitudes

COURTNEY WALSH
Thank you, Courtney, for your unending dedication to our work at The Kitchen over the past twenty years. You are the glue that holds this book together.

CHEF MICHAEL BERTOZZI
Thank you, Michael, for gathering all these recipes together, new and old. And testing them all, over and over again. Your dedication will be felt by every person who cooks from this book.

PHOTOGRAPHER LAURIE SMITH
Thank you, Laurie, for being our photographer for twenty years and counting. You capture the magic of The Kitchen through your lens.

PASTRY CHEF NATALIE MORALES
Thank you, Natalie, for your contributions to this book and The Kitchen. You've brought the perfect sweet tooth to this book.

MIXOLOGIST MATTY CARROLL
Thank you, Matty, for your amazing cocktails in this book.

THANK YOU, Sam Hallak, for your dedication to The Kitchen and the incredible team you have assembled. Thank you to our long-time guests Wendy Lea, Burgermeister, and Troy Omifray for giving us your time to be interviewed for this book. Thank you, Karla Shaw and Don Degnan, for your undying devotion to The Kitchen these past twenty years. Thank you, Chris Steighner, at Melcher Media for caring about this every day with the team.

Kimbal Musk is the co-founder of
THE KITCHEN, an American bistro with
restaurant locations in Boulder, Denver,
Chicago, and soon Austin. Now marking its
twentieth anniversary, THE KITCHEN serves
thoughtfully sourced, seasonal American
shared plates with global influences. Musk
is also the co-founder of Big Green, a phil-
anthropic organization devoted to getting
every American growing food. His personal
mission is to empower and invest in the next
generation who are building a healthier,
happier future. *The Wall Street Journal* has called
him a "cheerful crusader for real food," and
The Guardian has lauded how he "takes the tech
entrepreneur ethos and applies it to food."
Musk has been named a Global Social Entrepreneur by the World Economic Forum. Musk
currently sits on the board of Tesla Inc., and for-
merly served on the board of Chipotle Mexican
Grill and SpaceX. Follow him on X @Kimbal
and Instagram @KimbalMusk.